ANTONIO GRAMSCI

CRITICS OF THE TWENTIETH CENTURY
General Editor: Christopher Norris,
University of Wales, College of Cardiff

ANTONIO GRAMSCI

Beyond Marxism and Postmodernism

Renate Holub

LONDON AND NEW YORK

First published 1992
by Routledge
11 New Fetter Lane, London EC4P 4EE

Simultaneously published in the USA and Canada
by Routledge
a division of Routledge, Chapman and Hall, Inc.
29 West 35th Street, New York, NY 10001

Phototypeset and printed in Great Britain by
Redwood Press Limited, Melksham, Wiltshire

British Library Cataloguing in Publication Data
Holub, Renate
Antonio Gramsci : beyond Marxism and postmodernism. –
(Critics of the twentieth century)
I. Title   II. Series
335.4092

Library of Congress Cataloging in Publication Data
Holub, Renate
Antonio Gramsci : beyond Marxism and postmodernism / Renate Holub.
p.   cm.
Includes bibliographical references and index.
1. Gramsci, Antonio, 1891–1937. I. Title.
HX289.7.G73H65   1992
335.43'092—dc20   91–25881   CIP

ISBN 0–415–02108–1
ISBN 0–415–07510–6 pbk

Contents

Editor's foreword

The twentieth century has produced a remarkable number of gifted and innovative literary critics. Indeed it could be argued that some of the finest literary minds of the age have turned to criticism as the medium best adapted to their complex and speculative range of interests. This has sometimes given rise to regret among those who insist on a clear demarcation between 'creative' (primary) writing on the one hand, and 'critical' (secondary) texts on the other. Yet this distinction is far from self-evident. It is coming under strain at the moment as novelists and poets grow increasingly aware of the conventions that govern their writing and the challenge of consciously exploiting and subverting those conventions. And the critics for their part – some of them at least – are beginning to question their traditional role as humble servants of the literary text with no further claim upon the reader's interest or attention. Quite simply, there are texts of literary criticism and theory that, for various reasons – stylistic complexity, historical influence, range of intellectual command – cannot be counted a mere appendage to those other 'primary' texts.

Of course, there is a logical puzzle here, since (it will be argued) 'literary criticism' would never have come into being, and could hardly exist as such, were it not for the body of creative writings that provide its *raison d'être*. But this is not quite the kind of knockdown argument that it might appear at first glance. For one thing, it conflates some very different orders of priority, assuming that literature always comes first (in the sense that Greek tragedy had to exist before Aristotle could formulate its rules), so that literary texts are for that very reason possessed of superior value. And this argument would seem to find commonsense support in the difficulty of thinking what 'literary criticism' could *be* if it seriously renounced all sense of the distinction between literary and critical texts. Would it not then find itself in the unfortunate position of a discipline that had willed its own demise by declaring its subject non-existent?

But these objections would only hit their mark if there were indeed a special kind of writing called 'literature' whose difference from other kinds of writing was enough to put criticism firmly in its place. Otherwise there is nothing in the least self-defeating or paradoxical about a discourse, nominally that of literary criticism, that accrues such interest on its own account as to force some fairly drastic rethinking of its proper powers and limits. The act of crossing over from commentary to literature – or of simply denying the difference between them – becomes quite explicit in the writing of a critic like Geoffrey Hartman. But the signs are already there in such classics as William Empson's *Seven Types of Ambiguity* (1930), a text whose transformative influence on our habits of reading must surely be ranked with the great creative moments of literary modernism. Only on the most dogmatic view of the difference between 'literature' and 'criticism' could a work like *Seven Types* be counted generically an inferior, sub-literary species of production. And the same can be said for many of the critics whose writings and influence this series sets out to explore.

Some, like Empson, are conspicuous individuals who belong to no particular school or larger movement. Others, like the Russian Formalists, were part of a communal enterprise and are therefore best understood as representative figures in a complex and evolving dialogue. Then again there are cases of collective identity (like the so-called 'Yale deconstructors') where a mythical group image is invented for largely polemical purposes. (The volumes in this series on Hartman and Bloom should help to dispel the idea that 'Yale deconstruction' is anything more than a handy device for collapsing differences and avoiding serious debate.) So there is no question of a series format or house-style that would seek to reduce these differences to a blandly homogeneous treatment. One consequence of recent critical theory is the realization that literary texts have no self-sufficient or autonomous meaning, no existence apart from their after-life of changing interpretations and values. And the same applies to those *critical* texts whose meaning and significance are subject to constant shifts and realignments of interest. This is not to say that trends in criticism are just a matter of intellectual fashion or the merry-go-round of rising and falling reputations. But it is important to grasp how complex are the forces – the conjunctions of historical and cultural motive – that affect the first reception and the subsequent fortunes of a critical text. This point has been raised into a systematic programme by critics like Hans-Robert Jauss, practitioners of so-called 'reception theory' as a form of historical hermeneutics. The volumes in this series will therefore be concerned not only to expound what is of lasting significance but also to set these critics in the context of present-day argument and debate. In some cases (as with Walter Benjamin) this debate takes the form of a struggle for interpretative power among disciplines with sharply opposed ideological viewpoints. Such controversies cannot simply be ignored in the interests of achieving a clear and balanced account. They point to unresolved tensions and problems which are there in the critic's work as well as in the rival appropriative readings. In the end there is no way of drawing a neat methodological line between 'intrinsic' questions (what the critic really thought) and those other, supposedly 'extrinsic' concerns that have to do with influence and reception history.

The volumes will vary accordingly in their focus and range of coverage. They will also reflect the ways in which a speculative approach to questions of literary theory has proved to have striking consequences for the human sciences at large. This breaking-down of disciplinary bounds is among the most significant developments in recent critical thinking. As philosophers and historians, among others, come to recognize the rhetorical complexity of the texts they deal with, so literary theory takes on a new dimension of interest and relevance. It is scarcely appropriate to think of a writer like Derrida as practising 'literary criticism' in any conventional sense of the term. For one thing, he is as much concerned with 'philosophical' as with 'literary' texts, and has indeed actively sought to subvert (or deconstruct) such tidy distinctions. A principal object in planning this series was to take full stock of these shifts in the wider intellectual terrain (including the frequent boundary disputes) brought about by critical theory. And, of course, such changes are by no means confined to literary studies, philosophy and the so-called 'sciences of man.' It is equally the case in (say) nuclear physics and molecular biology that advances in the one field have decisive implications for the other, so that specialized research often tends (paradoxically) to break down existing divisions of intellectual labour. Such work is typically many years head of the academic disciplines and teaching institutions that have obvious reasons of their own for adopting a business-as-usual attitude. One important aspect of modern critical theory is the challenge it presents to these traditional ideas. And lest it be thought that this is merely a one-sided takeover bid by literary critics, the series will include a number of volumes by authors in those other disciplines, including, for instance, this study of Gramsci by a scholar whose interests range across the fields of feminism, philosophy, political theory and the history of ideas. Nothing could more clearly illustrate the benefits of this interdisciplinary approach when pursued – as here – with a sensitive regard for differences of critical perspective and cultural context.

We shall not, however, cleave to 'theory' as a matter of polemical or principled stance. The series will extend to figures like F. R. Leavis, whose widespread influence went along with an express aversion to literary theory; scholars like Erich Auerbach in the mainstream European tradition; and others who resist assimilation to any clear-cut line of descent. There will also be authoritative volumes on critics such as Northrop Frye and Kenneth Burke, figures who, for various reasons, occupy an ambivalent or essentially contested place in the modern critical tradition. Above all, the series will strive to resist that current polarization of attitudes that sees no common ground of interest between 'literary criticism' and 'critical theory.'

CHRISTOPHER NORRIS

Acknowledgements

This book deals with Gramsci as a critic of the twentieth century. Christopher Norris, the editor of the present series, was the first person to suggest the topic to me, and I would like to thank him here not only for doing so, but also for his unfailing friendship over the years and the many new ideas and ways of seeing he brought into my life. I would also like to thank Janice Price, the editor at Routledge, for her admirable patience. It was a great pleasure working with her.

Along the way, while I was working on the project, various friends have been supportive. Volker Gransow and Gregory Vlastos have listened, over lunch or coffee, to fragmented and disjointed mini-lectures on Gramsci, and they have always, and with kind words, encouraged me. Two very good friends, on the East and West Coasts respectively, have reminded me intermittently, and in no uncertain terms, that I 'should get it done'. Thank you for your advice and friendship, Peter (Carravetta) and Lucia (Birnbaum), which have served me well. Many sections of the book I had the opportunity to present at various conferences, and I would like to thank those friends who invited me to do so. Again, my thanks to Peter Carravetta and Lucia Birnbaum, and also to Anthony Tamburri and Tibor Wlassics. My students at UC-Berkeley in 'The Feminist Challenge to Critical Theory' (Fall 1989) and 'Gramsci, Western Marxism, Gender' (Spring 1990) got to know many of the ideas presented in the book, and their challenging questions, unsettling as some of them seemed at the time, have found their way, I think, in one way or another, into the final version of the project. I would like to thank Melissa Ptacek, Nadia Babella, Winifred Poster, Melissa Gum and Lisa Daniel; and also Liz Goodstein and Mary Foertsch, women whose practical feminisms have meant a lot to me.

There are two more very special friends I would like to thank here:

Bob Holub and Alexei Holub, both of whom had little choice but to live with me during the ups and downs of completing this project. I would like to thank both of you very much. In particular, I am indebted in many ways to my companion Bob, who listened to me on Gramscian matters on innumerable occasions and helped me with technical and not-so-technical problems alike, and, above all, whose solid knowledge of twentieth-century theory and intellectual history provided an excellent structure to my life-world within which it was a pleasure to construct my own version of Gramsci's critical theories. To you, Bob, and to Alexei, a big hug.

Part I

INTRODUCTION

1

Gramsci and critical theories: towards a 'differential pragmatics'

MARXISM AND MODERNISM

Gramsci had been in prison for almost eight years when Lukács, in 1934, published two essays which are crucial for understanding the state of Marxist aesthetics in the 1930s. The first, entitled 'Art and Objective Truth', displays the epistemological foundations of Lukács' aesthetic theory.[1] And the second focuses on what he calls the 'greatness and decline' of expressionism.[2] At issue in this latter essay were those cultural, artistic and literary forces which Lukács considered as having taken part in the rise of fascism, and not in its prevention. Expressionism he counted among such forces. For this reason, Lukács also polemicized against expressionism, as a form of modernism, in a famous essay entitled 'Let's Talk Realism Now', published in 1937, which would incite an unprecedented international debate (in the west) on the problem of realism and modernism among the left intelligentsia.[3] By that time Gramsci was, after eleven years in fascist prisons, no longer in a fit state to argue his case.[4] So when against the background of fascist cultural politics exiled intellectuals like Anna Seghers, Bertolt Brecht and Ernst Bloch, but also Walter Benjamin and many others, obliged Lukács to undertake a critical review of his verdict on expressionism, Gramsci was not among the interlocutors. Nor was he there when one of the largest international writers' conventions in defence of democratic culture took place in Paris in 1935 and when the anti-fascist popular cultural front was put into effect.[5] So when the realism/expressionism/modernism debate, as a response to the challenges of fascism, confronted the question of what kind of literature and art constituted an authentic anti-fascist politicality, and what kind of political status to assign to modernist art, when that debate raged among orthodox

3

and unorthodox Marxists alike, Gramsci did not take part in it and could not have taken part. And conversely, hardly known to anyone in the mid-1930s, Gramsci's contemporary writings were on precisely the same topics that preoccupied the participants in the realism/modernism debate. Like many of his contemporaries, Gramsci investigated, *inter alia*, in his notes written in prison, what constituted fascist and anti-fascist art, what kind of literature to support or reject in the class struggle, or to admit to a democratic cultural canon. Many of Gramsci's theoretical concerns indeed coincide with general questions of ideology and Marxist aesthetics, in particular as these have been addressed by one of the major protagonists in the realism/modernism debate: Georg Lukács.[6] In that Lukács is not only a pivotal figure in the context of the realism/modernism debate, but also one of the major Marxist aestheticians of our century, I have chosen to dedicate chapter 2 of this book to a comparative analysis of Gramsci and Lukács on Marxist aesthetics. At issue are their respective approaches to problems of realism on the basis of their reading of one of the major nineteenth-century Italian writers and novelists, Alessandro Manzoni.

To deal with Lukács and Gramsci in a literary context, rather than from the point of view of political or social theory, was particularly fascinating to me for a variety of reasons. Until recently, the Gramsci critical community showed little interest in his literary critiques and his aesthetics, not finding it particularly profitable, in light of the apparently fragmentary character of Gramsci's notes on aesthetics, to look at his stature as critic of the twentieth century.[7] As a result, it had become commonplace to deal with Gramsci, when evoked in conjunction with a major Marxist aesthetician such as Lukács, quite paradoxically, *not* in the context of literary criticism or aesthetics. Rather, when Gramsci does turn up in Lukács' company, usually it is in a context that addresses their pioneering work in the realm of western Marxism. There is surely good reason for understanding Gramsci in such a way. He was, after all, a major political activist around World War I, and one of the leaders of the Italian working-class movement in the early and mid-1920s, until his arrest in November 1926. Moreover, much of his work, whether it stems from his pre-prison years, or the research he pursued in prison, does indeed deal with questions of political and social Marxism. Against the background of the Russian revolution of 1917 and its European aftermath, the revolutions that failed in the west, Gramsci attempted, like many contemporary theorists, to correct Marxist dogma and strategy; particularly the kind of dogma which had been handed down by the Second International, a scientific and positivist form of Marxism, and a cognate view of history, which required, from Gramsci's perspective, a good deal of rethinking in light of the unprecedented historical developments unsettling the world around World War I. Historical realities called into question the orthodox theories of the Second International, with its understanding of historical change in terms of an economic determinism, where changes in the economic base would inexorably determine changes in the superstructure. The events of the Russian revolution, taking place, so to speak, before their historical time, and the failure of the revolutions in the west, not taking place, as expected, at their appointed time, required new approaches to politics, society and even history. The narrative of an evolutionary, natural, pre-destined trajectory of history within which one form of society (capitalism) would necessarily, without significant superstructural and ideological intervention, change into another form of society (socialism), had run its course. A new narrative awaited its turn. Like many critical theorists and political activists of his era, Gramsci contributed to the production of that narrative. He critically confronted the fact that the economic crisis situations in the various western countries had not led to a political crisis, as Marx had predicted. Rather, power and authority were still retained by the state and capitalism, in spite of the massive social and ideological upheavals currently taking place. The revolution, predicted for countries with more advanced capitalist economic formations, had not in fact arrived on time. Yet in Russia, in a country which was economically backward by most accounts and not ready, so it was reckoned, for massive economic transformations, a revolution had taken place. There was, as a result, much to rethink and reconsider in Marxist theory and strategy, from questions of the dialectic to theories of ideology, culture and the state. In Gramsci's work, the rethinking of these formidable historical events led to the conceptualization of key notions with which his texts were subsequently identified. I am referring to his notions of political and civil society, hegemony, as well as counter-hegemony, and, closely related to these two, his idea of the 'intellectual'. This latter notion is sometimes referred to as that of the 'organic intellectual'. I will rephrase it as 'critical specialist/non-specialist', for reasons explained in chapter 6.

Gramsci's concepts in general resist ready definition. Tending always to examine and interrogate phenomena from multiple points of view, from divergent angles and different sites, and in general in

5

slow motion, his concepts, designed to grasp some of the complexities present in social processes, are as manysided and multiple as ways of seeing. I will, therefore, introduce only provisionally here some of what Gramsci's notions, such as hegemony and counter-hegemony, can embody. Hegemony is a concept that helps to explain, on the one hand, how state apparatuses, or political society – supported by and supporting a specific economic group – can coerce, via its institutions of law, police, army and prisons, the various strata of society into consenting to the status quo. On the other hand, and more importantly, hegemony is a concept that helps us to understand not only the ways in which a predominant economic group coercively uses the state apparatuses of political society in the preservation of the status quo, but also how and where political society and, above all, civil society, with its institutions ranging from education, religion and the family to the microstructures of the practices of everyday life, contribute to the production of meaning and values which in turn produce, direct and maintain the 'spontaneous' consent of the various strata of society to that same status quo.[8] In this sense hegemony is related to both civil society and political society, and, in the last analysis, also to the economic sphere. And Gramsci's concept of the 'intellectual', which equally resists definition, is a way for Gramsci to begin to conceptualize, not perhaps primarily the production, but the directed reproduction and dissemination of an effective hegemony, a differentiated yet also directive and value-laden channelling of the production of meaning or signification. A counter-hegemony would, as a result, also depend on intellectual activities. These would produce, reproduce and disseminate values and meanings attached to a conception of the world attentive to democratic principles and the dignity of humankind.

With the invention of these concepts, Gramsci collaborates in the theoretical project of Marxist intellectuals of the 1920s who had witnessed the Russian revolution and its European aftermath, taking place despite and against the arguments of Marx's *Capital*. In this sense his text is indeed representative, along with those of Korsch and Lukács, of early western Marxism. It is not my intention in this book, however, to reinforce the received image of Gramsci as co-founder of western Marxism, legitimate though it is, or to probe deeply into Gramsci's political or social theory, his particular version of Marxism, that is. For one thing, there is plenty of good material on this issue already available.[9] And if I am not mistaken, this approach to Gramsci continues to be successfully pursued.[10] Rather, what attracts me more is to place Gramsci next to Lukács in the context of literary criticism, and in the context of Marxist aesthetics. This procedure has some advantages. It does not prevent me, on the one hand, from pointing to the many themes and interests Lukács and Gramsci share: their political, historical, biographical experiences, their emphasis on the superstructural rather than the infrastructural, their understanding of ideology, their attempts to come to terms with the rapidly diminishing revolutionary potential of western capitalism, their invention of new concepts with which to challenge that diminution. On the other hand, it is precisely by placing these two theorists not in a political but rather in a literary context, by analysing their approach to literary texts, that I can point to the differences which they display when it comes to their respective conceptions of the world. The life-world in which both thinkers are immersed, consciously or unconsciously, is structured by modernity. What I see inscribed in their critical analysis of a literary text is, to be sure, among other things, their respective understanding of modernity, their coming to terms, whether acknowledged or not, with the effects of technological modernization on the structure of the social, familial and, above all, cultural world. What I see emerging from their perspectives on modernity is not a view which would unproblematically settle them on common ground within the received category of western Marxism. What I see, and what I will discuss in chapter 2, is a significant differential that unsettles Gramsci's otherwise substantial affinities with Lukács. The Gramsci who emerges from my notes is not a supporter of Lukács' realism as it evolves during the realism/modernism debate, but rather a supporter of Lukács' opponents, of those intellectuals who supported modernism. Among these, as we will see, I count Brecht and Bloch.

That Lukács is not particularly fond of modernism can hardly be news to readers of his books. It is his trademark, so to speak, one that has cost him influence, credibility and theoretical force, in spite of his almost unmatched erudition, his clarity of style, his pre-eminent place in twentieth-century thought.[11] His controversial narrative is well known: attentive to epistemological models that are capable of accounting for all the parts in the whole, he rejects a vision of the world that finds delight in fragments rather than totality, in gaps rather than relations, in multiplicities of viewpoint rather than objectivity and truth. It is according to this standard that literary works are judged. What matters for Lukács is the totality the text evokes: the totality of relations in reality, between the economic base and the

7

superstructure, the totality of relations of historical forces, including the contradictory character of these relations, which a particular historical moment contains. Realism is the name of that mode of evocation, and of that mode of representation. In so far as Alessandro Manzoni's *The Betrothed* re-creates the fate of two lovers whose story mirrors the peculiar state of affairs of an uncentralized and fragmented Italy, that author pays his dues, whether consciously or not, to the requirements of realism, as Balzac, Tolstoy and others had done in the nineteenth century at the height of the development of the bourgeois novel. And in so far as twentieth-century writers such as Thomas Mann reproduce in literature, in the cultural and superstructural sphere, the mirror image of the decline of a once powerful class, the bourgeoisie, they also meet the requirement of realism. Authentic literature, the kind that ought to take its place in the canon, is that which reproduces the essentials of reality, which for Lukács, in the twentieth century, means the decline of capitalism and the class that carried it forward, the bourgeoisie, and by inference, and of necessity, the rise of an emergent world historical class, the proletariat. It is this kind of realism which Lukács pursues, as he rejects modernist literature and art. Modernism is, in his view, incapable of artistically reproducing the total view of the tensions and contradictions accompanying the teleologically necessary transformation from one society to another. What should count, then, as exemplary texts, in cultural politics, are not modernist texts, but those that adhere to the standards of realism. Or rather, what do count, for Lukács, as we shall see, are not primarily the readers, but mostly the writers of realist texts. The readers disappear somewhere near the horizon of Lukács' aesthetic expectations.

Now it is precisely when it comes to the reader, to the importance of the reception of a work of art as opposed to its production, that Lukács and Gramsci chiefly differ, and Gramsci and other modernists meet. Though Gramsci too expects the writer to show colours and take a stand in the world historical drama – Manzoni's condescending attitude towards the powerless, the marginalized, the poor, the subaltern classes indubitably bespeaks his partiality for those in power – the issue is not ultimately for him whether or not to put Manzoni on the cultural heritage list. Attentive, in many pages of his *Prison Notebooks*, to how much was read and by whom, running, so to speak, a 'private market research institute' from his prison cell that statistically discerns the modes of consumption of a stratified reading public, Gramsci observed that Manzoni had not been read by the

8

disadvantaged social classes anyhow. What people read instead were serial novels, trivial literature, popular novels, detective novels, and a lot of kitsch, forms of cultural consumption which no doubt play a role, so Gramsci reasoned, in the psycho-symbolic economy of the reader, in the production of social signification and in the reproduction of 'spontaneous' consent to the status quo. So understanding why people read what they read was ultimately of more importance to Gramsci than what Manzoni had to say and how he said it. It is here that Lukács and Gramsci differ most sharply. In an era that increasingly facilitates the reproducibility of literary and cultural texts, and thus the mobilization of systems of signification in the individual act of reading, Lukács' concern with a realistic, denotative depiction of reality, with its positing of a consuming rather than a meaning-producing reader, seems outdated, not ahead of but behind the times. So when Gramsci turns, in contradistinction to Lukács, not to the realism of the past but to the modernism of the present, to the reproducibility of cultural texts, then he intuits, contrary to Lukács, some of the powers emerging from the interstices of modern technologies. And when he reflects on the double-edged nature of these powers, when he intuits potentials and dangers alike in the gradual technologization and industrialization of culture, when he senses possibilities of manipulation and domination of the cultural sphere, the production and control of needs and desires designed for consumption of specific cultural and ideological goods, then Gramsci reveals an awareness of the complexity of modern reality which by far transcends Lukács' notion of realism.

So in my reading of Gramsci's treatment of realism in the context of Marxist aesthetics, I stress those theoretical assumptions which he does not share with Lukács. What I suggest is that his texts evolve against a background or a structure of concerns which he has in common not with Lukács, but with other major critical theorists of the twentieth century. Among these I count Brecht and Bloch, as well as Adorno, Horkheimer and Benjamin, but also the linguist and philosopher Vološinov, and the phenomenologist Merleau-Ponty. At issue then, in chapters 3, 4 and 5, are the ways in which Gramsci's work displays homologies with many pivotal twentieth-century ways of theorizing. When Gramsci relates the problems of realism and modernism to transformations in the structure of the modern life-world, when he examines phenomena related to the production and effect of the industrialization of culture, when he studies the production of meaning and signification in a linguistic and phenomenological

9

framework that in some ways anticipates a combination of structural linguistics and a kind of phenomenological critical theory, when he stakes out a critical practice which is suggestive in terms of a contemporary critical theory, in terms of what I would like to call a 'differential pragmatics', then he exceeds many concerns of received Marxism. He also goes beyond the way in which Lukács aesthetically and culturally confronted the immediate advent of fascism.

While Gramsci's contemporaries did not know what theoretical problems he addressed in his *Prison Notebooks*, he likewise did not know what theoretical problems they were addressing. Many of Gramsci's concepts replay the realist/modernist drama, enacted by Lukács on the one hand and by supporters of modernism on the other. Yet it is not only because Gramsci addresses – against Lukács – 'problems of modernism in the context of modernity' that I engage in a discussion of Gramsci and the Frankfurt School in chapters 3 and 4. It is also because of Gramsci's mode of approaching these 'problems of modernism and modernity', his way of posing questions and problematizing issues of technologization, that I have chosen to discuss Gramsci in conjunction with the Frankfurt School. For the way in which Gramsci, in his *Prison Notebooks* of the 1930s, analyses cultural problems of modernism, reflects an anticipatory sensibility to very complex cultural and social transformations. It also reflects his flexibility when it comes to adjusting old concepts, and experimenting with and inventing new ones, in order to begin to grasp new social and political realities. Both aspects of Gramsci's critical theory, his sensitivity to nascent social and cultural realities, and the unrivalled flexibility with which he adjusts, amends, transforms and reinvents conceptual frameworks, experimenting with ways of seeing in order conceptually to arrange new phenomena, need to go on record. So do the parallels not only between Gramsci's critical theory and many of the 1930s modernist theories of the Frankfurt School of the pre-war period, but also and in particular between some of Gramsci's ideas and some of those critical theories which would move to centre stage in the theoretical drama of the twentieth century, though not until the post-war period.

The polemics between Lukács and Brecht, on the one hand, and between Lukács and Bloch, on the other hand, were surely occasioned by fascism's inexorable seizure of political and cultural power. They simultaneously reveal, however, an awareness, to various degrees, of a background or the structure of a life-world that had been gradually emerging since the end of the nineteenth century. As liberal capitalism changed to monopoly capitalism, as free economies changed into more structured and regulated economies at times soliciting state intervention in crisis situations, as rationalization and technologization, new productive forces, affected the life-world of modern society and culture, new experiences broke through accepted limits and broadened the horizons of tradition and expectation. The new 'structures of feeling' that emerged from these massive and unprecedented transformations left traces in discursive formations and in processes of signification. In the writings of the most socially and politically engaged intelligentsia, these structures of a newly emerging life-world interfaced with visions of democratic cultures and societies capable of channelling the powers and effects of that inexorable march towards a new rationality, thereby countering Weber's imaging of an iron cage of total domination. So when intellectuals were taking a stand in the realism/modernism debate, they were, surely, first and foremost, responding to the cultural and political hegemony of fascism. Yet the most advanced intellectuals were contextualizing that debate in such a way that it reflects their interest in the historical forces which accompanied, perhaps produced, and would, in any event, survive fascism. The modernization of the life-world, constitutive of as well as constituting the rationalization of many spheres of experience and activity, offered new and unprecedented challenges to critical theory. Grasping the immensity of these transformations and intuiting their effects is the common ground Gramsci shares not with Lukács, but with Frankfurt School critical theory. It is the background within which, next to which and against which Gramsci writes his *Prison Notebooks*. These are filled with principles of pessimism, when it comes to the modernization of the life-world, but also and mostly with principles of hope.

MODERNISM, GRAMSCI AND THE FRANKFURT SCHOOL

What I argue in my study then is not that Gramsci should not be looked at as a founding figure of western Marxism, as someone who corrects Marxism in the area of political theory, social theory and a theory of the state. This is clearly one of the ways to look at him. However, since in many instances in his *Prison Notebooks* Gramsci examines questions of realism and modernism in the context of the modernization of the life-world, and frequently interrogates the effects of rationalization and technologization on the cultural

11

structure of that life-world, I have chosen to dedicate two chapters of this book to his notes on these matters, on his view and assessments of modernity, one of the effects of which constitutes the 'industrialization of culture'. My reading of the Gramscian text in these areas suggests that in many ways Gramsci's thought parallels that of critical theory in Germany of the 1930s, which is generally known as Frankfurt School critical theory. In my working definition of German critical theory of the 1930s, I include, however, not only Horkheimer, Adorno, Marcuse, Pollock, Lowenthal and others who are usually associated with the Institute for Social Research in Frankfurt, but also theorists and intellectuals who were not or only intermittently connected with that institute, intellectuals like Bloch and Brecht and Benjamin.[12] Part of this presentation is intended to indicate homological relations between Gramsci and the Frankfurt School, but also and again to evoke the complexity of Gramsci's *Prison Notebooks*.

Relating Gramsci's problematization of the effects of technologization and rationalization on the modern life-world to critical theory I found to be a fascinating task for a variety of reasons. For one, critical theory, as it evolved in the 1930s, in exile, as well as in the later post-war era of the 1960s, had made it its province to study critically the effects of rationalization on culture, society, the individual, values and knowledge, focusing in particular on problems of domination, alienation and reification of the modern life-world. And many of the themes and theoretical issues which are in general attributed to critical theory in these areas are indeed present in Gramsci's work. Let me cite a few examples: the way the young Gramsci critiques, as a theatre critic and cultural critic in Turin, the rise of the culture industry around World War I; the way in which he understands the cultural politics of the hegemonic social class, the gradual industrialization of culture, the increasing regulation, manipulation, surveillance and domination of the public and the private spheres; his theory of consciousness or of the subject, which points to his awareness of alienation and reification when it comes to the bourgeois subject, but which he apparently rejects when it comes to the proletariat; his theory of the political potentials inscribed in new technologies; his theory of human nature, his ontology so to speak, where humans always throughout the ages strive for freedom, displaying, thereby, an inherent principle of hope; and so on. While many of Gramsci's theoretical concerns parallel those of the critical theory of the Frankfurt School, not much of that parallel has been taken into account in the critical community. One of the few theorists who senses selective affinities between Gramsci and critical theory is Alfred Schmidt. In his *History and Structure* he has no doubts that Gramsci operates in the same theoretical, epistemological, critical sphere, as far as the 'objective content' of his work is concerned, as the critical theory of the 1930s: of Horkheimer and Adorno, and of Marcuse.[13]

It is not my intention to correct received intellectual histories of the twentieth century, to separate Gramsci from the Marxist crowd in order to identify him exclusively with German critical theory. Nor is it my intention to argue that Gramsci, who is of the same generation, roughly, as the founders and major representatives of critical theory of the 1930s, has not been given his due when it comes to his influence on or his anticipation of critical theory. 'Influence' is surely not an appropriate term in that configuration. 'Anticipation' may be applicable but should be used with care. It is difficult to say why the Gramsci/Frankfurt School paradigm did not get off the ground. In France, where Gramsci's works have been published and where they have had an impact, Althusser can acknowledge his debt to Gramsci, though not everyone seems to acknowledge the impact of Gramsci's conceptuality on their theories – I am thinking of Michel Foucault.[14] And in Britain, theorists like Raymond Williams readily speak of ways of seeing which they adopted from Gramsci, the most famous of which is possibly Williams' 'structure of feeling'.[15] In western Germany, where the critical theory of the Frankfurt School helped to enable an entire generation to take a critical stance towards cultural and social domination, many of the studies published on Gramsci and in the spirit of critical theory tend to study Gramsci against the register of Marxism, and not against the register of Frankfurt School critical theory.[16] In Italy, Gramsci's former leadership of the Italian working-class movement and his political theories have overshadowed, perhaps understandably, the various approaches to his work. While the Italian theoretical landscape in the 1960s and well into the 1970s owes much to the writings of the Frankfurt School, as does the German scene, and while Italian theory, perhaps due to its marginal and disempowered status in the global theory business, is occasionally more responsive to novel approaches and new connections, few attempts were made to retrieve Gramsci from an interpretive paradigm that validates only traditional Marxist associative relations, and to bring Gramsci into the vicinity of Frankfurt School critical theory.[17] In studies on Gramsci originating in non-hegemonic cultures – such as Latin America, where it seems to be more relevant than in the occidental academic world not merely to talk emancipation but to find conceptual and strategic ways of practising it, to resist power and domination – Gramsci's concepts, with all their potential, are expediently homologized with other forms of resistance theory or political theory.[18] And in some of the feminist searches for ways of challenging imposed structures of domination, Gramsci has been mobilized – in the company of other critical theorists – to support the feminist cause.[19]

If there has been, for whatever reason, a certain resistance to relating Gramsci to Frankfurt School critical theory, then that resistance should not keep us from investigating what insisting on such a relation might reveal. Gramsci and the Frankfurt School theorists probably never met. They probably never read each other's work. After their publication, following World War II, Gramsci's works and concepts are hardly, if at all, referred to by representatives of Frankfurt School critical theory.[20] Yet these factors should not prevent exploration. When apparently incongruous times and figures are placed next to each other, contemporary critical styles reveal more than they conceal. To deal with Gramsci, loosely, in the context of the Frankfurt School critical theory, in the context of modernism, is apposite. It helps to examine the contours of Gramsci's non-modernism as well, the ways in which he goes beyond modernism, and the possible applicability of some of his terms for a postmodern agenda.[21] Yet before we catapult Gramsci's conceptuality into the vicinity of the postmodern, before we investigate his penchants for structural linguistics and a phenomenological critical theory, not dissimilar to theoretical efforts we usually associate with post-World War II critical phenomenological theory in France, perhaps with Barthes and Merleau-Ponty, and before we interrogate some of his conceptualities in terms of their usefulness for our time and the issues that mostly concern us now, such as feminism and theories of power, I find it useful to probe some of Gramsci's views on industrialization of culture, against the background of the Frankfurt School. That Gramsci is sometimes commensurate with Lenin or Lukács surely cannot mean that he is not at times commensurate with other theories, and other times, as well.

In chapters 2 and 3 I discuss Gramsci's ways of leaving traditional Marxist aesthetics behind, of crossing modernist thresholds when paying attention not so much to the producer of a text, but to the receiver or the consumer of literary as well as cultural texts. What emerges from Gramsci's pages in the *Prison Notebooks* is sometimes, as in the case of his notes on Manzoni, a reading subject, who often knows what he/she wants and who refuses to be told what to want. Manzoni cannot impose his ideas on to the common people. The importance of the reception of the work of art, which marks Gramsci's aesthetic programme in general, anticipates, in some ways, Walter Benjamin's essay on 'Literaturgeschichte und Literaturwissenschaft' [Literary History and Critical Literary Studies], in which he argues for the need to understand a work of art not so much as a product of its time, but rather to interrogate it in terms of what it can show about the moment of its reception. Gramsci indeed fulfils the requirements of Benjamin's 'literary strategos', or of Horkheimer's 'critical theorist', for that matter, when he examines the work of art in terms of the social dynamics it resists or elicits, unravels or silences at the moment of its reception. What also emerges from Gramsci's pages is the notion of a culture industry, of the production and manipulation of needs and desires, of consuming subjects that are unable to define their needs, subjected to the powers that manipulate the public into acceptance of a static status quo. In this Gramsci anticipates later essays on the culture industry written by Adorno and Marcuse. There is, in addition, in the Gramscian text a discussion of perspectivism when it comes to a theory of truth, not dissimilar to Horkheimer's attempts in that area, and to the critique of the Vienna Circle enacted by the Frankfurt School. A critique of objectivity and truth is also at issue in Gramsci's discussion of social and cultural identity. There are glimpses, for instance, of the necessity of the 'inferior other' in the structuration of identity, which Gramsci relates to the need of the occidental world to conceive of the orient in the way it does, as an inferior other. In this he begins to problematize, long before Edward Said and contemporary theories of progressive anthropology, the predominant Eurocentricity in disciplines and knowledge.

So in the unsystematicity of his texts, Gramsci produces many theoretical insights which, whether they anticipate or not some of the work of the Frankfurt School, still enable us to establish points of contact between Gramsci and the Frankfurt School critical theory, particularly in the area of epistemology, theories of knowledge and the structuration of culture in modernity. Yet there are also moments in which Gramsci does not achieve the level of theoretical sophistication of the Frankfurt School. For instance, Gramsci's notion of the subject contains a configuration which separates or differentiates one collective subject from another collective subject, the proletariat and the non-proletariat respectively. The effects of the modernization of the life-world, of the industrialization of cultural and social spheres, are different for each group. From Gramsci's discussion of the playwright Pirandello it becomes clear that he tends to view reification and alienation, key concepts of the Frankfurt School in their analysis of modernity, not as intersubjectively valid experiences, perhaps known to people of all social classes as high capitalism moves towards late capitalism. Rather, here he seems to assume that the increasing rationalization of processes of economic and cultural production in modernity, intensifying experiences of alienation and reification, has the power to exempt some social groups, the non-bourgeois, while surely overpowering others. There is, then, in Gramsci's account of modernity, no clear-cut picture of how he conceives the structures of the life-world of the proletariat. Yet there is some indication, particularly in his essay on 'Americanism and Fordism', that he did not fully consider or accept reification as a by-product of rationalization.

It should be pointed out here that the generally acknowledged unsystematicities of Gramsci's texts do not lend themselves readily to pinning Gramsci down on specific issues. This is the more apparent when comparing Gramsci's treatment of problems with that of the members of the Frankfurt School, who often produce well-organized, disciplined and persuasive arguments. However, the trajectory of Gramsci's concepts can sometimes be made out. His concept of subjectivity, for instance, remains constant, throughout his writing, in its problematic relation to reification and alienation. It is not a universalizable concept, but contingent on particular social groups. His concept of technology, on the other hand, displays a distinct evolutionary trajectory. The younger Gramsci, the one of the pre-prison years, differs theoretically from the Gramsci of the *Prison Notebooks* when it comes to the application of modern technologies in the cultural sphere. While Gramsci rejected the cinematic apparatus in the writings of his Turin years around World War I, judging it negatively as a mode of cultural production designed hegemonically to manipulate and control the production of desire, he examines the cinema later, in his *Prison Notebooks*, around 1930, in terms of its technological potential for the production of a counter-hegemony. In this he is close to Benjamin (of the mid-1930s) and Brecht who, in contradistinction to Adorno and Marcuse, had welcomed new technological apparatuses and examined their potential for the production of meanings capable of challenging the status quo. It is indeed Gramsci's interest in and critical assessment of communicative processes, and in the deployment of technologies in these processes, which establishes his difference from the Frankfurt School. Or to put it differently: while Gramsci meets Frankfurt School critical theorists on many different grounds, while he anticipates some of their ideas and while he lags behind them in others, he also seems to differ from them in important ways. For his ways of seeing and examining problems do not neglect to take into account theoretical insights stemming from linguistic theories and structural linguistics, which leads him to examine the micro-conditions for the production of meaning in communicative processes, the structure of language, that is.

As is the case with Gramsci's concept of technology, his concept of communicative practice also evolves over a period of time. It is well known that Gramsci was a student of linguistics at the University of Turin before World War I. Yet his training or expertise in this area is not so apparent in his critical writings from his pre-prison years. Rather, his preoccupation with notions of the speech act, with performance, with productive readings of texts, as in his discussion of Dante, his penchant for a theoretical understanding of the production of meaning, notions of sign and signification which I find not in the early Gramsci but in the Gramsci of the *Prison Notebooks*, suggest that some experiences differentiate the older from the younger Gramsci. By the 1930s, Gramsci's texts had begun to shift from focusing on ideas and the power of the state to discussing their production, the production of hegemony, a move which involved him in investigating systems of signification and communication, and confronting the materiality of language. This tangential shift, however interstitially located in the unsystematicities of Gramsci's *Prison Notebooks*, reveals not Gramsci's complicity with Croce and idealism, as has often been assumed, or with Leninism and Lenin's notion of hegemony (though he does owe much to these two ways of seeing as well), but rather, I think, glimpses of an understanding of modernity which was maturing and continuously evolving as it made ready to find ways to counter, with ever-increasing complexities of conceptual apparatus and method, the ever-increasing complexity of rationalizing processes and structures of the modern life-world.

What chapters 3 and 4 then also indicate are Gramsci's shifts from an earlier lukewarm acceptance of forms of modernism, or a one-dimensional repudiation of it, to a position which superbly adjusts the tools of dialectical thinking to modernity. Indeed, the homologies between Gramsci and the Frankfurt School culminate in Gramsci's dialectical view of the dangers and the potentials of modernity. While

17

the younger Gramsci rejects many aspects of the modernist venture, by the time he is arrested, in 1926, and when he finally is allowed to do research and writing in prison, by 1929, he tends to have a more differentiated and matured view on what the critical potentials of modernist forms of cultural production might be. That differentiated view also includes a sensitivity to processes of signification which involves attention to linguistic and communicative structures and processes. I am not going to speculate in this book as to the biographical reasons for some of Gramsci's indubitable shifts, which would distinguish the older Gramsci from the younger one, and which would establish Gramsci as an early master, or an anticipator of a dialectical-structuralist merger. For one thing, I have not done the necessary research to warrant such speculations, and for another, I am not certain that much research in that area, on which I could have relied, has been done.[22] But let me say this: in the period from 1918 to 1926, Gramsci had a wide range of experiences. He had been one of the major leaders of the Italian working-class movement, not only organizing political struggles but, as editor of a major journal, the *Ordine Nuovo*, functioning as an organizer of the cultural and ideological struggle as well. He had been one of the top functionaries of the international working-class movement, which accorded him the privilege to intervene personally in strategic decisions at the centre of the international revolution: in Moscow.[23] Apart from this, and given his interest in cultural institutions such as the press, the media and the theatre, it is possible that he had had some encounters with the most advanced theories and performances in the realm of theatre and film during his stay in Moscow (May 1922–November 1923). The period 1922–4 in Moscow means the years of cultural and theoretical tension and excitement, the decline of the Proletkult, Sergei Eisenstein getting ready for his *Potemkin*, Vladimir Mayakovsky with his poetry, his plays, his left review *Lev*. The Moscow of these years also means the Russian formalist school with Victor Shklovsky, and the beginnings of Russian structuralism with Roman Jakobson. It means the era when many Soviet intellectuals – such as Bakhtin or Vološinov, to name but the now most famous ones – embarked on what I would like to call dialectical-linguistic-structuralist journeys, attentive to combining the synchronic with the diachronic in studies of the operations of consciousness and the production of ideology and counter-ideology.[24] It is also possible that Gramsci had the opportunity to continue his apprenticeship in 'dialectical-structural' thinking while sojourning in Vienna (December 1923–May 1924). Since there is some talk

18

of a possible encounter with Lukács, there might have been encounters with other theorists as well who experimented with a dialectical and pre-structuralist or structuralist merger.[25] And given the fact that his friend Piero Sraffa, who is known among Gramsci scholars for loyally providing Gramsci with much of his reading material while in prison, was later to have some close contacts with Wittgenstein in Britain, it is not out of the question that Gramsci could have been, in spite of his active political schedule, in contact in Vienna via Piero Sraffa with linguistically and structurally inclined intellectual and artistic circles, including those around Wittgenstein. It is surely possible that Gramsci had been exposed to the most advanced theoretical discourses on technological innovations in the arts and the avant-gardes of the time. Trotsky, after all, had written to him about futurism, and the answer Gramsci provides indicates a sophisticated and balanced view of the limits and potentials of this avant-garde movement which Gramsci knew very well.[26] Gramsci's prison notes on architecture in the context of modernism and rational planning, for instance, where he supports a moderate rather than radical functionalism, I find extremely interesting in relation to the fact that urban planning, as it was theorized and partially experimented with in Vienna in the early to mid-1920s, distinguishes itself from the more radical functionalism of the Gropius School: the urban planners in Vienna pursued, under a liberal city government, a moderate functionalism in architecture which did not impose rational and functional living spaces devoid of all ornament on the working class, but respected the differentials in the 'structure of feeling', or the 'structures of taste' of various social classes, and incorporated, therefore, received ornamental elements and spatial arrangements that allowed for traditional spatial experiences in architectural designs.[27] It is not impossible that Gramsci was aware of these architectural experiments in people-oriented functionalism carried out by progressive architects involved in urban planning in Vienna. Perhaps Gramsci was *au fait* with the latest developments in east and west when it came to the most advanced and challenging theories. Perhaps he was, as Marcia Landy suggests, 'no doubt aware that Lenin had discussed literature, and especially film, as part of the vanguard of revolutionary change, and possibly how Walter Benjamin had examined the role of newspapers and film in revolutionary and counter-revolutionary terms'.[28]

BEYOND THE MODERN: LINGUISTICS AND PHENOMENOLOGY

I have made it my purpose, in chapters 3 and 4, to show parallels of various kinds between German critical theory, primarily from the 1930s, and Gramsci's intermittent notes on aspects of modernization and technologization as they affect society and culture. While Gramsci theorizes the impact of modern technology on cultural production in ways that are often reminiscent of the Frankfurt School and those intellectuals who loosely identify with critical theory, Gramsci differs from that tradition on one crucial count: his interest in and knowledge of linguistics, which, along with his attention to the phenomenological interaction between language and the structure of the life-world, bring him close to those forms of critical theory that we know from the Soviet Union as well as from France. The names and concepts I would like to evoke in that context are in particular Vološinov, as he is known to us for his theory of ideology based on the sign, as well as Roland Barthes' semiology and theories of reading, and finally Maurice Merleau-Ponty, with his phenomenological theory of perception. I argue then, in chapter 5, and on the basis of Gramsci's literary analysis of Canto X of Dante, that this possibly 'insignificant' piece of literary scholarship develops a theory of reading and interpretation with great relevance for those modern schools of thought where a theory of the sign and of perception intersect. In this, Gramsci moves in the orbit of both pre-war and post-war critical theory, reflecting on linguistic and structuralist issues which would not move centre stage until the 1950s and 1960s. My intention is not, however, to speak of a Gramsci who anticipated theories of the later twentieth century, or to catapult him out of the modernist into the postmodernist camp. Nor do I intend to neutralize the political, the critical content of Gramsci's concepts. By aligning him with theories or intellectual positions that range from Barthes and Vološinov to the later Merleau-Ponty, I am interested in pointing to Gramsci's sensitivity to and complex interactions with questions of semiotics, linguistics and phenomenology. I think that this aspect of Gramsci's critical theory has often been marginalized, and sometimes even eliminated, in those studies that either emphasize his place in the history of western Marxism, or examine his conceptual apparatus in the context of political and social theory. By discussing Gramsci's nascent semiotics, his proto-structuralist understanding of linguistics, his relational-pragmatic dialogics, as well as his tangentially phenomenological perception of processes of knowing, I am interested both in balancing the Gramscian account and pointing to the difficulty and complexity of the Gramscian texts. What I would like to see emerge is an appreciation of the complexity of the *Prison Notebooks*, of Gramsci's conceptual framework, which squarely situates him in the context not only of modernist problematics, but also tangentially – albeit inadvertently on his part – of some postmodernist problematics as well.

It should not come as a surprise to anyone, however, that when Gramsci engages in a set of problematics which we might identify as 'postmodern', when he examines the structures of language relative to the conditions of possibility for enunciation, and the production of meaning, then it is not in order to stake out the boundaries of linguistic processes but rather to interrogate the conditions of the operations of hegemonic processes in the production of meaning. What is also important for Gramsci, in this context, is to guarantee that freedom of movement in enunciation which is crucial for the construction of counter-hegemony, be it imagistic, conceptual, or linguistic. I indicate, therefore, in my discussion in chapter 5, how Gramsci examines the structure of interpretation of a literary text. In Gramsci's analysis, the reader's production of meaning is pre-ordained, contained and conditioned by the structural and semiotic elements of the text, thereby being rendered unable to produce alternative meanings. While Gramsci could have extended this insight to all knowledge-producing processes, thereby potentially embracing a structuralist cause, he stops quite abruptly short of such an inference. There is no indication as to why he does this. Yet it is clear from his way of creating a world for himself in prison, from his insistence on the need and possibility of autonomously producing images and imagistic objects in prison, that the imagistic and enunciative freedom of movement of individuals, or of the subject, is of utmost importance to him. For this reason I dedicate the second part of chapter 5 to a brief discussion of the phenomenology of the prison-world in which Gramsci lived.

What I discuss in that section is Gramsci's attempt to remain always in a position that allows him to produce meaning. The production of meaning is contingent on a relation between a subject and an object, which a subject achieves by a conscious or intentional entertainment of relations with an object. Gramsci often indicates a need for objects with which to begin to entertain and to continue a relation. By citing letters I show how Gramsci insists on the interaction with the largest possible number of phenomena surrounding him, as if he

21

senses that the moment in which he forfeited such relational interaction would see him reduced to a simple I, no longer speaking as a subject, no longer producing meaning, no longer meaningfully living. Often Gramsci is adamant about stating who he is and what he experiences, contrary to what his correspondents (most often Tatiana and Giulia Schucht) think he experiences and how he feels. This insistence on the validity of his own portrayal or perception of his life-world in prison, on the value of his consciousness, his subjectivity, his way of seeing things as they emerge from his position in and interaction with his life-world, and aided by his immense propensity for seeing detail in the presence and absence of relations, as well as his insight into the impact of detail and relationality on the production of meaning and value, all of this places Gramsci, I think, with little qualification, in the vicinity of Merleau-Ponty's phenomenological project.

TOWARDS A 'DIFFERENTIAL PRAGMATICS'

If chapters 2 to 5 of this book place Gramsci in the context of a series of twentieth-century critical theories, the last two chapters are designed to examine the possible usefulness of Gramsci's thinking in the context of contemporary critical theory. In so far as I hold the position that many of Gramsci's ideas have evolved as responses to the problems and complexities of his own time and place, I do not view Gramsci's text as 'a manual', to borrow Anne Showstack Sassoon's term, from which to extract ready-made concepts for a contemporary critical theory responsive to political questions of power and domination in our place and our time.[29] Rather, what I would like to adopt in the last two chapters is not Gramsci's response to a particular set of problems, but the structure of his response. I understand that structure first of all as Gramsci's way of seeing and assessing problems of power and domination, of doing analysis, and of critically developing that analysis in his critical theory. By way of example I discuss his analysis of intellectual activities and functions, his theory of the 'intellectual'. The structure of Gramsci's theory of the intellectual I understand, and this I would like to emphasize, as a political and historical response, as a response to the power relations in Italian society and culture during what we might roughly call the modernist era. I would like not only to examine the structure of Gramsci's analysis and theory of the intellectual, but also to explore the possibility of pragmatically adjusting, altering, negotiating, transforming that structure to meet our political challenges and to experiment with analytical and theoretical frameworks that respond to relations of power and domination in our place and our time. In this context I would like to propose the minimal contours of a new critical project, and a new critical practice. This practice I would like to name 'differential pragmatics'.

Beginning to trace the possibilities of a 'differential pragmatics' in the context of chapter 6 means that this chapter represents a break with the previous three chapters. While chapters 3, 4 and 5 were designed to examine some of the homologies between Gramsci's thought and major critical theories of the 'modern' era, to suggest multiple relations between his thinking and many forms of critical theory including neo-Marxism, Frankfurt School modernism, Marxist linguistics and critical phenomenology, chapter 6 and the concluding chapter 7 probe the possibilities of experimenting with some of Gramsci's categories in response to political questions in what is often called the 'postmodern' era. No doubt, the practice of 'differential pragmatics' is inspired by the structure of Gramsci's critical projects, and it is for this purpose that I delineate the four major models of his analysis and theory of the intellectual in his various writings. However, 'differential pragmatics' is also an attempt to go beyond Gramsci. Against the background of many different theoretical models, which include Lyotard's position as propounded in his *The Postmodern Condition*, as well as Habermas' notion of a universal pragmatics, I attempt to outline some of the political questions that seem to be important for us as intellectuals as we enter the 1990s.[30] So chapter 6 briefly examines intellectual activities in the western hegemonic spheres in their relation to the presence and absence of global power, intellectual functions in their relation to developed and developing cultures and societies, that is. Chapter 7 briefly focuses on the notion of power with respect to feminism, and concludes my first tentative exercise in 'differential pragmatics'.

Gramsci's analysis of relations of power and the function intellectual activities perform in the complexity of these relations leads him to formulate a theory of the intellectual. This theory contains four major models. I have enumerated them as 'The traditional intellectual: artist, philosopher, poet' (Model 1), 'The "structure of feeling" and "intellectual community"' (Model 2), 'The "organic intellectual", the "new intellectual", the "critical specialist"' (Model 3) and 'The "universal intellectual"' (Model 4). With Model 1 Gramsci accounts for the presence in Italian society of intellectuals who, particularly as public figures, as academics, artists and publishers, represent moral and ideological positions in the cultural sphere. As such, they incorporate instances of power. This Gramscian model is not unrelated to both an idealist and a Marxist account of the social function and political possibilities of the intellectual. It speaks of the non-neutrality of ideas and knowledge, of the partiality, that is, of the producers and disseminators of knowledge, of the political role of the intellectual as part of a system of relations that is inscribed by power and domination. Model 2 is in my view the most complex and simultaneously most productive Gramscian account of intellectuality. I have used the terms 'structure of feeling' and 'intellectual community' in order to describe this model. In some ways it theorizes the conditions of possibility of mobilizing 'traditional intellectuals' for the democratic cause. Yet it also analyses the conditions of possibility of mobilizing resistance to democratic change, not only on the part of the intellectuals as a sociological group, but also, and more importantly, on the part of the subaltern social groups. These conditions of possibility are constituted by various substrata and subsystems of intellectual activities within class society, activities which are carried out in churches, in educational institutions, in cultural spheres, and which arouse the 'spontaneous' consent of large masses of subaltern social groups to the social and political and cultural inequities of the status quo. Doctors, pharmacists, teachers, priests and all sorts of professionals and semi-professionals take part, so Gramsci found in his analysis of social relations, in the dissemination of values and ideas that support inequities in relations of power and, with their partial propounding of how things are and why, legitimate the interests of one social class over another. With their value-laden intellectual activities, they produce hegemony and reproduce the status quo. The effectiveness of the legitimatory activities of the semi-professionals in a complex of relations is contingent on the corporeal proximity of various social bodies. In the practices of everyday life, the impoverished and exploited peasants of southern Italy encounter the priest or the pharmacist, and it is in these dialogic encounters, where the parties do not speak a common language but share a 'dialect' or some elements of a common 'structure of feeling', that the priest or the pharmacist proposes a world-view which the peasants find difficult to negotiate, given the privilege and prestige the priest and the pharmacist embody in their respective community. In this sense, the semi-professional strata mediate between the masses of the people and the predominant class, and without their mediation in the cultural and

24

social realm political hegemonization would remain an empty project. Yet political counter-hegemony can be produced on the same
grounds and by way of similar structures. If the dialogic encounter
between the professionals and the subordinate social classes is always
also an encounter where one world-view, that which legitimates
unequal social relations, triumphs due to the prestige attached to the
social power embodied in the professionals and their institutions, a
different view of social relations which does not legitimate unequal
social relationships can also be advanced. Yet Gramsci does not
suppose that it is only the intellectuals who can work to promote such
a relation. Every person, so he finds, is capable of such reasoning, in
as much as every person is a philosopher and a legislator at once, one
who has the power, in the practices of everyday life, to propose views,
to impose them on others, to insist on imposing them, or to refuse to
impose them. This universal condition of exchange of ideas and
values is at issue in Gramsci's account of the 'universal intellectual',
which I named Model 4.

Model 3 expounds a notion of the intellectual which is fairly well
known in the Gramsci community. I am referring to the 'organic
intellectual'. Gramsci differentiates between at least three forms of
organic intellectuality. In that every major social and economic formation produces its intellectuals, among other things functioning as
legitimators of values and of the conditions on which an economic and
social formation rests, feudalism and capitalism as well as socialism
have each produced a category of organic intellectuals. For his own
era, moving towards a form of high capitalism challenged by the
working-class movement, Gramsci distinguished two forms of organic intellectuality. I shall give these the titles 'new intellectual' and
'critical specialist'. The new (also 'organic') intellectual of capitalist
formations is a specialist, a technocrat who knows his or her role but
not necessarily how that role is related to other aspects of a complex
system of relations. The critical specialist, on the other hand, is able to
understand his or her activity as a partial activity, yet in addition the
critical specialist understands that precisely because the activity is
partial, it is related to other activities in a system of social, political
and economic relations.

To what extent the four Gramscian models of intellectuality outlined above are useful for analysing relations of power in our societies
in the west, and for formulating practices that challenge these
relations, is the main point at issue in the second part of chapter 6. It
also provides the title for that chapter, 'Gramsci's intellectual and the

age of information technology'. Since I hold that Gramsci's time and place are not identical with ours, so that a good deal of his cultural theory responds to his time rather than to ours, I present a brief descriptive account of our time in order to provide at least some terms for distinguishing Gramsci's time from ours. This involves a schematic view of the major transformations marking western society as it apparently moves from predominant forms of industrialization towards what has been called informatization. Indeed, it has been argued that a 'mode of information' has displaced a 'mode of production'.[31] What emerges from my schematic view is that processes of transnationalization in the area of finance and production have apparently led to the installation of a global assembly-line effectively organized with the help of information technology. Moreover, the transnationalization of production and its organization, while expanding into many regions of the developing world, contracts under the control of a few financial centres in the developed world. Since informatization, the production and dissemination of information and knowledge, appears to further this process of economic transnationalization and financial contraction, strengthening the western advanced capitalist and informatized nations while weakening the developing world, I raise the critical question as to how we, as producers and disseminators of knowledge and information in the west, relate to these forms of hegemonic power. I also entertain the question of how minimally to challenge these relations from a democratic point of view, against the background of Lyotard's understanding of the ubiquity and irresistible presence of global power and Habermas' model of universal pragmatics.

There is good reason to believe, with Lyotard, that the symbolic realm, increasingly colonized by all-pervasive and powerful transpersonal communicative apparatuses, succumbs to the determinative laws of the system itself. Hereby all action, the material as well as the linguistic, cognitive and ethical, inexorably moves within the orbit of an informatized technological order directed by no one but the systemic and self-regulative nature of the system itself. In this scenario, we as western intellectuals cannot but reproduce the inherent laws of the system when engaging in the reproduction and dissemination of knowledge. Yet there is also reason to believe, with Habermas, as well as with the experiential knowledge tied to feminist practices, that the symbolic realm participates not only in the production of actions or practices but also in their suppression. The symbolic production of practices and their suppression are not necessarily

26

interlaced with the determinations of self-regulative systems. In his theory of communicative action, Habermas distinguishes between system and life-world. Each sphere produces, enables and delimits specific sets of action. Whereas the system produces and enables action contexts which resemble Lyotard's assessment of self-regulated and integrated action contexts, whereby individual choice and action become obsolete, the life-world is capable, according to Habermas, of producing contexts in which agents meet in order to negotiate differences and inequalities against the background of a reciprocally accepted normativity. In Lyotard's interpretation, the systemic and all-pervasive nature of power makes it difficult for producers of knowledge to put up any real or meaningful resistance. In that sense most intellectuals are implicated in this state of affairs. Habermas' theoretical model does take into account the systemic nature of power. A self-regulative system orders functions and positions unaffected by and independent from individual preferences, choices and actions. The subject disappears in these systems of relations. Yet Habermas also reserves a realm from which to challenge inequities. It is a realm of dialogics, of social, political, cultural and private interaction, where, against the background of a communicative ethic, individuals negotiate their needs and desires.

Lyotard's assessment of the systemic nature of power is useful. It points to the global extent of the hegemonic structure and the function information technology fulfils in that inexorable extension. I propose that a contemporary theory of the intellectual will examine the limits and the possibilities of this scenario for intellectual activities. With Gramsci, for instance, we can raise the question of whether technology exclusively determines our intellectual activities and our function in the hegemonic global structure, or whether information technology can be examined in terms of its applicability for challenging the global hegemonic net. The 'Community Memory' movement, as it is under way in various parts of the USA, points to immense possibilities of democratic communication, of ways of challenging the inequities that currently exercise hegemony. If information technology has participated in hegemonically structuring global relations, it should be interrogated in terms of its powerful potentials for democratically restructuring these global relations.[32] Examining those potentials and experimenting with information technology I consider an important aspect of a critical theory of the intellectual. There are already some signs that via Deep Dish tv and satellites, alternative ways of seeing and evaluating things will soon be, if they are not already, available to and retrievable by any global tv set. Free computer terminals, with information data bases on issues relevant to democratic communities, will enable electronically monitored dialogic interaction between the most diverse and geographically distanced cultural groups, communities and individuals. In addition, a contemporary critical theory of the intellectual activities and functions between the developed and developing world can experiment with the formulation of a new dialogic model. This model I do not see as a 'universal pragmatic', but as a 'differential pragmatic'.

Habermas' 'universal pragmatic' focused on the possibility of negotiating differences against the background of a universally accepted communicative ethics. The agents Habermas had in mind were mostly citizens involved in the societies and cultures of western advanced industrialized and informatized nations. In this sense Habermas positions himself in the western developed world. What I, in contradistinction, propose are the practices of a 'differential pragmatics'. These investigate the possibility of telecommunicatively and electronically mediated dialogic interactions and negotiations not exclusively between individuals or groups in the western world. A contemporary critical theory of intellectuals would, so it seems to me, examine the possibilities of dialogic interaction between western and non-western individuals alike. It would investigate and help to coordinate the technological possibilities of listening to and reading and seeing non-western points of view, and of processing information and knowledge which challenge, from a non-western perspective, hegemonic power relations. Critical theory of intellectuality as well as critical theory in general, it seems to me, will be critical to the extent that it interrogates its function in a gradual hegemonization of the global life-world. As information technology exponentially increases these processes of hegemonization, it simultaneously exponentially increases possibilities of global democratization. *Pace* all pessimistic predictions, there is still, I would contend, an opportunity for critical thinking to challenge forms of power and domination. The *quid pro quo* of such a challenge is the critical use of information technology and knowledge of the ways in which it can be applied to counter global hegemony.

In lieu of a conclusion, I briefly discuss Gramsci's relation to feminism, feminist theory and women. As a critical feminist, I find it difficult not to engage in such a discussion. In this context I point to Gramsci's problematic relationship to two women, Tatiana Schucht and Giulia Schucht. Yet I also point to Gramsci's fascinating microhistory of sexuality which he, long before Foucault, unearths in his archaeology of power. The centrality of sexuality in women's oppression is one of the aspects of Gramsci's understanding of the woman question. In this sense he anticipates the slogan of second wave feminism, 'the personal is political'. However, Gramsci tends to relate woman's inalienable rights of control over her body to processes of production and the rationalization of production. These, he reckoned, would play a role in future forms of sexuality, forms of disciplining the body, and a consciousness of these disciplines would encourage the formulation of specific sexual ethicalities. Contrary to Foucault, Gramsci does not understand the production of sexual ethics, or these discourses on sexuality, as discourses of power and domination. By participating in these discourses, agents reproduce, not as in Foucault's account, consent to the status quo, but the conditions for a social context that promises equality and freedom for men and women alike.

Foucault and Gramsci agree, however, on one issue: that power is not imposed from above, but that the operations of power and their success depend on consent from below. For both Foucault and Gramsci, power is produced and reproduced in the interstices of everyday life, and for both, power is ubiquitous. However, contrary to Foucault, Gramsci does not evoke the imagery of unqualifiable and unquantifiable ubiquities of power. If power is everywhere, it is not everywhere in the same form and to the same degree. Adjectives figure in Gramsci's account of powerful relations. The power a father exercises over his children is a specific form of power, paternal power, which is not identical with the disciplinary power the state exercises over the body via the institutions of police, army and law courts, and it is not identical with the disciplinary power that culture and society exercise over the mind. Some social groups possess more economic, social and cultural power than others, and since this imbalance of power is neither easily challenged nor readily changed, there is a directedness to power relations. So while Gramsci agrees with Foucault in his assessment of the ubiquity of power relations, he differs from him when he specifies the equally ubiquitous uneven relations of power. What I suggest then in the last few pages of my study is the usefulness of both Foucault and Gramsci for a feminist agenda. From Foucault we can learn for one thing that we are all implicated in power, that, in many ways, power is gender-blind. As well-to-do members of western economic and political communities, most of us women theorists and writers are in some ways implicated in the power these communities hold over the non-western and underdeveloped or developing parts of the world. From Gramsci's complex analyses we can adopt, on the other hand, the notion that we are indeed part of many different 'structures of feeling', of many different loci which inherently carry diverse functions and effects in relation to other sites of power or powerlessness. As members of the 'western structures of feeling' we are implicated in global power relations. As women of specific social classes, we are often discriminated against by the male establishment of a specific social class. As women of a privileged social class, we are less discriminated against than other women of less privileged social classes. As white women we belong to 'a structure of feeling' that enjoys privilege over and against non-white 'structures of feeling' or women's communities. Drawing relevant lessons from Gramsci and Foucault, we can engage and mobilize our feminist knowledge of power relations. As feminists, we can contribute to a broader analysis and understanding of global power relations. Feminist theory has been astute in deciphering microcosmic power relations: the way specific experiences, forms of knowledge, ways of seeing or epistemologies, ways of judging or ethics, have been silenced or marginalized or partially represented in the discursive and symbolic realm of our reality. These feminist insights, part of a body of knowledge which has been accumulated over the last two decades and which continues to expand, have the potential to become powerful tools in the deconstruction of global power relations. I hope that this book may encourage collaborative theoretical and practical efforts in the dismantling not only of power but also of the many forms and disguises of power, and may encourage critical thinking in the direction not only of a 'universal pragmatics' but also of a 'differential pragmatics'. I shall then have achieved much more than I originally set out to do.

Part II

FROM REALISM TO MODERNISM

2

To realism farewell: Gramsci, Lukács and Marxist aesthetics

CRITICAL PRACTICES

In a section entitled 'Questions of Method' in one of the prison notebooks dedicated to cultural problems, Notebook 16, Gramsci discusses methodological approaches to vast bodies of work of specific thinkers. I loosely paraphrase the argument. Some texts, so goes Gramsci's contention, do not offer systematic explanations as to the specific perspective or conception of the world of their respective author. If that is the case, the essential coherence of the author's world-view should not be sought in each individual text or in a series of texts but rather in the development of that entire body of work with all its various aspects, in which the elements of that conception tend to be implicit. And moreover, Gramsci argues that if a critic is out to study the beginnings or the genetic trajectory of that world-view, it would be wise to begin with preliminary work: with minute and detailed philological exegesis, undertaken with greatest care and to high standards of accuracy, with scientific integrity, and without partiality, preconceptions, prejudices and apriorisms. What critical work should seek in a text is not casual and individual affirmations, or disconnected aphorisms, but rather leitmotifs, the rhythms, the dynamics of thinking in motion, of specific texts. And there are many other suggestions, at times tending towards the pedantic, which Gramsci offers here as to how methodologically to approach a vast body of knowledge attributed to a single author.[1]

From the context of this note it appears that Gramsci was primarily thinking of a determinate body of knowledge, of the writings of Marx and Engels, that is, as well as of the obsessively anti-Marxist reception of these writings by a philosopher who represents the most eminent and influential figure in twentieth-century Italian cultural

33

history: Benedetto Croce. This is surely the way the initial editors of Gramsci's texts thought of it, when they included this note, in the first edition of Gramsci's works they put together, in the volume on historical materialism and the philosophy of Benedetto Croce.[2] For reasons that bypass Gramsci's obsession with Croce's obsession with Marxism, legitimate or understandable as both, one, or neither of these obsessions might be, this passage is extraordinarily suggestive to me. What I am referring to is its heuristic usefulness when it comes not only to Gramsci's own critical practices in relation to problems of knowledge, culture and society, but also to the way in which I would like to approach Gramsci's position in relation to critical theory. Let me first deal with the latter. At issue here are the leitmotifs in Gramsci's thinking, not only the rhythms of his thought but also the structures of his thinking in motion, of his narrative, in relation to Marxist aesthetics.

Until recently, until the mid- to late 1970s to be more precise, attempts to deal with Gramsci's aesthetics in general were somewhat problematic, judging from the apologetic tone in which studies of Gramsci's aesthetic theory regularly tended to be introduced. The post-war managers of the Gramsci trust, mostly located in Italy at the time, were not innocent in this state of affairs. They had announced, with not much ado, their position on the issue of Gramscian aesthetics when they emphasized in no uncertain terms the importance of Gramsci's writings for a systematic theory of politics, for ways of strategizing the trajectory of the Italian traditional left, and of legitimating the *terza via*, Italy's original third road to socialism. With this intransigence they had contributed to a climate of critical uncertainty when it came to the place and significance of Gramsci's aesthetics. The fragmentary and unsystematic nature of Gramsci's work composed in prison, an amalgam of notes, sketches, drafts, research plans, aphorisms, seemed particularly apparent when it came to poetic and aesthetic matters and did not facilitate the entire business. It seemed problematic to attempt an evaluation of Gramsci's aesthetic apparatus in the context of a self-contained, autonomous and organic theory of aesthetics, of the kind Croce had produced. Nor were they of much help when it came to indicating their place, proper or improper, at a distance from or in the vicinity of Gramsci's political, cultural, or economic theory. In short, the status of Gramsci's aesthetics was uncertain for almost three decades in the predominant Gramsci scholarship, and the legitimacy of the issue was timidly fought for in the cultural courts.[3] The rhetorics inscribed in Giuliano Manacorda's project, one of the first to attempt a more complete reconstruction of Gramsci's aesthetic fragments under the general heading of 'Marxism and literature', well indicates the concern and influence brought to bear on him and others, which they respectfully endured when insisting not only on Gramsci and Marxism, but also on a system of semi-autonomous literary aesthetics. He writes:

> The attempt to present Gramsci's writings on literature in and by themselves, in a complete and organic way is, no doubt, somewhat arbitrary. This is so for two reasons: Gramsci's ideas on literature are closely related to his entire intellectual production, such that a correct reading and interpretation of his writings on the subject would have to take into account his other writings, in particular his view on the relations that obtain between literature and other spheres of human activity. And secondly, it is problematical to assign his literary criticism to the critical-aesthetic realm exclusively, a procedure which has justifiably been criticized. While I am aware of the fact that a 'literary' approach to Gramsci's work renders inevitable some mutilation of his thought, I believe, none the less, that such a project is not illegitimate.[4]

And Sabine Kebir, an astute reader of the Gramscian text and extraordinarily knowledgeable when it comes to Gramsci's linguistic and literary theories, reveals through her choice of terms a tonality that confidently accommodates both a non-negotiable high pitch alliance between Gramsci's literary criticism and his strategy of popular front alliance politics, and a basic melody of the fragmentariness of Gramsci's research programme on aesthetics.

> Even though Gramsci indeed bequeathed to us fragments of an aesthetic programmatics, the greater part of his notes on culture and literature must be understood as part of an approach to cultural politics, as a result of his politics (or strategy) of alliance which he developed and practised before his imprisonment.[5]

Surely, things have changed rapidly since these words were written when it comes to discourses on unsystematicity and fragmentariness, on the autonomy or contingency of the aesthetic, both in relation to Gramsci and critical theory. And some things have not changed that much. Among the events which come readily to mind as effecting changes in critical demeanour next to many others that have played major and minor roles in the cultural transformations of critical practices are first, the advent of poststructuralism, and second, the publication of a new critical edition of Gramsci's prison writings issued in the mid-1970s, the so-called Gerratana edition. Let us first turn to the latter event. The Gerratana edition attempted to present most of Gramsci's prison writings in an edition which respects the original order and arrangement of Gramsci's notes. One effect of this was to show that the fragmentariness often attributed to Gramsci's research on aesthetics and literature surely also characterized his notes on political theory, cultural theory, philosophic theory and economic theory, to stay with his larger and in general more popular research programmes. Indeed, the first impression one gains from studying Gramsci's prison notes is that of being overwhelmed by the sheer quantity of research programmes Gramsci pursued in prison, by the way in which he proceeds, and by his manner of presenting his material. Deciphering Gramsci's fragmentariness is often not easy, nor are his language, his concepts, the structures and the motions of his thought. Most commentators have remarked on it, and I see no reason to break with this pattern. A recent publication puts it well:

> Any interpretation of the *Prison Notebooks* is faced with two difficulties. First, the scope of Gramsci's thought is far too wide for any specialist to assess his contribution.... Second, the *Prison Notebooks* consist of 2353 pages of unfinished notes, with no apparent order or overall structure.... Given, then, both the scope of the notebooks, and their unfinished and inconsistent character, the interpreter is put in the difficult position of evaluating the relevance of many passages whose meaning is obscured and of dealing with topics of which he or she knows little.[6]

The publication of Gramsci's prison notebooks, still unfortunately largely unavailable in non-Italian editions, surely then did not make things easier for interpreters of Gramsci's political or cultural theory.[7] It does clear up, though, the question of the textual unsystematicity in relation to Gramsci's aesthetics. And so does the other event I am about to mention: the rise and institutionalization of a new style in critical theory, poststructuralism.

In the course of this new critical practice many a hitherto cogent, rigorous and unified conceptual system was subjected to dissecting philological operations which would unearth unsuspected inconsistencies, contradictions, paradoxes and illogicalities of the dominant rhetoric informing the text. And many a text from disciplines which had insisted on validity claims, on referential meaning, on universal rationalities, logicalities and truths, was rigorously interrogated in terms of textual strategies which appeared to legitimate the tyranny of the concept of logocentricity, of the domination of one way of thinking over another. Ultimately, every textual performance, including rigorously structured philosophical and scientific texts, was seen as contextual, and as such contingent on the never-ending play of a never-ending chain of signifiers. The end of the identity of subject with object had arrived. The poststructuralist agenda is by now well known and I do not intend to explicate its assumptions, teleologies and programmes here. What matters rather is to indicate that the cultural climate of recent years as it manifests itself particularly in the discursive formations of postmodernism and poststructuralism allows for, or even welcomes, modes of rationalities which opt – in what is understood as a subversive gesture in relation to conceptual domination – for unsystematicities, disjunctures, discontinuities, fragmentariness. If a rigorously structured text such as Hegel's *Phenomenology* may be enlisted in the poststructuralist cause, in that it presumably narrates in and with its very narrative the inexorable structure of alienation, of fluid phenomenology, of non-substantive referentiality of all experience and deferring of meaning, it surely is not illegitimate to enlist a text the unsystematicity of which had already been successfully scrutinized for its possible usage in the destruction of received and 'systematic' bodies of knowledge, Marxism, non-Marxism and anti-Marxisms alike.[8] And if all disciplines, methods and modes of writing are ultimately texts that follow the arbitrariness of the sign, if all texts are kinds of writing that reveal metaphoricities and poeticities, the matter of writing, that is, then Gramsci's literary texts should not be differentiable from his non-literary texts, from his political, economic and cultural theories, that is.[9] The question of whether it is legitimate to speak of Gramsci's aesthetics as an intrinsic part of his vast body of work is thus no longer relevant. Indeed, as new critical practices stand on the brink of being entered into the data base of theoretical legitimacy, the question of the legitimacy of Gramsci's aesthetics, which seemed to inconvenience Manacorda in the 1970s, has, by the 1990s, in itself become illegitimate.

There is a third observation I should mention here. Notwithstanding poststructuralism but very much because of the new edition of Gramsci's writings in 1975, it has become obvious that in prison

Gramsci seems to return to aesthetic and literary matters. That is to say, what the *Prison Notebooks*, coupled with the publication of many of his *Letters from Prison*, reveal is that Gramsci in prison renewed interests which we know had occupied his youth and his years as a political journalist around World War I: his interests in linguistics, in literature, in theatre and the arts.[10] These interests are of long standing. As a student at the university of Turin, he had studied philology, literature and philosophy, subjects in the humanities and not in the natural sciences. When he first became involved in political activism, he left the university, yet he seemed always to have taken time to write on literary matters, and to work as a theatre critic. Clearly, during his most active political period, as one of the major leaders of the Italian working-class movement, he wrote on political matters. Yet after his incarceration, when he finally was allowed to spend some time writing, and when he decided on a research programme that was workable under prison conditions, he was quick to include literary and philological matters on his study list. Indeed, of the sixteen main arguments he outlines for his research project, more than a third pertain to literary and philological matters. And when, in 1931, after what is known to scholars as his physical and mental 'crisis', he shortens and condenses his study plans to ten arguments, literary and philological issues still constitute a third of his research programme.[11] So the Gerratana edition once and for all testified to the non-negotiable presence of literary and aesthetic matters in the Gramscian text. Manacorda's apologetics, though understandable, have lost their force. Yet there is something else this critic offers which has not lost its relevance for today. In one of his footnotes, from the margins so to speak, that attempts new readings of a text held zealously captive by the knights of the Gramscian Grail, he intuits, still respectfully, a potentially subversive record. It reads in translation something like this: 'One could though legitimately hold that [a study of Gramsci's literary writings], a partial study of his work [that is] should not prevent an integration of such a study into a larger discourse, into a larger unified and political discourse. In fact, such a study would prepare such a discourse [would become its condition of possibility].'[12] I will not comment here on this marginal yet radical message from the then critical underground, speaking of the literary conditions of political possibility, correcting the image of a political Gramsci in favour of a Gramsci whose literary, aesthetic and linguistic interests give shape and form to his political interests. There will be a place for that later on. What I will do here instead and first is commence my search for leitmotifs and rhythms of Gramsci's thinking, structures that graph Gramsci's relation to Marxist aesthetics.

PREDICAMENTS OF HISTORY

With this in mind, I have decided to place Gramsci next to a twentieth-century intellectual with whom he perhaps in multiple ways intersects: I am referring to Georg Lukács. He is, next to Adorno and Marcuse, but also next to Benjamin and Brecht, one of the major Marxist aestheticians of our century. His intransigent stance on aesthetics provoked, as mentioned in the introductory chapter above, the realism/expressionism debate.[13] One of the questions that I pursue is to what extent Gramsci developed new categories, new ways of seeing and understanding the literary and artistic process, how he advances, that is, Marxist aesthetics. So a brief balance sheet between Gramsci, and this most controversial Marxist aesthetician, Lukács, is in order. What makes this procedure particularly inviting is that on first sight, and indeed not then only, Lukács and Gramsci, these two extraordinarily important theoreticians of western Marxism, seem to display an impressive array of selective affinities.

Indeed, it has become a commonplace in much of the scholarship on twentieth-century Marxism to mention Gramsci next to Lukács and Korsch when speaking of the founding fathers of western Marxism. I follow this trend, in order not so much to reveal what is common to their respective Marxisms, but more to point to differences in their respective aesthetic theories. For who would want to distort that which speaks plainly from the historical record and suggest that Gramsci was primarily an aesthetician and literary critic, interested in questions of poetics and aesthetics, driven by issues of canon formation and literary heritage, obsessed with universal relations of aesthetics to ethics and ontology, or of the historical relation of literary genre, collective unconscious and economic production. This is what Lukács' interest for most of his life ultimately was. Gramsci was also and always interested in literature, but primarily he was a militant, a critical and pragmatic one, to boot. So to the extent that fate made him a political activist in Italy and not in some other country he organized his theoretical work around multiple problems concerning the factors that led to certain political configurations in Italy: the long prevention of Italy's unification; the events that led to its unification in 1870; the 'passive revolution', and the rise of fascism in the 1920s. Answers to these problems he sought in the study of the history of Italy and of the history of the Italian intellectuals, as also in the function of popular culture in its relation to official, or 'high', culture, and to fascism. Lukács approaches problems of realism and modernism as part of his overall philosophical and aesthetic system, which is his project of realism. Gramsci seems to approach the literary sphere both as part of his overall project and in relation to it. This project I would like to call, for lack of a better term, his philosophy of praxis. No doubt, Lukács organizes his work around an aesthetic and Gramsci around a cultural and political critique. And they both develop a theory: Lukács' is aesthetic, and Gramsci's is mostly cultural as well as political. Perhaps Lukács' research programme was to write the definitive Marxist aesthetics. And perhaps Gramsci's research programme was, if one is to judge from the current Gramsci scholarship, to write a definitive Marxist cultural theory. So if there seems to be a difference in the importance the literary and the aesthetic play in their overall research designs, and if there is, as we shall see in the next section, a radical difference in the way in which they conceive of and apply Marxist aesthetics, there is also a compelling similarity: both theoreticians deploy their skills in an attempt at mending Marxist theory in areas where it was most deficient and vulnerable. What I am referring to is the troubled and troubling relation of the superstructure to the infrastructure in Marx's metaphor, the paradox that haunts the nature of the relations of the forces of production to the relations of production. From its very inception, this metaphor was unsettling for an approach to Marxist aesthetics as well.

Marx's predominant metaphor figures history as a progressively and teleologically moving process and the historic moment as a dynamic structure in which an economic base (forces of production) dialectically relates to a social, cultural, political superstructure (relations of production). Though Marx and Engels merely interspersed and scattered unsystematic remarks on literature and art in their vast body of work, hardly a match, I would say, for their complex and systematic analyses of economic and historical processes as Marx addresses them in his *Capital*, and hardly comparable with Lukács' system of Marxist aesthetics, they were certain to assign a place to literature and art in their metaphor.[14] This assignment looks something like this: as part of the cultural sphere, where many forms of ideologies are produced, re-produced, maintained, legitimated, marginalized, and silenced, literature and art function in specific and in interested ways. As part of that cultural sphere, literature and art entertain relations not only with the philosophical sphere, with intellectual history, with the realm of ideas and the realm of consciousness, but also with the political, and ultimately with the economic as well. Literature and the arts, as part of the superstructural relations of production, function in the context of these relations. These relations produce ideological practices which legitimate the values and normativities of the social class in power, commanding the forces of production. In the context of capitalism, the bourgeoisie represents the social class in power. The ideological practices embedded in the relations of production are employed to wrap in mystery the most basic fact of capitalist economy: that one social group exploits another. However, since 'at a certain stage of their development, the material productive forces of society come into conflict with the existing relations of production', to quote Marx from the famous preface to the *Critique of Political Economy* (1859), initiating an epoch of social revolution, literature and art as part of these relations of production embody, figure and perhaps prefigure the tensions, contradictions and paradoxes inherent in the processes that relate superstructural legitimations to the material productive forces of society.[15]

There was a problem, though, in this narrative. The problem was not so much the purported nexus or the relationship between literature, culture, politics and economics: Marx's claim that the literary sphere did not function autonomously or independently from other spheres in society, that literature was a social practice. What presented a problem was not the relatedness of literature to other spheres of human practices, its sociality and politicality, but rather the more precise nature of the operations of that relationship. Caught in the cause and effect logic in spite of their rhetorics to the contrary, which would insist on a dialectics obtaining between the base and the superstructure, Marx and Engels were in this respect more of an obstacle than a help. The inventors of the Marxist metaphor tended ultimately to posit primary or first causes in historical motion, which would relegate the rest to a secondary, accidental, contingent and dependent status. Engels tends to stand squarely for one explanation, which posits the productive forces of society or the economic base as primary: 'In every historical epoch, the prevailing mode of economic production and exchange, and the social organization necessarily following from it, form the basis upon which is built up, and from which alone can be explained, the political and intellectual history of the epoch.'[16] Marx, particularly the early Marx, tends to favour a similar explanation, but less uncompromisingly. There are, however, textual sites where both spheres of the metaphor, the infra- as well as the superstructural, are, if essential, still inequitable partners in that relationship. In the above-mentioned preface to *A Contribution to the Critique of Political Economy*, he relates base (forces of production) and superstructure (relations of production) as follows:

> The sum total of these relations of production constitutes the economic structure of society, the real foundation, on which rises a legal and political superstructure and to which correspond definite forms of social consciousness. The mode of production of material life conditions the social, political and intellectual life process in general.[17]

This positing of the primacy of the material foundation of society, which seems non-negotiably to propose not only that, but how, base and superstructure are related, was ultimately more problematic than expedient for Marxist aesthetic theory.

Problems in Marxist aesthetics focused on such questions as the following. How does this relation between base and superstructure operate, what are its practices, its possibilities, its limits? If there is a definite connection between art and the totality of the relations of production, between art and the material base, what kind of a connection is it? What is the relation between art and social class? Is authentic art the art produced by the dominant class or by the ascending class? In what way do changes in production relations affect changes in art? If art embodies a site of ideology, does art anticipate new ideologies, new insights, new forms of knowledge, or does it, like Hegel's Owl of Minerva, always lag behind? What are the functions of the writer and artist? Should they merely artistically record what they see and feel, or should they consciously take part in the class struggle, opting for the interests and needs of the emergent class? What is the correct form of art? Can art, as ideology, affect relations of production, and thus power relations in society, or is it merely a passive reflection, unable to influence anything effectively? These and other questions would turn up regularly at the drawing boards of political activists and armchair Marxists alike, intent on complementing or correcting Marx in such matters. Classical Marxism was deficient when it came to examining the multiple ways in which the superstructure with its culture, politics and ideology relates to the base, beyond simply calling this relation dialectical, and it was deficient in examining the multiple ways in which culture and politics or the state produce ideology, authority and power. Lukács' and

Gramsci's interest in the realm of the superstructure, rather than the base, indeed, their privileging, in their studies, of one area of Marx's dialectical relation, the superstructural realm of ideology, culture and politics rather than the relation of base to superstructure, was thus an attempt at correcting Marxist theory in areas where it was very deficient. It was also an attempt at advancing Marxist theory, perhaps to adjust it to new historical, theoretical and political realities. In the following pages I will point to some of these new historical, theoretical and political experiences which Gramsci and Lukács both share.

As critical thinkers drawn to Marxism, Gramsci and Lukács were interested in participating in a historical process which they thought would lead to a radical social, political and economic revolution. This participation was for both of them theoretical as well as practical. Lukács and Gramsci wrote on issues pertaining to the success and failure of socialist revolutions and as members of political parties they participated in the organization of movements which from their perspective would lead to revolutions. Moreover, as members of a generation that had witnessed the Russian revolution and its European aftermath, both taking place against the arguments of Marx's *Capital*, they examined in their writings some of the factors which led to an unanticipated revolution in Russia and to the failure of a predicted revolution in some countries of the west. These included rigorous interventions, on the level of theoretical writings as well as party politics, in what we might call 'the contest of the Marxist faculties', the contest between the various theoretical and political factions purporting to dialectical materialism or to historical materialism respectively. This contest had already since the 1890s and under the irrevocable impact of positivism in the scientific sphere, as well as under the impact of gradual social, economic and political gains, carried the day for Marxist and anti-Marxist alike through the turn of the century and beyond. In the context of Italian culture, Benedetto Croce's influential repudiation of Marxism would be a case in point.[18] With the failure of a socialist revolution in the west, active intervention in that contest by the leftist intelligentsia had literally become unavoidable. At issue was the scientificity of Marxism, or, to put it in other words, the interpretation of what Marxism is and what it is not. Were there, as some traditional Marxists claimed, laws of history, comparable to natural laws, which were discernible, describable and inevitable, so that the future course of events would be predictable? Did Marxism fulfil the requirements of a fully-fledged science, stating laws of inevitability and predictability? Were these laws based on the motions of economics, the forces of production in society, which would, independently of human will, shape relations of production and generate economic and social crises in advanced capitalism? Was the economic factor the decisive one in the shaping of revolutions? These were some of the questions marking the 'contest of the Marxist faculties' and Gramsci and Lukács dealt with these theoretically and politically, as did many other leftist intellectuals, such as Korsch, for instance. The most important question to examine was why power and authority remained with the state and capitalism in countries in which social and economic crises had indeed occurred. The revolution had not taken place, either in Italy or in Germany or in Hungary, so that one had to conclude that it was not the economy that determined all of social life. The political events of the early twentieth century had defied the laws of history and the primacy of the economic factor as defined by classical Marxism.[19]

Lukács and Gramsci both examined as a result and independently from each other factors which might play a role in propelling or arresting historical change. For both of them, this meant, as mentioned above, shifting their attention away from the material or economic or objective factor of Marx's dialectic to the so-called theoretical or subjective or superstructural factor. With this shift, Lukács and Gramsci marked the beginning of what is known as western Marxism.[20] In the context of the Marxist paradigm that dialectically relates the economic base to the superstructure of culture, politics, ideology and law, Lukács and Gramsci are interested in privileging an understanding of the complexity of the superstructural realm in its relation to the economic basis. So Lukács, in his *History and Class Consciousness* (original German edition 1923), critiques traditional, or scientific, or economist, or orthodox Marxism on two grounds: one, that the structure of society is different from the structure of nature, such that the laws of nature are not applicable to or identical with the laws governing social and thus historical life;[21] and two, that the economist assumption, that consciousness or ideology follows the motions of the economic sphere and is ultimately determined by the economy, was not correct. Moments of crisis, dissolution and consolidation taking place in the realm of the economy were not necessarily reflected on the level of consciousness and ideology. In fact, Lukács believed at the time of the composition of his essays in *History and Class Consciousness* that the general intensive tendency towards rationalization and Taylorization of twentieth-century capitalism tended to produce a consciousness that accepted rather than reacted to the general conditions of life. This notion Lukács described as the reification of consciousness. So he reflects on the possible laws governing society, attempting to define the realm of ideology, class consciousness, culture and so forth, and the role that consciousness or the subjective factor might play in historical processes which tended towards increased rationalization and bureaucratization. If social revolutions were still to be won, knowledge of what moves people and what arrests their motion, of how ideas move individual and collective wills, was an urgent necessity. Gramsci, similarly, reflects in his *Prison Notebooks* on the way in which ideology governs and controls political processes and thus, ultimately, also the organization of economic processes. Hegemony is the term Gramsci is best known for in the context of a critique of traditional, scientific, or orthodox Marxism. It is a concept which attempts to capture the complex nature of authority, which according to Gramsci is both coercive and dependent on the consent of those who are coerced into submission. Gramsci examines on many pages of his *Prison Notebooks* the way in which political society, or the realm of state power and authority, creates and maintains as well as manipulates systems of beliefs and attitudes in civil society; how the predominant class not only creates hegemony, but can also depend in its quest for power on the 'spontaneous' consent arising from the masses of the people. This consent is carried by systems and structures of beliefs, values, norms and practices of everyday life which unconsciously legitimate the order of things.

Lukács and Gramsci both attempted to come to terms with the rapidly diminishing revolutionary potential of western capitalism first and foremost by countering that reality with the creation of new and more adequate concepts. A revolution could still be achieved if one were to understand the precise workings of the ideological sphere, of the subjective and cultural factor, that is. Surely, one might argue that as students and proponents of the work of Antonio Labriola they were both already predisposed towards privileging the subjective factor in Marx's dialectic. Labriola was one of the foremost Italian Marxists who, against the theoreticians of the Second International, had opted for a Hegelianized interpretation of Marx's dialectic, for an understanding of history that indeed stresses the subjective and self-creative component in the making of history over the objective or economically determined, or again the scientistic and reductive strain.[22] So it is possible that they were already theoretically predisposed towards privileging the superstructural moment in Marx's dialectic at the expense of the economic one. This does not explain, however, why they should both have pursued that legitimation with such particular rigour, though in different superstructural areas, and to different degrees. Throughout his work, Gramsci would be more intent on studying the broader cultural and ideological realm, the complex relations between civil and political society, to use his terminology, and the way in which hegemony or directed power relations are produced, maintained and legitimated in these two major superstructural realms. Lukács ultimately would be more intent on studying problems of aesthetics and the way in which literary practices as part of the superstructure are sometimes capable of reflecting forms of knowledge concerning the totality of the historical process long before other disciplines or other areas of intellectual activity begin to perceive and conceptualize them. This Lukácsian position has entered literary discourses under the name of reflection theory and is related to Lukács' Marxist notion of the law of uneven development as part of the dialectic.

Yet perhaps what is most important, when it comes to similarities in Lukács' and Gramsci's critical theory, is this: that as Marxist intellectuals interested in literary problems, Lukács and Gramsci both refused to understand literature as a sphere unrelated to other spheres of social and political activity. So when they re-examined the function of literature in its relation to politics, to the revolution that failed on the one hand, and to the rise of fascism on the other, they proceeded from the most basic premises of Marxist aesthetics: problems of culture are not separable from the realm of politics, so that the production and circulation of specific cultural goods, such as literature, are not separable from but related to the production and circulation of political, ethical and moral values and norms. Literature, *qua* cultural expression, constitutes for Gramsci as well as for Lukács a terrain where certain moral and political values and attitudes are propagated and others are silenced and marginalized. In their teleological vision of a history which progressively moves forward towards a classless future with a good life for all, literature, like all human activities in a social context, has a significant ideological and thus political role to play. What kind of ideological functions specific literary practices assume, whether they exert a progressive or regressive influence on historical change, is something both of these theoreticians are intent on determining in their confrontation with literary practices of the past, the present and the future.

So while Lukács and Gramsci share similar political, historical and biographical experiences, and while their attitudes to literary production reveal some common Marxist ground, it is nevertheless uncertain to what extent these two Marxist theoreticians knew about each other. It is also uncertain whether they ever met. There is some indication that Lukács and Gramsci might have met in Vienna, when they both sojourned in that city in the early 1920s. According to one of Lukács' biographers, Fritz J. Raddatz, there are sources which would suggest that much, even alluding to a friendship between these two men.[23] Gramsci seems to have been aware of Lukács' influential *History and Class Consciousness*, or at least of some of the essays contained in that volume. In his *Prison Notebooks*, specifically in 'Quaderno 4' focusing on a delineation of his own philosophy of praxis, Gramsci refers to Lukács' repudiation of Bukharin's understanding of the dialectic while simultaneously and quickly adding that he is only superficially acquainted with Lukács' theories.[24] And indeed this is probably the case. For Gramsci's brief reference to Lukács' theories privileges only one aspect of Lukács' argument: namely his notion of a dialectic that includes only human history in dialectical processes while excluding nature from such processes, as Engels, many proponents of the Second International, and also Bukharin had attempted to establish in their version of Marxism under the name of dialectical materialism. Thus, while focusing on the problem of the Marxist dialectic, Gramsci made not much use of or perhaps was not aware of what seems to be the cornerstone of Lukács' famous essays in *History and Class Consciousness*: I am referring to the concept of reification, the adventures of which are well known. This concept influenced the work of many critical thinkers, in particular the members of the Frankfurt School such as Horkheimer, Adorno, Marcuse, and others. In this context, this concept was productively integrated in reflections on the culture industry, consumer economy, industrialization and the commodification of culture. It also plays a role in Marcuse's call to resistance and revolt in a consumer society which equally reifies the mind and the body, as well as consciousness and desire. Reification is also dealt with by Gramsci himself, in his notes on 'Americanism and Fordism', albeit from a different and less critical angle, as compared to Horkheimer, Adorno and Marcuse.[25] Surely, that in the context of his notebooks on philosophy Gramsci should be interested in participating in a discussion on dialectical versus historical materialism, and not on some other topic, is not so very surprising. After all this problematic had been raging among economists and critical Marxists alike since the beginnings of the

Second International, and in Gramsci's own lifetime Korsch contributed his outstanding *Marxism and Philosophy* to that same ongoing debate.[26] And moreover, it is also a problematic which persistently accompanied Marxist thought and critical theory well into the 1960s and 1970s. Louis Althusser, with his intervention in the humanism versus anti-humanism debate, is a case in point, for one, and the current debates on system theory, the most famous being probably the ones carried out between Habermas and Luhmann on the one hand, and the followers of Habermas and Lyotard on the other, is another.[27] Yet that Gramsci would miss what is perhaps most relevant, and what was certainly more influential in Lukács' *History and Class Consciousness*, his attempt to formulate a new theory of class consciousness, his definition of reification, his critique of reification underlying specialization, rationalization, Taylorization and bureaucratization, all of which are in any event relevant to the polemic between historical and dialectical materialists, leads me to conclude that Gramsci was not aware of the range of the essays included in Lukács' unsettling collection. I consider it unlikely that Gramsci would have bypassed a critical discussion of the concept of reification which he not only specifically addresses in his essay on 'Americanism and Fordism', but which also plays a significant role in his formulation of hegemony. I presume, then, that Gramsci simply did not know about the extent of Lukács' collection.

It is also uncertain on the basis of my research whether Gramsci knew of Lukács' 'Blum Theses' (1928). These theses, by pleading for a democratic dictatorship over the dictatorship of the proletariat, by opting for political alliances with non-proletarian forces, unceremoniously ushered in the end of Lukács' political career, at the orders of the Komintern. Gramsci had, as far as I can ascertain, in parts proposed similar strategies in the last essay he wrote in freedom, 'On the Southern Question' (1926), where he began to plead for an anti-fascist democratic popular front. Indeed, there is some critical evidence that for both thinkers the political strategy of an anti-fascist popular front is strongly related to their respective notions of aesthetics. I will return to this in a moment.

It is, in addition, unclear whether Lukács ever read Gramsci's *Prison Notebooks*. Lukács was fluent in Italian and one might hypothesize that he knew of their publication, particularly since Lukács himself and his work on Marxist aesthetics were well received in Italy throughout the 1950s and also in the 1960s. There is some research which suggests that Lukács referred to Gramsci and his notion of hegemony in conversations.[28] So if Gramsci and Lukács perhaps never read each other's work, perhaps even never knew much about each other, and if perhaps they never even met in the early 1920s, in some café in Vienna, they did meet on the very real fictional grounds of the Italian realist novelist, poet and dramatist: Alessandro Manzoni. Indeed, it is on these Manzonian premises that Lukács' and Gramsci's understanding of literature emerges against the background not only of the impact of fascism on critical thinking, but also, and more importantly perhaps, of the impact of the immense processes of industrialization on the production of culture, leading to the very industrialization of literature itself. In their respective analysis and evaluation of Manzoni's realism, Lukács and Gramsci meet, only in terms of theory to depart from one another. And it is with Manzoni that one of them says farewell to realism.

GRAMSCI'S MANZONI: AN INTELLECTUAL WITH CLASS

That Gramsci should draw up a special balance sheet on a literary figure such as Manzoni need perhaps not be considered an extraordinary move on his part. After all, one might propose that Manzoni had already been staked out by national and international organizers of cultural canons, by de Sanctis and Croce, that is, as one of the more prominent figures of Italian intellectual history, and this for good reason. With his historical novel, *I promessi sposi*, or *The Betrothed*, where protagonists from a variety of social classes had critiqued the imposition of a foreign culture on Italian soil, Manzoni had consciously participated in the creation of a national dream direly needed in the first few decades of the nineteenth century. Manzoni represented a great figure of Italian culture, one who had a programme, controversial as it might have turned out to be, to incorporate problems of different Italian languages and dialects into cultural politics. That much had been recorded in the collective consciousness of most historically inclined Italians, attentive to emancipatory and not so emancipatory causes, and Gramsci was no exception. And given Gramsci's great admiration, probably not so much for Croce, but surely for de Sanctis, the latter's double-edged judgement on Manzoni should also have played an initial role in Gramsci's Manzonian interests.[29] De Sanctis had viewed Manzoni as a proponent of a romanticism that in spite or perhaps because of its being intrinsically Italian rather than European, taught the majority of Italians to

49

think politically, to acquire, as citizens, a sense of the limits of their political practices, as well as a sense of their possibilities.[30] Moreover, Gramsci was, as already pointed out, not an outsider to literary matters. He had pursued a degree in the humanities at the University of Turin; he had worked as a rather innovative theatre critic during the period roughly corresponding to World War I and in that context he had produced pioneering insights into the complex relations that obtain between Pirandello's theatrical and structural innovations and the changing aesthetic and philosophical expectations of the theatre audiences at the moment of the gradual insertion of the movie industry into Italian society; and when Gramsci, well over two years into his prison sentence, was finally allowed to do some writing and began his prison notebooks, he outlined sixteen areas of study, two of which address literary problems directly.[31] One concerns popular literature, and the other Dante's *Divine Comedy*. Manzoni is also mentioned in this study plan, yet not in relation to literature or literary theory, but rather to the 'Questione della lingua in Italia', that major concern of Italian intellectuals attentive to their national history, and to the problems of promoting a hegemonic national language at the expense of the specific cultural content of dialects, some of them marginal, others more widely used.

So when Gramsci chooses Manzoni as a topic of inquiry, he seems to do so for apparently non-literary or semi-literary reasons. Manzoni will be studied in his relation to the 'Questione della lingua', and not *qua* poet, novelist and dramatist. We will see in a moment whether this is indeed what Gramsci does, or whether there is a discrepancy between his express intentions and actual performance. I hope to point this out in my exposition. Gramsci's methodology, his critical practice, appears to be both 'archaeological' and 'pragmatic'. No matter which phenomenon he chooses to interrogate, he organizes his examination of a problem in such a way that he arrives at a large amount of information concerning his object of study. Or to put it another way: he chooses to interrogate a phenomenon on the basis of multiple relations, whether apparent or not so apparent, or to use contemporary *koine*, whether present or absent, multiple relations a particular phenomenon entertains with other phenomena. In this way he not only sheds light on the motions and dynamics that accompany the complex relatedness of one phenomenon to other phenomena, he also, and perhaps more importantly, proposes a critical practice which makes generous allowances for new insights and the formation of new information. So when Gramsci announces that he will deal with Manzoni in the context of the 'Questione della lingua', a reader does well to anticipate that Gramsci will also deal with Manzoni in contexts which have little to do with the troubling question of the Italian national language. And this is what occurs.[32] Manzoni and his texts, including his famous epic novel *The Betrothed*, are 'archaeological' sites, where numerous inquiries are unearthed and intersect. And, perhaps more importantly, Manzoni's text is not only a ground which allows for specific 'archaeological' work to take place, apparently pertaining to the traditional categories of the historical, the literary, the philosophical, epistemological, aesthetic, ideological and the political. It is used as a pretext for such interrogations, but not in isolation. It is by relating the Manzonian text to a series of phenomena, objects or texts, or shall we say to a series of elements that are arrangeable in a structure, that the elements of that series or structure comment on each other, as well as on the Manzonian text. This, I believe, is one of the keys to Gramsci's critical practice, which I would like to call here a 'relational pragmatics', or perhaps a 'homological pragmatics'.

I will exemplify Gramsci's 'homological pragmatics' briefly with this: the index of the Italian edition of the *Prison Notebooks*, the *Quaderni del carcere*, lists fifty to sixty entries on Manzoni.[33] There are probably many more entries than that on Manzoni in the *Quaderni*, not because the index was incomplete, but rather because it is likely that Gramsci intermittently offers information on Manzoni, as is his practice with other authors, without expressly stating his name. I am not concerned about these 'invisible' sites, since the 'visible' ones are already more than are necessary for my argument. Indeed, I will begin by commenting only on the first six. In all of these six entries, as in the remaining fifty or so, Gramsci consistently relates Manzoni to other phenomena, textual bodies, archaeological sites, forms of knowledge. Entry 1: here Gramsci relates Manzoni to one of Manzoni's contemporaries, Ascoli. Entry 2: Gramsci points to the fact that in a French study on romanticism, Manzoni is only mentioned in a footnote. Entry 3: here Gramsci relates Manzoni to the problematic of the non-existence of a national language. Entry 4: here Gramsci relates Manzoni to Lorianism. Entry 5: in this entry Gramsci comments on Manzoni's opinion of Victor Hugo. Entry 6, the last entry on my list: Gramsci records Manzoni's opinion of Napoleon III. Each entry represents an element or a byte of information that can become part of or be easily assimilated to many additional series or structures of larger sets of information. Or to put it another way: each entry refers to information which in turn refers to an additional body of information. So entry number 1, the relation of Manzoni to Ascoli, can be useful information for a series of discourses. I mention those which come readily to mind:

1 The question of a national language.
2 Intellectual history of Italy in the early nineteenth century.
3 Political history of early nineteenth-century Italy.
4 Manzoni's understanding of language and dialects.
5 The relation of dialects to grammar.
6 Manzoni's relation to and validation of the spoken language.
7 Manzoni's relation to and validation of the written language.
8 Manzoni's understanding of language as compared to Ascoli's.
9 Manzoni's view of cultures and languages other than his own.
10 The possibility or impossibility of imposing a national language on to a culture.

I will stop here, although this list is surely extensible. How is one to grasp Gramsci's critical practice? Is there a logic, a rationality, or perhaps a rhetorical strategy that orders the multiplicity of these numerous informational sites, seemingly squaring to many powers with algebraic precision? Are Gramsci's practices intentional or arbitrary? Are they symptoms of his preference for unsystematicities and fragmentariness over systematization, symptoms of his preference for differentiation, for complexity and multiplicity over simplicity and reduction? Are we seeing here signs of analytical techniques which seem to tend towards destabilizing, decentring and unsettling rather than ordering common relations, towards deconstruction rather than reconstruction, towards seeking out that which is multiple, marginal, arbitrary, discontinuous and subaltern rather than that which is centred, necessary, dominant and linear? Are we confronted with texts and contexts that, by adhering to decentralization and dissemination, seem to defy organicities, totalities and hierarchical structures in which each component has a well-defined place and value?

Gramsci's practice lends itself to propelling him into the orbit of structuralist or even poststructuralist thought. Before we attempt to do so, let me point to this. While many of the entries seem to refer to or signify references or signifiers which in turn seem to refer to or signify new references and signifiers, similar to the unending play of signifiers we know from the critical work of Derrida and Lacan, there are also many entries that can be more readily ordered than others in what we can call a series of distinct 'homologies', or 'structures', or 'narratives'. The editors of the *Quaderni*, who were indexing not only names and concepts but also conceptual contexts, suggest contexts which are not dissimilar to what I am calling here Gramscian 'structures'. I cite at random: there is, for instance, a structure in which Gramsci compares Manzoni to other significant realist novelists of the nineteenth century; there is a comparison between Tolstoy and Manzoni expressly, and between Manzoni and Balzac indirectly. There is also a structure in which Manzoni is examined in relation to the problem of providence, of evolutionary and revolutionary motion in historical, political and philosophical terms. In addition, there is a structure that comments on Manzoni's relation to the proverb 'the voice of the people is the voice of God', to the problem of a collective psychology, which great Italian Hegelians such as Spaventa had attempted to frame in a Spinozistic key.[34] Manzoni is also related to empiricism, to the formation of the rise of a new bourgeoisie at the beginning of the nineteenth century. There is a structure that seeks to relate Manzoni to the question of a national language; to Machiavelli and to Thierry; to the attitude Italian intellectuals have displayed towards the economic and cultural problems of Italy throughout its history; Manzoni is also related to the problem of the Romans and the Longobards, to Germanic and Roman law, and finally, to the notion of common sense and good sense, common sense as the site of unexamined prejudices, values and normativities governing the practices of everyday life founded on inequality and discrimination, versus good sense, which would demand a human life for all people.[35]

What I wish to argue, then, is that many of these multiple entries may be organized along various homological lines of relationship. Even fragments, such as Gramsci's notes on the difficulties of translating those passages of Manzoni making specific reference to the assimilation of French cultural practices in Italy, and even his fragmentary notes on the reception history of Manzoni's novel in France, which is largely a non-reception, are somehow relatable to the larger narratives that Gramsci constructs in prison. In the case of the two notes mentioned here, I would relate them to Gramsci's narrative on Italy and France, which resembles a comparative culturology. I think that just as the multiple entries on Manzoni are to a large extent relatable to a set of narratives or structures, these structures themselves tend to coincide with – or can at any rate be accommodated by – the sixteen principal arguments of Gramsci's research programme as he outlined it at the beginning of his *Prison Notebooks*.

Is there a thread that links these diverse inquiries together? Is Gramsci's approach and presentation, his critical practice, in its fragmentariness, its discontinuities, with its aphorisms and impressionisms, perhaps dictated by the difficult circumstances under which he was writing in prison, ultimately built on a rigorous foundation where co-ordination coexists with subordination? I should like to assure the reader that I do not raise this question in pursuit of a grand unifying principle which would either seek to deduce all of Gramsci's interrogations from a massive and non-negotiable foundation or would attempt to discourse on the irreducible multiplicity of Gramsci's texts. Yet the fact of the matter is that in the multiplicity of his interests and studies, which span many disciplines and forms of knowledge, all of which bear upon his investigation of Manzoni, Gramsci seems to think that he is focusing primarily on one question. Let us look at one of his letters addressed to Tatiana Schucht, a letter which is quite renowned among Gramsci scholars, written on 19 March 1927, four months after his arrest. I will quote excerpts from it:

> It seems I am plagued by a notion, common among prisoners, that one has to accomplish something *für ewig* [for eternity] . . .
> I'd like to set up a plan for the intense systematic study of some subject that would absorb and concentrate my inner life. . . .
> Four ideas have come to me so far. One is research on the history of Italian intellectuals, their origins and groupings in relation to cultural events. Second, a study of comparative linguistics, nothing less. Third, a study of Pirandello and the transformation of theatrical taste in Italy that he represented and helped determine. Fourth, an essay on feuilletons or 'serials' and popular taste in literature.

And he adds in the next paragraph:

> Really, if you look closely at these four arguments, a common thread runs through them: the popular creative spirit, in its diverse phases of development, is equally present in each.[36]

I would like to repeat the point that seems crucially important to Gramsci: the popular creative spirit, in its diverse phases of development, is equally present in each aspect of his project. What Gramsci remarks upon in this letter is what he considers the leitmotif of his research, a leitmotif that runs through his notebooks, that combines the most diverse inquiries over a period of eleven years. Perhaps we should take a cue from Gramsci and attempt to deploy his understanding of this leitmotif, 'of the popular creative spirit', as a possible point of entry into his complex and difficult textual and conceptual universe, and use it as an organizational tool for his reading of Manzoni. Yet this is more easily said than done. For what is the 'popular creative spirit'? Surely, like any of Gramsci's terms, it will be a complex one, one that resists easy definition, one that problematizes the 'is', one that links and does not link the opposite sides of the predicate. I will make the following attempts: the popular creative spirit is not exclusively a universal class, the proletariat, or a subaltern social group, or the common people, or the wretched of the earth. At points in Gramsci's narrative, the popular creative spirit embodies all four of these groups and others as well. What the popular creative spirit is surely not is the 'directing', 'directive' and predominant social and political group, it is not the group that holds political and cultural power. The popular creative spirit is majorities as well as minorities of any historical period whose practices are present in spite of the silence imposed on them by the hegemonic drives of dominant groups, dominant classes, or dominant cultures. The popular creative spirit is subject to domination, discrimination, marginalization and oppression not because it consists of objectifiable subjects, but because it consists of subjects which are, *qua* subjects, capable of producing a consciousness, a consensus to their state of subjugation. Conversely, the popular creative spirit is capable of producing an alternative or counter-cultural consciousness to the predominant or high culture, capable of rupturing the continuity of the flow of domination, capable of rupturing the silence which is imposed. The popular creative spirit is the object of desire of hegemony not because it lacks desire, but because it is, as collective and individual, subject of desire itself, human beings that desire something more than they have and are. The popular spirit reproduces 'spontaneously' consent to domination that is the product not of their creativity but of that of the dominant class, and it can invent practices which, by meeting personal fantasies and desires, can simultaneously transcend the boundaries of domination. Italian intellectuals, claims Gramsci, have seldom taken into account the existence, the power and the legitimacy of popular desires, they have ridiculed the humble people, distanced themselves from them, ignored their symbolics, marginalized their cultures, exoticized their labours, underestimated the powers of their feelings and wills. They have not spoken their language and not written their histories. They have treated them as inanimate objects rather than as subjects with powerful and sometimes historically

55

fateful desiring bodies, as fascism had irrevocably reiterated. In short, Italian intellectuals had not understood that the political and economic fate of the Italian nation at the brink of modernity is irrevocably linked not only to external but also to internal relations. It is linked internally or organically to the relation of intellectuals or high culture to the practices and their functions of that 'popular creative spirit', which I would like to paraphrase here as 'the languages and practices of popular culture'. And it is linked externally to the political and historical function of the relations that obtain between the 'practices and languages of popular culture' and the 'practices and languages of Italian intellectual high culture' with non-Italian cultural practices. What Italian intellectuals had not understood is the more than double-edged politicality that becomes operative when the historical needs of a culture aspiring to be a sovereign and democratic nation are met with attitudes that ignore the presence and the dynamics of 'popular collective psychologies', of 'popular cultural practices'.[37] Manzoni's position on that problem, as it emerges from his great epic novel, *The Betrothed*, fits part of that Gramscian bill.[38]

There is some question as to whether Manzoni's political reformism or liberalism had led him to incorporate poor and weak members of the society into his creative work – servants, artisans, peasants and other popular characters animate his plays and his novel – or whether his major historical novel, *The Betrothed*, required for reasons of historical accuracy the representation of specific social classes, including the very poor. In *The Betrothed*, the common people, the fourth estate in eighteenth-century political terms, are, next to the aristocracy, the clergy and the entrepreneurs, well represented here: both as principal characters – Renzo, Lucia, Perpetua, Fra Galdino – and as the masses: the Milan rioters, the country people, the sailors. Yet Gramsci does not simply go by numerical representation. He applies his practice of relational thinking to Manzoni's masterpiece as well. What matters is not that members of the lower social classes find some form of representation; rather, what matters is the way in which the uneducated, the undereducated and the poor appear in their relation not with but to the nobles in the narrative. There are some epic models and morals Manzoni has to muster: Tolstoy and Dostoevsky are two of them. And when compared to these two novelists, in particular the way they treat ordinary people, Gramsci finds that Manzoni falls short. So contrary to Tolstoy, where the 'naive and instinctive wisdom of the people, even when uttered casually, enlightens and brings about a crisis in the educated person', in Manzoni there is not one common person who is not laughed at.[39] Only the nobles have an inner life, a complex psychology, a desiring body. The wretched and the poor are deprived of such qualities. Magnanimity, great feelings, noble thoughts belong exclusively to members of the upper classes.[40] In his attitude towards the undereducated and the poor, Manzoni is elitist. He displays an irony towards the poor, the nuances of which are perceptible only to the initiated, the educated, the cultured reader. In short, Manzoni takes sides. He represents the 'humble' not in the manner of Dostoevsky, where the characters are not called the 'humble' or the '*umili*' but rather the '*umiliati*', the ones who are humiliated, insulted, offended and injured.[41] By his choice of grammatical construction Dostoevsky shows that the characters are subject to insulting and offensive treatment and become its object. Or to put it another way, his choice of '*umiliati*' or the offended ones presupposes an agent who acts unjustly to a person. Manzoni semantically chooses an adjective that qualifies a state of being rather than an adjectivized past participle of a verb which structurally contains the residues of an action. Hereby he neglects to point to transitivities taking place between various agents, and he obscures directed power relations taking place between subjects and objects. He evokes staticity rather than motion, and authorial knowledge of rather than dynamic interaction with the way things might be. This also points to Manzoni's selective affinities with 'the traditional attitude of Italian intellectuals towards the people', towards the undereducated and the poor, an attitude which is intrinsically paternal in its unexamined superiority.[42] For Gramsci, Manzoni belongs to a genealogy of intellectuals that embraces the Italian Jesuits as well, who, as representatives of the Church, have always made sure of the hierarchy that severs the common people from God. In Manzoni, the voice of the poor is not the voice of God – between God and the people, there is always the Church.[43]

The above passages do not do justice to the richness and complexities of the issues Gramsci raises with respect to Manzoni. It should also be pointed out that precisely because Gramsci does not proceed logically in the traditional sense, in a linear and reductive fashion, but rather what we might describe as 'structurally' or 'topically' as well as 'relationally', 'differentially' and 'dialectically', it should come as no surprise that the many relations Manzoni is placed in also consist of contexts in which he is not judged by Gramsci as severely as above. Indeed, there are notes where Manzoni, compared to more conservative figures of Italian intellectual history, such as the followers or the

57

progeny of the Catholic writer Father Bresciani, easily gets off the hook. Though Gramsci does insist that Manzoni belongs to a tradition that is reformist in nature rather than revolutionary, that is elitist rather than democratic, Gramsci does also differentiate between Manzoni and Foscolo. With his anti-romantic realism, Manzoni demonstrates greater sensibility than Foscolo for social and political transformations taking place in the wake of modernity.[44] From Gramsci's pages there emerges also a Manzoni who deserves praise for his dialectical thinking, as well as a Manzoni whose irony towards the ordinary people is surely not identical with the sarcasm of second-rate Jesuit writers.[45] Indeed, Manzoni had presented a threat to Catholic ideology.[46] In short, when dealing with Manzoni in the context of a brief history of Italian intellectuals, Gramsci tends to separate him from conservative, reformist, elitist and undemocratic traditions. When he deals with Manzoni in the framework of a larger cultural history and critique, however, there are difficulties for Manzoni in meeting the requirements of Gramsci's cultural politics. This is particularly the case in the context of a 'History of the Subaltern Classes', which for Manzoni does not exist in that the subaltern classes have no traces in documented history.[47]

What is interesting in this context is the way in which Manzoni's unexamined attitude towards the common and ordinary people, his paternalism marked by a mix of irony, distantiation, devotion and contempt, is a factor that influences not only his choice of language, but also his very theory of language, his theory of history, perhaps even his epistemology and his ethics. His lack of interest in the ordinary people, his lack of respect for subaltern groups, his inability to sense the presence of creative forces latent in marginal and subaltern groups alike, lead him to the assumption that a national and unified language can be imposed, from above, on a geographic space consisting of multiple and diverse cultures and languages. This assumption does not take into account the effects of such an imposition, namely the effacing of cultural and linguistic differences. When Manzoni exchanged the first version of his *The Betrothed*, which included passages written in various dialects, for a second version, all written in a unified language, he changed only the lexicon, and not the syntax. Gramsci doubts that changes in the lexicon without changes in the syntax could create a unified language, a unified country, a unified frame of mind. Yet what Manzoni above all did not understand with his contribution to the 'Question of language' in the opinion of Gramsci is this: 'L'unità della lingua è uno dei modi esterni e non esclusivamente necessario dell'unità nazionale, in ogni caso è un effetto e non una causa.' And I translate: 'A unified language is an external factor, and probably not even a necessary instance of a national language; it is above all an effect of national unity, and not its cause.'[48]

A unified language is not the only measure Manzoni would like to implement aristocratically in a reality consisting of many languages, diverse ways of seeing and judging and cultural preferences. In his theory of history, so writes Gramsci, he tends towards a concept of motion that values natural evolution over 'artificial' revolution, a concept which – against the background of Giorgio Cabanis' and Hyppolite Taine's materialist theories of nature and morality – considers 'egalitarian democracy a monstrosity in light of the laws of nature'.[49] And furthermore, linked to this notion of natural and artificial processes in history are Manzoni's principles of moral philosophy, opportunely assessed in his understanding of predestination and free will. In this context, free will stands as desiring or consenting to the natural, and not the artificial or human-made, order of things.

In Gramsci's reading of Manzoni, then, there are cultural differences that are being played out in the context of Manzoni's work. By comparing Manzoni to the work of various French historians or writers, Gramsci underlines microcosmic aspects of Manzoni's work which again point to Manzoni's class consciousness and even to a relation between class and race. Gramsci evokes in that context Augustin Thierry's studies on the racist component as an intrinsic aspect of the class struggle.[50] And the popularity of Eugène Suë's popular novels where the democratic-Gallic is played out against the Nordic, Germanic, or non-Gallic upper class, also contains a race-related component. Gramsci commands in that context attention to the fact that people know when they are racially discriminated against, and when they are linguistically or culturally devalued. Thus, it should come as no surprise that Manzoni's class consciousness, his ultimately condescending attitude towards the powerless social classes, is felt by the people as the expression of express class and race superiority. So Manzoni's master novel, *The Betrothed*, Gramsci laconically remarks, has never been popular among them.[51]

Although Manzoni represents one of the most important writers of post-Renaissance Italian culture, Gramsci appears to be determined to eliminate him from the cultural literacy list. Even though Gramsci occasionally credits Manzoni with some historical sensibility, such as the distinction Manzoni observes in chapter 32 of his novel between common sense and good sense, whereby good sense, as in Gramsci's own conceptual system, stands *qua* historical and progressive reason as a social practice that aspires to subvert common sense, prejudice, traditional beliefs and superstition – even though Gramsci cannot but credit Manzoni for such insights, his final verdict is irrevocable. Manzoni represents the typical Italian intellectual who had not bothered either to bond with the real people, or to contribute to political designs which would lead to a democratic rather than a bourgeois Italian state. He had not constructed moral and cultural models which insisted on the dignity of all people, and which would contribute to a popular and unified culture. He had not contributed to democratic historical roots which would have prevented fascism. Manzoni's aristocratic attitude was transparent to the humble and the poor: thus, his novel was not popular among them. One wonders: if Gramsci had lived to have a say in Italian cultural politics, would Manzoni have made the cultural canon? But who, or what, one might ask, would then be allowed in Gramsci's aesthetic politics, given the fact that Manzoni is something of a national monument to the collective memory of the Italian people? Some sort of socialist or populist realist, as it had been propagated by Zhdanov and the post-war cultural politics of the left in Italy?[52]

Critics knowledgeable in Manzoniana and with or without progressive leanings have attempted on occasion and as a corrective to Gramsci to rehabilitate Manzoni by putting him on the nineteenth-century political activist list, and by placing his presumed philosophical and moral limits, as unearthed by Gramscian archaeologies, in a historical context.[53] Manzoni's programme of cultural politics as it permeates his novel is thus not seen as regressive with respect to the possibilities of Italian culture in the early nineteenth century. To the contrary, some of these critics see in what Gramsci described as Manzoni's critical limitations the critical limitations of the very history of Manzoni's Italy. Its economic backwardness compared to other European countries produced a consciousness which could not transcend the limits the economy imposed on political, social and philosophical thought. This includes the sphere of art as well. This position is not dissimilar in parts to Lukács' reading of the Manzonian text, and it is to this reading that I will now turn.

LUKÁCS' READING OF MANZONI

In the 1930s, when Lukács polemicized in the context of the realism/modernism debate against expressionist literature in particular, and against Bloch and Brecht in general, he simultaneously staked out the ontological and epistemological groundwork of a design which would occupy much of his subsequent work in the 1940s and 1950s, and which would make him famous and infamous at once: his well-known work on European realism.[54] The problem was crystal clear to Lukács on the eve of Hitler's takeover of power: expressionism, the favourite child of the decadent Weimar bourgeoisie, which had, in place of direly needed economic concessions to the people, lavishly endowed the bourgeoisie with artistic and literary avant-gardes, that expressionism, with its representations of a dissolute and fragmented reality, is the artistic expression of an intellectual elite that refuses to see the total political picture.[55] What he proposes instead is a literary current, such as contemporary realism, which includes novelists like Maxim Gorky, Thomas Mann, Heinrich Mann and Romain Rolland.[56] These writers are in Lukács' assessment neither openly anti-realist nor pseudo-realist, and most importantly they are not defensive and apologetic of the present political system, fascism. They do not distance themselves from present anti-democratic politics, but seek its liquidation. This they achieve, so Lukács avers, by installing in their narrative the figure of a great individual who is not merely representative of fragmentation, alienation and dissolution in contemporary society but who mediates between appearance and reality, between form and content, between the subjective and the objective, between *Schein* and *Sein*. This mediation occurs by pointing to the appearance of fragmentation and dissolution in society, by relating these to social relations, and by relating both to a historical force, motor or essence which in Lukács' account creates fragmentation. In doing so, realist writers represent a progressive tendency in contemporary literature and political life.

While the fascist takeover was something of an event that incited the realism/expressionism debate, it is apparent from the development of that debate that more was at stake than the question of what kind of literature to write against fascism and under the sign of progress. For the major protagonists of that debate, for Lukács, Bloch and Brecht alike, the problem was ultimately more tied to other preoccupations than to fascism proper. Brecht, sensitive to the impact of technological advances on the environment into which social relations are built and in which they are changed, the environment in which individual lives are lived, experiments in his theatre with technical forms and devices by means of which he hopes to change people's consciousness for and not against a better future for all. This

61

includes the struggle against fascism. So in his rebuttal of Lukács, he critiques him on the ground that the great individuals whom Lukács retrieves from the realist literature of the nineteenth century are unrealistic individuals in a reality that does not afford much space for such individuals any longer.[57] If we talk realism, notes Brecht, then let us acknowledge that reality requires a different kind of real representation. The great individual has shrunk, magnanimity has turned into mediocrity, courage into neurosis, the hero is dead.

Bloch, Lukács' great intermittent theoretical antagonist throughout his life, epistemologically reflects what Brecht theatrically detects.[58] Bloch is aware, perhaps better than any other theoretician, of the tension in Lukács' theories between an account that grounds knowledge in the impossibility of fully or totally knowing the object, and an account that grounds knowledge in the possibility of fully knowing it, the replay of a historical tension between Kant and Hegel taking place in a different social reality in the early twentieth century. That tension is replayed – under the alienating impact of increasing rationalizations in processes of production, bureaucratization and social systematizations – in terms of ontological alienation, as in Heidegger's *Sein und Zeit*, as well as in terms of system-produced alienation, as in Lukács' *History and Class Consciousness*. Both works are in any event ways of dealing with that tension.[59] The later Lukács will provide a historical explanation of that condition of alienation marking modernity.[60] Bloch, whose problematization of alienation as partially anthropological reveals a philosophical and political critical awareness as well as his points of contact not only with Adorno's epistemology but also with Heidegger's ontology, is sensitive to the underlying tension in Lukács' argument. Is Lukács on the verge of laying to rest a disturbing affair when he condemns as decadent, neurotic and politically regressive those artistic practices that focus on the fragmentary, on discontinuities, on atonalities, on the uncommon, on the differential, thereby problematizing the norm, the common, the whole, the total? Has Lukács crossed the anti-modernist Rubicon by intransigently gesturing to an option which would propose one epistemological solution over another, which would fold the subject into one with the object, which would insist that the totality of reality, of base and superstructure, can be grasped by the idea, is consummate with its powers, and can transcend appearance? Perhaps Bloch makes a last-ditch effort to divert Lukács' decision when he proposes this: why, he asks, should ruptures, fragmentation, dissolution, the incomprehensible and the confused as artistically produced by expressionist writers and artists not be viewed as an experiment with dissolution rather than political dissolution itself?[61] What if one finds new insights in the interstices of fragmentation, what if new knowledge is born from these interstices, what if ruptures create the new? Why should only Goethe and Homer and all the rest of the classics be respectable, true at the expense of the new, the avant-gardes? What if true reality is not the totality of the base and superstructure, of the identity of the subject and the object, but rupture, discontinuity, filled with interstices which perhaps are capable of being filled? And what about expressionism? What about its non-petty-bourgeois tendencies to search for the new, for the silenced, for the under-represented? Did expressionists not search for motives in popular art, in folklore, particularly the painters? Can one indeed just argue on the basis of literature and overlook the history of art of the past eighty years? And so Bloch argues.[62]

Lukács seems not to have been disturbed by Bloch's fundamentally epistemological objections, which might have been attractive to a thinker who liked to regard himself as thinking dialectically. What counts as political correctness, he counters, is a literature to which not an elite but the reader from the broad masses of the people has access: to Cervantes and Shakespeare, to Balzac and Tolstoy, to Grimmelshausen and Gottfried Keller, to Gorky, to Thomas and Heinrich Mann.[63] To these authors the reader from the broad masses of the people has access because these texts reproduce the most diverse aspects and experiences of life. And some years later, when Lukács engages in the elaborate construction of his grand system of European realism, he will add Manzoni to this list.[64]

Manzoni is for Lukács a superb example not only of politically correct great literature, worthy of being entered in the data base of the great classical canon, but also of an epic writer in the early nineteenth century chosen by the world spirit to record, whether consciously or not, both the totality of the historical rise of the bourgeoisie and the art form that alone and eminently captures the trajectory of that total evolution: the historical novel, where historicity and sociality fold into one. Manzoni met, next to Sir Walter Scott, Balzac, Tolstoy and others, the aesthetic requirements of Lukács' realism. Manzoni was, as English, French and Russian novelists were, aware of an historic experience of which he was part, the aftermath of the French revolution and the Napoleonic wars, an experience of clashes between unprecedentedly huge masses of people and forces which opposed these masses. This had made it difficult to overlook the connectedness, historical necessities and contingencies, the historicities, that is, of things, ideas, events, customs and traditions when writing in a genre that tended to paint the broader rather than the smaller social picture. Yet in contradistinction to the French and the British novelists, whose narrative power is linked to their awareness of a progressively evolving class struggle internal to their national histories, Manzoni's epic venture was from the start caught in the specificity of the Italian situation.[65] Lucia and Renzo's trajectory, moving from love to separation to reunification, is one concrete episode of Italian popular life which, in the course of the narrative, evolves into the general tragedy of the Italian people in a state of national humiliation and fragmentation. The fate of Manzoni's lovers paradigmatizes the tragedy of the Italian people.[66] That Manzoni wrote only one novel of the kind is to his credit. It is also not separable from the history of Italy itself, the only narrative closure of which was its very unification. Yet the lack of a grand historical and national narrative, which Italy shares with Germany, affected not only the Manzonian theme; equally affected are, according to Lukács, the artistic choices the author has. The world-historical atmosphere, which Lukács feels in Sir Walter Scott's epic novels, is absent in Manzoni's depiction where somewhat more limited desires mark the horizon of expectation of the protagonists. Lucia's fate seems, after all, not much more than an idyll threatened from the outside, and the negative characters are somewhat tainted by a certain pettiness. This does not lead, in spite of their negativity, to a demystification of the historical dimension and limits, their negativity, that is, is not consummate with an equitable positivity, and does not unfold the process of a dialectic. In the final analysis then, Manzoni depicts specific historical events negatively, writes Lukács in his *The Historical Novel*. As in the history of Italy, historical events are disturbances in the life of ordinary people, rather than events that further the national cause. Tolstoy, in contradistinction, wrote his epic novels from a more fortunate point of departure, in that in spite of the economic, political and cultural backwardness of Russia, the absolutist regime of the tsars had created a national unity. The peculiar pettiness or mediocrity of the Italian condition, re-emerging in the great Italian historical novel of Manzoni, is absent from the historic backgrounds against which the Russians portray their epic heroes, true heirs to Ivanhoe and Sir Walter Scott. Manzoni could not resist, as could neither Sir Walter Scott before him nor Balzac after him, the emanations of a historical world-spirit placing itself somewhere between the unconscious and the consciousness of these great nineteenth-century novelists and directing, as it were, their understanding and conception of the world. Their epics are great precisely because they capture a specific non-repeatable moment in the progressing history of humankind. As such they are inimitable, their forms gone for ever.[67]

Lukács' Manzoni is caught, involuntarily, almost as a function of, and not as an individual in, the inexorable determinacies that move history. And he is caught in Lukács' version of Marxist aesthetics, where Marx's metaphor of the dialectic of structure and superstructure is read in favour of the determinacy of the structure. As part of the totality that images the relationship between the relations of production and the forces of production, of superstructure to structure, Manzoni but reflects and reflects on, indeed, is only able to reflect and to reflect on the state, the feelings, the sensitivities of his class at a specific moment in the history of the peoples of Italy. In the context of Lukács' logic, Manzoni's condescending attitude towards other social classes is thus adequate, authentic, dictated by the logic of its time. Hegel's Minerva is here resuscitated, she begins her flight of knowledge not before but after the fact, not at dawn but at sunset, for Lukács' Manzoni can record only what there is but not what there should be. The dynamics of the forces of production, virtually alone and burdened by the superstructure, inexorably grind forward towards the realms not of slavery and irrationality but of reason and freedom, such that a writer's task can be but only to record that motion in its totality. That is what makes a writer progressively move with emancipatory politics. Manzoni is thus a political activist in his passivity, an ally of the new and ascending class in his partiality for the old, fit for the revolutionary business in terms of Lukács' Marxist aesthetics.

Gramsci's Manzoni, on the other hand, is not subject to the inexorably natural social laws, a position which the later Lukács exchanged for his earlier one, where he separated the laws of nature from the laws of society in his *History and Class Consciousness*.[68] Gramsci's Manzoni is not invested against his will in a structure, but with a will which enables him either to resist or consent to these determinacies. In other words, Gramsci, intellectual pupil of Sorel, of Labriola and of Croce as well, and who, in prison, under very taxing circumstances, keeps professing an optimism of the will next to a pessimism of the spirit, that Gramsci does not let Manzoni off the hook. He is held accountable for his condescending attitudes towards the ordinary people, paradigmatic of entire groups of intellectuals while

65

non-conducive to the formation of a democratic national history in Italy. His usefulness for a progressive cultural agenda is called into question, his decision to opt for his class rather than an authentic alliance with the ordinary people makes him unsuitable for Gramsci's Marxist aesthetics.

So what does Gramsci want? A literary canon consisting of writers who have passed the lifetime revolutionary activist test? Writers who have indicated their unconditioned partiality with the working class, who diffuse an anti-capitalist ideology, who create a counter-hegemony capable, as part of the relations of production, of effecting changes in the forces of production? Does Gramsci believe that literature, as ideological site, changes history, that, indeed, it is the subject that makes history? Are these the pillars of Gramsci's Marxist aesthetics? Not quite. Contrary to Lukács, who, dogmatic utterances to the contrary, buried his face in the realisms of the past, Gramsci was a pragmatist and a realist, who non-negotiably challenged the uncertainties of the future. So ultimately, the issue was not for him whether or not to read Manzoni, whether or not to accept him as a progressive or reject him as a politically regressive writer. Gramsci's Marxist aesthetics follow the logic of different rationales. Manzoni had not been read, and was not going to be read, by the masses of the people anyhow. This, I think, is an important leitmotif in Gramsci's critical theory, where aesthetics intersect with his political agenda. To create a democratic future meant for Gramsci not to keep insisting on great classical literatures of the past, on the great masterpieces of high culture of the western world. Rather, what it meant was to understand what the ordinary common people liked to read, and, more importantly, why they liked to read what they read. What kind of needs and desires are being met by specific kinds of literature and art is one of the most important questions of Gramsci's critical project. And to this issue Gramsci dedicates many pages of his *Prison Notebooks*, discussing the structure of serial novels, detective stories, and the way technology began to have an impact on the processes of production and reception of popular taste, popular literature, popular culture and mass culture. Understanding why people overwhelmingly chose to read certain texts, including kitsch, and why they refused to read other texts, even nationally monumental texts, such as Manzoni, meant for him to understand the structure of their fantasies and their desires; and addressing that structure, with a different, more democratic content, would contribute to changes in consciousness, would contribute to what he called the moral reform. The author and the reader are in Gramsci no longer timeless individuals who write and read a novel, but twentieth-century producers of texts, the production of which is linked to processes of increasing modernization and rationalization. In Gramsci's Marxist aesthetics, both author and reader become producers of social texts.

So in contradistinction to Gramsci, Lukács, who was aware of the impact of technology on the structure and structurations of consciousness, was not aware of the impact of technology on the production of literary practices. With this attitude, he said farewell to reality as it began to unfold, and not to his form of realism. Gramsci, on the other hand, says farewell to realism, as Lukács understood it, but perhaps not farewell to new, unfolding, technologizing realities. How that reality in its shift from classical capitalism to high and late monopoly capitalism affected literary culture and his view of it is at issue in the next chapter. Chapter 3 will comment on Gramsci's homological relations not only to those theorists who, against Lukács, reflect on the applicabilities of new technologies for progressive cultural politics, but also to those theorists who bypass Lukács in their assessment of the effects of the new technologies on the production of literature and culture. Among both groups are intellectuals such as Walter Benjamin, Ernst Bloch and Bertolt Brecht, as well as Theodor Adorno, Max Horkheimer and Herbert Marcuse.

3

The industrialization of culture: Gramsci with Benjamin, Brecht and the Frankfurt School

MODERNIST THRESHOLDS

In Gramsci's aesthetic programme, which accommodates the cultural representations of the past as well as a sketch for a new culture to come, one of the greatest Italian writers, Alessandro Manzoni, was not admitted to a progressive cultural heritage list. Manzoni's attitude towards the marginalized and the poor, his inability to forge a nexus between art and many forms of social life, meant that he was not well disposed to enter a democratically perceived cultural programme. His art reveals, so Gramsci reasons, the political and philosophical intentionality of an Italian intellectual of the nineteenth century, who did not, as de Sanctis, Gramsci's preferred model, had required it, elaborate a 'new attitude towards the popular classes and a new concept of what is "national"'.[1] As such Manzoni had contributed not to the formation of an Italian Risorgimento moving towards a nation based on authentic democratic principles, but to the prevention of such a formation. And he had contributed to the prevention of a genuine symbolic link between the poor and the privileged, such as the novels of Tolstoy and Dostoevsky had managed to forge. From this perspective, Manzoni was at best material for a 'high culture', for the upper class, but not for Gramsci's cultural politics.

In terms of the logic that informs his discourse on the function of the intellectuals in Italian cultural and political history, one of the most pronounced discourses in the *Prison Notebooks*, Gramsci's critique of Manzoni makes sense. The predominant attitude of Italian intellectuals was, throughout the history of Italian culture, double-edged in its significant lack of sympathy towards national-popular values when compared to intellectuals from other European cultures, such as Russia or France. What Gramsci seems to mean by 'national' and 'popular' is this: on the one hand, the feeling of belonging to a specific national collective, a unified geographic site and history; and on the other hand, the feeling of identification with this history or this collective not only in terms of the ruling groups or classes that seemed to guide it, such as dynasties or national heroes, but also in terms of the conditions of possibility for these very ruling classes, who are themselves dominant by virtue of the existence of non-ruling or dominated classes: the subaltern classes, the marginalized, the poor, the peasants, the ordinary people. In Italy, Gramsci contends, intellectuals with few exceptions liked to view themselves as cosmopolitan or international rather than national, citizens of the world rather than of Italy, and their relation to the common people was one of condescension, rather than of comprehension.[2] Intellectuals in Italy had little understanding of their function in the trajectories of a national history. A unilinear national history could not have been written. In France, on the other hand, Gramsci argues, historians, novelists and artists and other intellectuals have in general helped to shape a culture where the national-popular, the 'people-nation', has a well-prescribed function, emerging in effect as protagonists of French history.[3] 'There is nothing of the sort in Italy, where one must search the past by torchlight to discover national feeling and move with the aid of distinctions, interpretations and discreet silences.'[4] Manzoni thus exemplifies in some ways an attitude quite typical of the Italian intellectual towards his generation and his environment, the function of which was to slow down the process of Italian unification. More specifically, he represented one of those intellectuals for whom unification was to be carried out under the distinct aegis of an ideology and a government that did not sufficiently and adequately represent the economic and cultural needs of large masses of the Italian people: those not prepared for the industrial revolution, those living in the poor rural areas on the margins of the industrializing centres, the unskilled agricultural workers, the peasants, the small farmers, most of them on the islands and in the south.[5]

Gramsci's rejection of Manzoni makes sense in terms of his particular reading of Italian history, of his largely unexamined belief in the intentionality of an author, and of the specific function ascribed to intellectuals in a national history. It seems to make less sense, however, in terms of the strategy of alliance he pursued on the political level, which was, in his own time, an alliance with the progressive and anti-fascist segments of the bourgeoisie. Those segments were no doubt uninterested in ousting figures such as Manzoni from their cultural histories. Yet as I will indicate, this apparent problematic is to some extent resolved when one takes into account Gramsci's metaphors of reality, his images of the conditions of possible political transformations, his belief in the effective presence of a popular will. As it turns out, both strategy of alliance and attention to the conditions of political strategy point to Gramsci's rigorous reading of the presence of a collective will and consciousness that in his view resists direct, unmediated impositions of different norms and values by intellectuals. A strategy of alliance between a variety of social groups, conditions of transformation, and the presence and functions of a collective will, in its relation to hegemony, are addressed intermittently throughout the *Prison Notebooks*.[6] Here, however, I would like to point to a text Gramsci composed shortly before his arrest, his famous essay 'On the Southern Question', where all three issues interlock.[7]

Against the background of a capitalism which had not vanished in Italy with the working-class movement, the factory council movement of Turin and the revolution in Russia, a capitalism which had not changed naturally into socialism but rather solidified in a phase of unprecedented fascism as northern industrialists and bankers, allied with southern landowners, managed to mobilize a politically vacillating urban petty bourgeoisie for its cause, Gramsci elaborated the political counter-strategy of a north-south bloc, of an alliance between the country and the city, which would unite the rural peasants in the south with the industrial workers of the north in an attempt to wrest control from fascism and capitalism alike. In Gramsci's conception of that alliance, peasants and workers would also seek the support of anti-fascist progressive and liberal forces in Italian society. Both strategies, the anti-fascist and the anti-capitalist historic bloc, pursued an alliance and collaboration with liberal intellectuals, such as Piero Gobetti, for instance. As promoter of a 'liberal revolution', Gobetti could agree with Gramsci's anti-fascist cultural programme. It is unlikely, though, that Gobetti and the social groups he represented would go along with the elimination of a liberal bourgeois tradition from Italian cultural history. Manzoni figures prominently as a progressive Italian in that history, and one wonders to what extent Gramsci would have been successful in negotiating this point.

It is interesting in this context to remember that Lukács' aesthetic programme is also not unrelated to the cultural and political strategy of an anti-fascist popular front which he helped to shape in the 1930s alongside other western European intellectuals.[8] Lukács' participation in the cultural politics of an anti-fascist '*Volksfrontpolitik*' (popular front politics) aimed towards eliminating avant-garde literary and artistic experimentation in favour of the great literature inspired by enlightenment ideologies and the revolutions of the eighteenth and nineteenth centuries. The canon of classicism and romanticism, the literature of a bourgeoisie that in opposition to a resistant pre-capitalist feudal and aristocratic world and in its progress towards economic and cultural power promoted liberal values and philosophies of romantic heroism in the service of equity, tolerance, harmony and reason, are the literary models which Lukács chooses for the literary production of anti-fascists and anti-capitalists alike.[9] So in their respective understanding of the cultural effects of an anti-fascist popular alliance, Lukács believes that it is possible to impose on to the members of that alliance a bourgeois culture from above, while Gramsci rejects this premiss by apparently relying on the point of view from below. Manzoni was not, in spite of Gramsci's anti-fascist alliance with liberal democrats, admitted to the progressive cultural canon.

There are passages in 'On the Southern Question' which offer a kind of subtext of argument on the basis of which Manzoni's cultural 'misfortune' becomes integrated into an inexorable logic that by far transcends Gramsci's authorial judgement of Manzoni. What emerge from this subtext are traces of a philosophical programme within which Manzoni's rejection is not contingent on the personal whims of a cultural critic, such as Gramsci. For Manzoni was not going to be imposed as a literary, moral and intellectual model on the ordinary people, because he could not have been imposed. Acceptance is not enforceable. 'No mass action is possible unless the mass itself is convinced of the ends it wants to reach and the methods to be applied', writes Gramsci in 'On the Southern Question'.[10] It is unwise, unrealistic, to assume that intellectuals can impose their will, their politics, their aesthetics, on to the people in an unmediated fashion. So it is Gramsci's belief that the desires, habits, feelings and customs of the common people and of the most marginal social groups do count, indeed that they fulfil a function on a larger social scale. What matters then is not only what Manzoni, this nineteenth-century Italian intellectual, was or was not with respect to the Risorgimento or Italian history. What matters is also what and how his text does. That text had, in Gramsci's estimation, not done well. It had not been well received, indeed it had not been accepted, by the popular masses. Yet those popular masses, deprived of self-determination and political power, marginalized by predominant cultures and structures of feeling, are not deprived, however, of personal, intrinsic powers of their own. They have bodies and minds, desiring energies that are capable of attracting and repulsing their objects of desire. 'The popular creative spirit' had rejected Manzoni.

In Gramsci's assessment of Manzoni, then, there is not only a critique of Manzoni's intentions, but also a hint of those conditions which enable and resist the formation of cultural and political hegemonies. The norms and values of one social group cannot be simply imposed on to another. A highly sophisticated process of production of acceptance or 'production of consent' is required. Neither collective nor individual will can be imposed, at whim, arbitrarily, without preparation, on the collective will of the people. So Gramsci's rejection of Manzoni is not simply based on ethical standards, which would accuse Manzoni of being prejudiced in favour of the ruling class (though that is part of it). What also emerge from Gramsci's pages are traces of a complex philosophical model, a Spinozistic universe of materialist immanence, a cosmology almost, where space is not a void but filled with energies or forces, which, in perpetual motion, not only affect the energies they encounter in motion, but also always encounter energies already in motion. Intellectuals can attempt to impose their views on the people, just as a social group can attempt to impose its views on another. Yet to assume that the desire of a group, or desire itself, a field of energy, imposes itself on nothingness, that power, when placing itself, does so in a void that can be filled with its designs, that assumption is something Gramsci refutes.[11] In Gramsci's universe, matter in motion will find already existing matter present and in motion. Intellectual practices will find existing practices already present. There is always something there already. With this I have attempted to sketch another of Gramsci's leitmotifs, which points towards relations that obtain between Gramsci's ontological, epistemological and political programmes. These are traces of a philosophical materialism, of Spinozistic immanence, and of his reading of the conditions of possibility, of the operational limits of subjective and collective will.[12] These traces relate Gramsci to a theory of materialism and power, to a Foucauldian world order, perhaps to a phenomenological materialism, or to a phenomenological Marxism. What I would like to stress at this point is simply this: that Gramsci not only tends to view reality as a field in motion occupied by various forces, no matter how invisible or visible in their immanence; he also proposes that these forces must be accounted for

73

when making strategic cultural and political moves designed to change their overall arrangement. So in his cultural critique he proposes not only that one should begin from what there should be – Gramsci assuredly works from ethical premisses as well – but that one should begin from what there is.

'Realist' is the term Esteve Morera uses in her study of Gramsci to describe this style of Gramsci's thinking. She writes that Gramsci 'clearly rejects a conception of historical reality as dependent on a transcendent world as well as the view that the will can arbitrarily impose itself on reality and create a new world'.[13] So in the 'creation of a new world', a new culture and a new theory, the cultural critic does well to look at what there is. What Gramsci seems to see are not first and foremost autonomous poets or writers, pieces of literature or texts independent of a context, but texts that are written by someone and for someone. Texts, authors and audiences function in relation to one another. Authors and audiences are seen here as related in the production and the reception of texts, which turns them into producers of social texts. So Gramsci is interested not only in the structure of the reception of a text, as seen in his reading of Manzoni, but also in the structure of its production. In this Gramsci moves away from the orbit of idealist as well as traditional Marxist aesthetics, either where the text is first and foremost its own and only reality, or where the text first and foremost reflects a reality. Gramsci views texts as processes of production that involve producers and consumers within a social context. That context has been marked, since the turn of the century, in Italy as well as in other western countries, by significant changes in the modes of production. Modernizing technologies change instruments and modes of production, rationalizing the overall processes and mode of production, including the very relations of production themselves. New ways of producing and processing material goods, new technologies, that is, also effect new ways of producing and processing cultural goods, unsettling the world of received norms and values. Whereas idealist aesthetics tended to measure, as did Croce, for instance, new forms of cultural production against received aesthetic norms, Marxist aesthetics, particularly in the Lukácsian version, tended to ignore new cultural formations when measuring art against a new set of aesthetics. Gramsci does both and more. He not only interrogates traditional norms against the background of these new developments, but also interrogates these new developments against the background of traditional aesthetics. In this, Gramsci also departs from the orbit of traditional idealist aesthetics, such as Croce's, who, like Lukács, preferred the classicisms of the past, with its neat separation of what constituted true poetry and what did not, to the challenges of the future. Yet it should also be pointed out that Gramsci's openness towards technological production and its effects on the cultural sphere, which inexorably places him in the modernist camp with Benjamin and Brecht, that openness simultaneously marks his distance from other emancipatory aestheticians and modernists of the twentieth century: I am referring, for instance, to Adorno and Marcuse. While Gramsci shares their discontents with the culture industry, he does not share, and perhaps could not have shared, their response to that discontent: an aesthetic dimension that, fixing its claims on the autonomy of art, hopes to activate a dialectic capable of vindicating the effects of mass culture.[14] Surely, and these are points I hope to make in the next sections of this chapter, Gramsci is a modernist, standing beside Marcuse and Adorno, as well as Horkheimer, to the extent that he examines the operations and effects of the culture industry. And alongside Brecht and Benjamin, at least the earlier Benjamin, he is a modernist who appropriates elements of modernity for his own cultural and political programme. What problematizes Gramsci's modernism is his apparent naïvety about commodification and reification, not only when it comes to culture but also to industry. Perhaps it is this naïvety which best marks the sharp distinction between Gramsci's cultural critique and that of the Frankfurt School. To some of these and related issues, I will now turn.

GRAMSCI, TURIN AND CULTURE INDUSTRY

While Gramsci lived in Turin and in the years preceding his activities as one of the great leaders of the Italian working-class movement, he worked as a militant journalist, columnist and theatre critic and a cultural critic for a variety of progressive journals, including *Avanti*.[15] During those years, roughly from 1915 to 1920, he wrote many theatre reviews of plays staged in Turin. As a cultural critic attentive not so much to the maintenance of the status quo but to the structures that maintain and diffuse social, cultural and political hegemony, he critically reviewed these performances against the background of a predominant bourgeois culture in power, as well as against the aspirations of a newly emergent culture: that of the working class. Though the bulk of these writings take their point of departure from actual performances, Gramsci simultaneously reflects on the institution of the theatre and on the structures that enable the content and form of specific productions. What permeate his pages are issues we have in part already encountered in his treatment of Manzoni: the attitude of the author towards the marginal social classes, and the reception of a work of art not only by the dominant social class, but also by the new and emerging social classes. So, for instance, Gramsci is fond of a performance of Pirandello's *Liolà*. The characters here, though belonging to what by bourgeois standards are surbordinate social classes, the classes of the peasants, of the undereducated, of those subaltern classes living at the margins of predominant culture, are not represented from an ironic, condescending or morally superior point of view, as we know it from Manzoni and as in Gramsci's account it resurfaced in the 'Catholic' literature of various periods, including his own.[16] What Pirandello theatrically reproduces are neither nostalgically tainted pastoral images of an idyllic agricultural past, nor naturalistically documented social details mirroring the lot of the wretched of the earth, nor again exoticizing sketches of peasant life as folklore.[17] What he offers instead are efflorescent images of a naturalistic paganism, where 'life, all life, is beautiful, work is joyful and irresistible fecundity springs from all organic matter'.[18] Gramsci's appreciation of Pirandello's play is thus not only based on Pirandello's presentation of peasantry and work which, when compared to that of Manzoni, he finds more acceptable. What Pirandello also achieves, according to Gramsci, is that in *Liolà* the peasants, their customs, their norms and their work, do not, as in most Italian literature of the nineteenth century, function as the alien other in an exoticized or a pitiable otherness. They do not fulfil the objectificatory desires of a middle-class audience, but rupture these desires for otherness. The peasants are depicted as a source of value, of strength, of alternative and more natural ways of being.

Gramsci's understanding here, in the context of his review of Pirandello's *Liolà*, of an intrinsic need and desire for otherness, of the constitutive function of the other and otherness, as marginal as it might appear, in the processes of self-constitution of social classes or social groups, as well as in the production of collective meaning, identity and 'truth', reveals his interested awareness of something of a binary structure of social and cultural life. This interest is quite apparent in other Gramscian pages, particularly in his *Quaderni*, as he problematizes the structures informing collective imageries of city and country, for instance, or the structures that enable notions and relations of orient and occident. With respect to the notions and relations of orient–occident he surmises that they are constructed in terms of centre and otherness, a construction which is cultural and arbitrary, as it is historical and conventional. That constructedness is contingent on the 'point of view of the European upper class who, by exercising hegemony, made sure of the ubiquitous acceptance of their point of view'.[19] What Gramsci addresses here indirectly is the twentieth-century battle between positivists and critical theorists, between science and social science, between value-ladenness and value neutrality on the issue of methodology and methods. When he points to the conditions of 'objectivity', to the contingencies which are operative when establishing a 'universal truth' or an 'objective fact', then he reveals his solidarity with an early project of the Frankfurt School, namely Horkheimer's, Marcuse's and Adorno's struggle against the logical positivism of the Vienna Circle. Gramsci proposes with Horkheimer that there is no point of view without a perspective from which the taking of it occurs.[20] Yet when Gramsci relates this problem to the production of cultural values in relation to the European or the western world and the orient, when he begins to relate and extend the problematization of truth and value, though in a marginal note, to the ways in which ethnocentricity and ethnomarginality are constituted, then he begins to introduce a discourse the political ramifications of which had hardly been tapped by the Frankfurt School theorists at the time. Even the younger descendants of the Frankfurt School, Jürgen Habermas, for instance, have problems with a non-Eurocentric perspective, with cultural relativity, with non-western forms of logic and truth. In Gramsci's critique of universality and factuality, traces of the legitimacy of non-western ways of seeing begin to emerge. Was it his analysis of Pirandello's play which led him to such insights? Does Gramsci's literary criticism reveal the point from which his politics takes off, as Manacorda surmised in his subversive footnote?[21] Perhaps. I do not think, however, that there is much point in trying to establish a hierarchical order when it comes to Gramsci's rationality, and inquire whether his analysis of a literary text, such as Pirandello's, which lends itself to a critique of the value-laden production of universality, identity and truth, becomes the inexorable point of departure for an analysis of the conditions of possibility of class and of ethnocentricity. Given the unsystematicity of the Gramscian text, an unsystematicity which almost always, however, seeks to establish relations, I prefer to follow suit and proceed by analogies and homologies. The result is something like this: just as the west or the occident needs, in order to constitute its identity of superior reason and

77

morality, the imagery of a morally or culturally inferior other – the orient – thereby simultaneously contributing to and legitimating the orient's economic inferiority, the middle-class audience of Pirandello's play needs the imagery of a culturally inferior subordinate class in order to ground and legitimate its own cultural identity. This process perpetuates the actual inferior economic and political lives of peasants. Cultural hegemony labours to maintain an order of privilege of which marginality or the 'other', most often considered inferior from the point of view of hegemony, is both condition and effect.[22] It should come as no surprise, therefore, that the negative reception of *Liolà*, its non-popularity, cannot but reflect the psychic structure, structures of feeling and consciousness, of the hegemonic class. Faced with a life-affirming peasantry outside the boundaries of petty-bourgeois moral and aesthetic norms, a peasantry which Pirandello unearthed from Sicilian residues of a pre-Christian moral world and which he brings to life against the horizon of expectation of the middle class, when neither murder nor marriage resolves the action in *Liolà*, the audience is at an aesthetic, moral and psychic loss. It did not and could not applaud Pirandello's portrait of the Italian peasant.[23]

The importance of taking into account the reception of a play or a work of art, which marks Gramsci's critical evaluation of Manzoni's *The Betrothed* and Pirandello's *Liolà*, is very much part of his aesthetic programme in general. As usual, Gramsci will operate with an analytically relational structure that allows for the identification of more than one level and relation. Manzoni's novel was examined from the point of view of the marginalized people, and Pirandello's play from the point of view of the petty bourgeoisie and the middle class. In his review of Ibsen's *A Doll's House*, Gramsci adds another level to his analytic structure, an analytic subtext as it were: here he distinguishes not only between dominant and dominated cultural structures, between, let us say, bourgeoisie and ordinary people, but also and in addition between the women of these respective social classes. So it is not only class but also gender that constitutes the reception history of Ibsen's play. Whereas the women of the bourgeois middle-class audience were 'bewildered and deaf' after Ibsen's third act, proletarian women, so argues Gramsci, understood Nora's decision.[24] Bourgeois women were unmoved by sympathy before the profoundly moral act of Nora Helmer who was giving up her home, her husband and her children to look after herself and to live, on her own, an authentic, non-parasitic life. Proletarian women on the other hand felt solidarity with Nora's struggle for emancipation from patriarchal and bourgeois laws that stifle women and their creativity, laws which make women into slaves and 'submissive even when they seem rebellious'.[25] To the women of the bourgeoisie not used to freedom, self-determination and autonomy but only to the 'freedom of coquetry', the drama of Nora Helmer is necessarily incomprehensible.[26] To the women of the working class, on the other hand, Gramsci contends, Nora represented a 'spiritual sister', whose actions were essentially moral. She symbolized the 'aspiration of noble souls to a higher humanity', whose standard is the fullness of inner life.[27]

What some of Gramsci's theatre reviews disclose, then, is his insistence on the importance of integrating into a cultural critique not only the attitude of the artist or the writer to the social environment, but also the reception history of a play or a work of art. His notion of cultural critique thus focuses on the producer of the text, the author, and also on the reception of that text. In this Gramsci anticipates, by a good fifteen years, one of the pivotal issues of Walter Benjamin's essay 'Literaturgeschichte und Literaturwissenschaft' (1931), which we might translate as 'Literary History and Critical Literary Studies'.[28] Benjamin emphasizes in this essay, in which he attempts a definition of the domain and function of literary studies, not only the historicity of all sciences and disciplines, including the discipline of 'literary history', but also the potentially cultural, educative, progressive function of literary studies. That function, Benjamin proposes, criticism best fulfils when dealing with the work of art not so much in terms of its genesis, but more in terms of its reception history, and what that reveals and conceals. Indeed, the life of a text, its effects, its destiny, its success, this is what should be considered primary when dealing with literary works. In dialectical parlance, so dear to him as well as to Bertolt Brecht, and to the Frankfurt School in general, Benjamin puts it like this, and I translate freely:

> The problem is not, so it seems to me, to interpret literary texts in terms of the historical moment in which they are created; rather, what needs to be done is to relate our time, in which we interpret literary texts, to the moment in which these texts were created. [Denn es handelt sich ja nicht darum, die Werke des Schrifttums im Zusammenhang ihrer Zeit darzustellen, sondern in der Zeit, da sie entstanden, die Zeit, die sie erkennt – das ist die unsere – zur Darstellung zu bringen.][29]

Benjamin's contention, which rephrases, on a different terrain, Horkheimer's call for a critical theory which, in contradistinction to traditional theory, reflects on the social function of its project, corresponds to Gramsci's programmes as well.[30] As remarked already, Gramsci makes a point of setting up a structure which allows for difference among the various reactions to a specific performance on a Turin stage. By insisting on differences that mark the reception of a play, on the difference in feelings, sensibilities, normativities and aesthetic tastes that carry the social and cultural day, Gramsci contributes towards graphing, on the basis of the theatrical apparatus, a micrological picture of a society which, in its complexity, dynamics and contradictions, points to a social and cultural order where both cultural hegemony and an emerging counter-hegemony coexist. In this he fulfils the desiderata of the Benjaminian 'literary strategos', or the Horkheimerian 'critical theorist'. The play or the work of art is viewed not so much in terms of its origins as in terms of the social dynamics it elicits and resists, unravels and silences, affirms and denies, reveals and conceals, at the various moments of its reception.

Gramsci's sensibility to modernist ways of pursuing a cultural critique is not limited to his complex notion of the structure of reception, however. What also issue forth from his cultural critique of the theatre are critical reflections on the institutional character of the theatre, on the ways in which the theatre *qua* institution produces plays and disseminates social and political values. From a perspective which I would like to call 'a perspective of critical sociology', Gramsci interrogates the funding policies of theatrical institutions, their technical organization of the ideological contents of the repertoire, and their concomitant function in shaping, manipulating, surveilling and controlling public opinion. Morality, sociality and politicality intersect in the theatre. So Gramsci interrogates the relation of the theatre to the political and cultural hegemony of the social classes in power, as well as the theatre's relation to those classes or groups without significant social and political power. In this he parallels, to the very coining of his terminology and conceptual apparatus, and again from a distance of a good fifteen to twenty years, some of the efforts of the Frankfurt School. Gramsci examines, as would Adorno, Horkheimer and Marcuse, the phenomenon of the culture industry, with its concomitant manipulation of sensibilities, of the psychological needs of large masses of people, and with its tendencies to fabricate mass cultural one-dimensionality, for manufacturing consent to a political status quo. To be sure, Adorno and Horkheimer, writing their essay on the culture industry some twenty years after Gramsci, do not focus on the institution of the theatre as Gramsci does. Their interest lies with more modern forms of communicative technology, with the cinema and the radio, which by the mid- to late 1930s had testified, particularly in Germany and the USA, to an unprecedented usefulness for purposes of mass manipulation.[31] The cinematic apparatus and communications systems in general had by far superseded the manipulative or controlling powers of the theatre. And Adorno and Horkheimer had, due to their empirical studies of the psychic structure of the authoritarian personality, its relation to the modern family and to the formation of authoritarian states, in contradistinction to Gramsci, apparently a far better theoretical map of the relation of psychology and authority in modern civil society. That map included reflections on the crisis of the subject, and the trend of modern consciousness towards one-dimensionalization, with premonitions of a perhaps inexorable involuntarism which marks, in the minds of many people, many social sectors in postmodernity. In addition, the Frankfurt School had enormously profited from Lukács' theory of reification as proposed in *History and Class Consciousness*, and from Reich's investigations into the problem and structure of class consciousness. From Max Weber they had learned, so it seems, to become more sensitive to the effects of new technologies on the structure of modern community life, to the '*Vergesellschaftung der Gesellschaft*', the effects of an increasingly administered society. And from Benjamin they had learned about the effects of these new technologies on forms of communication, and perhaps even perception, and with it possibly the relation of perception to the structure of consciousness; on the replacement of communication by information, on the displacement of active intersubjective experience and bilateral reciprocities by unilateral information resting on active producers and passive receivers.[32] Thus it seems that the members of the Frankfurt School, working out their theories at a time when Gramsci was forced to slow down, could profit far more from the most advanced cultural, theoretical and political experiences and processes of their time than Gramsci could. Yet some of the operations of the culture industry and its relation to technology as examined by Adorno, Marcuse and Horkheimer are similar or homological in kind to those uncovered by Gramsci's examinations. And so are some reflections by Benjamin and Brecht on the relation of technology to art, similar in important aspects to the ones described by Gramsci in the context of his critical study of the theatre. By pointing in the following discussion to some homologies between Gramsci and these twentieth-century theorists in matters of the culture industry, I was also able to pursue one of the leitmotifs of this study: the question, that is, as to how Gramsci, compared to major theorists of the 1920s and 1930s, stands with regard to the 'modernization' of the cultural business, the industrialization of culture, that is.

Some of the articles which critically and conceptually link Gramsci to the writings of the Frankfurt School on the culture industry deal with theatre as an industry, and were written in the summer of 1917 for *Avanti*.[33] Some, though not all, carry the programmatic title 'The Theatre Industry'. These rather brief pieces – there are, according to a recent edition of Gramsci's pre-prison writings from that period, about seven of them – are framed by a series of reviews of what could at the time have been considered highly experimental and avant-garde theatre: these include the Chiarelli play *La masquera e il volto*, composed in the genre of the theatre of the grotesque, something of an Italian version of expressionist and surrealist theatre, and many other plays, in particular by Pirandello, such as *Cosi è si vi pare* [*Right You Are*].[34] In these reviews Gramsci addresses the authority of the public sphere, of centralized social normativities, of received ways of seeing, of validating and judging the actions of private individuals. Unexamined moral and philosophical norms authoritatively govern thoughts and actions, dictate ways of being and feeling, uncompromisingly closing the door on the issue of the legitimacy of difference before it has commenced. Even minimal gesturing of difference in will and perspective cannot but ultimately succumb to the ubiquitous domination of the social cage. While Gramsci understands the critical potential of these avant-garde plays, the power of their negativity to call into question dialectically the moral and epistemological status quo, he is somewhat undecided when it comes to a final aesthetic verdict. In the case of the Chiarelli play, for instance, he is unconcerned by its metaphorics of stifling unalterabilities, its failure to propose alternatives to decadent social and moral structures. Its negation of bourgeois decadence and hypocrisy is apparently enough. Yet in many of his reviews of Pirandello, he critiques this contemporary Italian playwright for focusing on the socially unalterable, on what we would now call, yet what he never calls, 'alienation' and fragmentation, for not proposing alternative, more positive, energetic, self-determinative and life-affirming modes of personal and collective experience. What Gramsci himself seems to pursue with his articles on the 'theatre industry', with his rigorous demystification of the power structures inscribed in that industry, and with his relentless call for social and cultural change, is a point of view he does not always put on his critical agenda when it comes to the most advanced Italian theatre practices at that time. So in some sense the divergence of interests emerging from some of these reviews seems to clash with the critical militancy of his notes on the 'theatre industry'. And indeed it does. We will see in a moment how critical Gramsci's critique of the theatre industry indeed is.

What Gramsci addresses in these articles on the 'theatre industry' are the activities of the 'Chiarelli Firm', which had monopolized and commercialized a series of Turin theatres.[35] Under the management of the 'Chiarelli Firm', the profit principle, as in modern industry, gradually began to shape and determine the quality of the product. This strategy was achieved among other things by competing, in content and in form of the performances, with the variety shows of the city, thereby cornering the most lucrative category of the theatre audience. Moreover, Gramsci argues, the owners of the theatre, by paying their actors lower wages – variety artists received lower wages than the regular stage actors – make out doubly well. Who or what does not profit, contends Gramsci, from the efficient implementation of the profit principle is the theatrical and cultural scene of Turin as a whole. The 'theatre industry', by ruthlessly lowering its artistic and aesthetic standards, by streamlining its performances in triviality, banality, pornographic indecorousness and rubbish, not only had endangered the existence of high-quality theatre companies and actors, but also had begun a process that viewed the audience as manipulable consumers. In addition, the 'theatre industry' had begun to cut Turin off from the national and international theatre movement. It had turned into a pleasure industry. Gramsci expresses his concern like this:

> The theatre has a great social importance. We are concerned by the degeneration which threatens it at the hands of the industrialists and we would like to react against this as best as we can. There is a large public that wants to go to the theatre. The industry is slowly conditioning it to prefer the inferior, indecorous show to one which represents a positive need of the mind.[36]

With this reaction to the gradual industrialization of culture Gramsci signals his attentiveness to the crisis and the transformation of the Italian theatre in the early twentieth century as northern Italy, with its industrial cities, slowly shifted from a stage of liberal capitalism towards monopoly capitalism, marked by a planned economy, increasing rationalization and technologization, as well as bureaucratization, and the eventual advent of state intervention in economic crisis situations. His notes on the 'theatre industry' reveal the extent to which Gramsci reflected on the principles of competitive efficiency that dictate the quantity and quality of theatrical commodities, how he understands the changes in his social and cultural environment, and how he proposes to intervene. As in his critique of Manzoni, human agency, human will, decision making and self-determination are some of the forms of rationality that structure events and their transformations, that enable, support, maintain, guarantee, legitimate and change the specific course of a phenomenon. So it is no surprise that Gramsci will first attribute this crisis of the Italian theatre to human agency, to the actions and decisions of specific individuals, the industrialists. The general tendency towards monopolization and rationalization of the theatre industry is not contingent on 'natural' but on 'artificial' processes, not related to a systemic rationality which, with self-regulating principles of expediency and profitability, governs economic, social and cultural transformations, but the results and effects of decisions made by concrete and autonomous individuals, the theatre owners. By consorting, monopolizing, commercializing and profiteering, the owners of the theatrical means of production have applied the 'Taylor method' to the realm of art. When directly addressing and polemicizing against the 'Chiarelli Firm', a monopoly consisting, it seems, of two brothers, Gramsci holds individuals and not anonymous systems or larger socio-historical processes, with their introduction of the profit principle, accountable for the 'Taylorized' state of the arts. What could change such a state of affairs, Gramsci proposes, is a collective agency, namely direct state intervention.

With his notes on the 'theatre industry' Gramsci intuits a relation between the modes of rationalization or 'Taylorization' applied in industry and those applied in the theatre. In industry as well as in the theatre, the basic structure of the commodity exerts a pervasive influence. In this he not only diagnoses the theatre crisis according to economic criteria, but also prescribes the kind of political solution generally applied to a crisis in the economy: he calls for state intervention. What Gramsci does not seem to intuit here is the relation of the rationalization of economy and culture to the rise of new rationalities, of what I would like to call 'new structures of knowing, seeing and feeling', capable of affecting the production and reception of art. A transformation of cognitive and affective structures is not envisaged in Gramsci's critique at this juncture. Furthermore, what Gramsci also does not seem to acknowledge in his critique of the 'theatre industry' is the relation of the rationalization of economy and culture to new technologies. The silent film, the product of new technologies, was one of the conditions that affected the commercialization of the theatre. And finally, what Gramsci also does not recognize at that point is the way in which new technologies could lead to new cultural experiences and progressively participate in the production of new cultural and political formations. In short, the divergences which I noted earlier in the juxtaposition of Gramsci's notes on the theatre industry with his theatre reviews reappear in his critique of the theatre industry.

While Gramsci is able to discern the commodity principle as the major motivating force behind the crisis of the theatre, he is reluctant to relate this principle to larger changes in the realm of socio-economic processes, to the new rationalities, new structures of feeling, seeing and knowing which these economic and organizational changes produce. That is to say, whereas he had asserted in his review of Ibsen's *Doll's House* that the sensibilities of proletarian women corresponded to those expressed by Nora, sensibilities which are differentiable from those of the middle-class and bourgeois women, perhaps related to the different place and function proletarian women occupy and carry out in the process of production, and perhaps related to a different consciousness, Gramsci seems reluctant, in his critique of the theatre industry, to entertain the logic of a possible emergence of new sensibilities, or perhaps new psychic and cognitive structures, next to the formation of new rationalities informing, affecting and resulting from the gradual rationalization and modernization of processes of production. In so far as Gramsci critiques the commodification and commercialization of the realm of art, where art no longer remains an end in itself, but engages in the establishment of a competitive, expedient and efficient theatrical apparatus, he apparently maintains that the commodified sphere of culture can be the subject of criticism. Yet nowhere does he critique the processes of rationalization and technologization as they evolve in the sphere of economic production. The extent to which Gramsci refused to see, or was still unable to see, by 1917, the impact of new technologies, in themselves not unrelated to the rationalization of the economic sector, on received forms of culture and tradition is apparent from an article written roughly a year before the 'theatre industry' pieces and entitled 'The Theatre and the Cinema'.[37] What is also apparent from this article is Gramsci's inability to see the political potential of new technologies in the construction of a new culture.

This article suggests that some critics had apparently attempted to understand, and with hindsight correctly, that the crisis of the theatre was an effect of the emergence of new and powerful technologies on the cultural market, such as the silent film. It had also been argued that the rise of the movie industry made the commodification of the theatre virtually unavoidable, if it wanted to survive as an institution. So in its competition with the movie industry, the theatre was keen on offering to the paying public sensations and experiences commensurate with those provided by the new medium of film. Gramsci is adamant about seeing this situation from his point of view. There is no point in arguing, he suggests, that the theatre is competing with the movie industry. Rather, the theatre, in its degenerate and decadent state, already offers a series of sensations which are identical with the ones offered by the movie industry. Or to put it rather differently, what the cinema offers is exactly the same banality and triteness as contemporary theatre, 'the same sensations, but under better conditions, and without the choreographic contrivances of false intellectualisms, without promising too much while delivering little'.[38] What audiences get in the commercial cinema, then, is precisely what they get from the commercial stage, only more economically:

> The most commonly staged productions are nothing but fabrics of external facts, lacking any human content, in which talking puppets move about variously, without ever drawing out a psychological truth, without ever managing to impose on the listener's creative imagination a character or passions that are truly felt and adequately expressed. Psychological insincerity and lame artistic expression have reduced the theatre to the same level as pantomime.[39]

The future of the theatre lies consequently not in competing with the cinema and the technologies of the future, but in readjusting its artistic standards to rationalities of the past. Should the theatre refuse to compete with the movie industry, Gramsci reasons, this does not mean, as some have argued, the end of the theatre. On the contrary, low-quality film experiences could help the theatre to get back on its high-quality feet.

What Gramsci noted, then, is the application of the profit principle in the cinema industry. Just as in the economic sphere the application of rational technologies enables the production of commodities, and the triumph of exchange-value over use-value, thereby generating greater profits, in the sphere of culture the deployment of cinematic technologies enables the production of greater pleasure. Yet Gramsci stands firm. That there is or might be more pleasure, perhaps of a different kind, means little. The point is that it is not adequate to what Gramsci perceives as the psychic and cultural needs of the audiences. The cinematic apparatus produces a 'low' mass culture and manipulates, controls and corrupts the audience. By 1916–17, the cinema is, in Gramsci's account, not an instrument for political and cultural struggles. The audiences are here, as in his critique of the theatre industry, passive objects of the manipulative desires of the theatrical industrialists. Gramsci's insistence on the responsibility of the owners of the means of theatrical production in the formation of public taste potentially keeps him from viewing the crisis of the theatre as part of complex economic, social and cultural transformations. In this he underestimates the power of new technologies in effecting, engaging and even intervening in existing forms of culture. He seems to vacillate, in those years, between a position that affirms the productive force of new technologies and a position that applies uneven evaluative principles to economic production and cultural production. In that new machinery and new technologies had contributed to the formation of the machine age with its working class, the working class as protagonist of history is entitled to demand and expect not 'low-quality culture' but 'high-quality culture'. The image Gramsci creates is that of a public that knows what it wants, and this is certainly the impression he put forth when reviewing Pirandello's *Liolà* and Ibsen's *Doll's House*, as well as Manzoni's *The Betrothed*. On the other hand, in that he condemns the theatre and the cinema for offering low-quality cultural products to a manipulable audience, he creates the image of social groups who do not know what they want and how to get it. In this he merely attests to the manipulative powers of technology, and not to their potential use in subverting an old culture and in creating a new one. He thus offers several readings of technology, as well as several readings of the notion of consciousness, some of which join forces in his cultural critique. In one reading, new technologies, new ways of organizing processes of production and their distribution, including cultural production, impinge upon the 'affective and cognitive structures' of a social group. The proletariat, knowing what it wants, reveals a class consciousness of its own. In another reading, the public appears as an anonymous, unstructured,

87

class-less mass which, apparently without a practical consciousness of its own, without awareness of its needs and desires, succumbs to the powers of old and new technologies. So the predominant images that emerge are those of a consuming public that is both incapable of projecting and producing its own needs and desires, and capable of so doing. Those who, throughout Gramsci's cultural critique, know the means for producing and satisfying desire are the owners of the means of production of the theatre industry, who, as profit-hungry producers, sell their cultural products to a product-hungry public. The feelings, needs and interests of the audience have been assimilated to the theatrical apparatus. Mass manipulation is here, by 1916 and 1917, thematized in Gramsci's critiques of the theatre industry, well over twenty years before Marcuse's startling essay on 'Some Social Implications of Modern Technology' (1941), and thirty years before Horkheimer's and Adorno's *Dialectic of Enlightenment* (1947).[40]

Gramsci the theatre critic and Gramsci the critic of the 'theatre industry' diverge when it comes to the issue of economic versus cultural rationalization. As a theatre critic writing reviews, Gramsci evokes a public whose 'structures of feeling' are affected by the tendencies towards economic rationalization. That is to say, the reception of specific plays points to a society divided into social classes that relate antagonistically to each other, classes that are capable of voicing their respective aesthetic desires, of saying yes or no to a play, of creating their own diverging cultures. As a critic of the 'theatre industry', Gramsci evokes a public whose 'structures of feeling' seem to be affected not so much by economic rationalization but rather by tendencies towards social and cultural rationalization. The audience which emerges in this depiction is one without desire. It is not clear, however, what the precise status of this lack of desire is, whether the audience consents to the manipulations directed by theatrical industrialists (and by their cinematic counterparts), or whether it is coerced in this direction. The operations of hegemony, and their conditions of possibility, are not clearly explained. What is certain, though, is the status of the desire of the owners of the means of theatrical production. In their pursuit of self-interested profit, they have driven the Italian theatre into a crisis.

So much for the complexity of Gramsci's cultural critique by 1917. Bertolt Brecht has also addressed the crisis of the theatre, and the poor quality of the cinema, from the point of view of a playwright and producer, in one of his early writings.[41] Brecht is, as Gramsci was, interested in raising the quality of theatrical performance, and in using the stage as a vehicle for emancipatory and liberatory adult schooling. Yet in his analysis of the causes of the theatre crisis, he does not look for just one party dancing the tango. On Brecht's account, it is not only the banality-producing theatre that deserves contempt, but the public also, for both are implicated in that crisis situation. While the current theatre prefers a certain public, one that 'consists of people who either lose their naïvety when entering the theatre or one that never possessed naïvety in the first place', it is hopeless to presume that the theatre would be able to keep such a public by 'making more allowances'. It is difficult to accommodate the public, Brecht writes, 'since one cannot know how to accommodate it. It has no appetites whatsoever.'[42] Brecht's solution to the problem is a new factor on stage, the producer, whose responsibility it is continuously to make attempts towards the creation of a theatre that involves the public as much as the stage, the actors as much as the audience, stage design as much as the producer. What Brecht has in mind is his very own epic theatre, which in its reliance on the points of view that arise from the great western drama of production of the time, evokes a world in which the owners of the means of production do not alone set the tone, but the producers of goods and value, the working people, actively engage and perhaps even intervene in the production of cultural values. By the same token, Brecht does not reject, as Gramsci did by 1917, the cinematic apparatus, but interrogates it against the background of what it can do. In some of his earliest notes on film, dating back to 1922, Brecht was not, like Gramsci, dogmatically refusing to see the other side of the coin, but already dealing in dialectics. He writes, and I freely translate: 'There are effective movies which do have an effect even on an audience who considers these movies kitsch; however, effective movies which are made by people who consider them kitsch, these kinds of movie do not exist.'[43] While Brecht can think, in contradistinction to Gramsci, of politically beneficial effects of a certain cultural product on a public, in spite of that public's understanding of that particular product as 'kitsch', he can also think, with Gramsci, of the politically detrimental effects of a cultural product conceived as kitsch by its producers.

By 1917, Gramsci's position and his approach to cultural problems indicate a series of indeterminacies. This is so with his notes on the theatre of the grotesque, the Pirandello plays in general, and with his critique of the theatre industry. All this has not gone unnoticed by predominant Gramsci scholars. For some these indeterminacies serve as convenient vestiges of what is considered Gramsci's persistent

Crocean heritage. So be it.[44] These tendencies no doubt call into question Gramsci's otherwise impeccable credentials, of whatever kind they might be. Yet tensions in Gramsci's accounts do exist, and it is therefore tempting to evoke, in *concordia discors* with the critical community, the terms 'antinomy', 'dualism', 'paradox', and so forth, and speak of the Crocean/idealist/subjectivist presence in Gramsci's theory.[45] In my case, I prefer to stay away from such categorizations, particularly since his militant performance on the stage of twentieth-century critical theory can more than stand and coexist with his indeterminacies. If anything, they do not disturb, but emphasize, by contrast, the complexity, the manysidedness, of Gramsci's cultural critique.

It should now be pointed out that Gramsci's activities as theatre critic and journalist in Turin were soon displaced by his political activism as one of the major leaders of the Italian working-class movement. When he returns to writing on the theatre and on film, when in prison, that is, by the late 1920s, many of his attitudes on the ways in which the audience interacts with the stage have changed. And so have his anti-modernist assessments of the subversive potential of the cinema and his modernist-Adornian rejection of mass culture. At the time of the *Prison Notebooks*, audiences rise from their one-dimensional passivity to dialectical engagement with producer and play, they perform as they participate in a performance. The notion of a dialectical theatre, in general and for good reason attributed to Brecht, is, by the early 1930s, decidedly anchored in parts of Gramsci's theoretical design. So it should come as no surprise that his understanding of the cinema, of the immense communicative potentials of the cinematic apparatus, has also changed by the early 1930s. He no longer dwells on a negative critique of the theatre industry, in polemics against profiteering producers of mass culture and their attempts to manipulate, control and surveil the aesthetic and moral sensibilities of the populace for benefits of money and power. Rather, Gramsci shows more of an interest in issues related to new communication and film technologies in their relation to mass culture. So, for instance, he argues that film not only reproduces the preferred melodramatic taste of large strata of the Italian public – that the cinema indeed functions as a successor to melodrama[46] – or that for this reason the cinematic apparatus holds an eminent place in the production of mass culture. He also argues that the structure and the function of the melodramatic element must be taken into account in a cultural critique and theory.[47] And precisely because the cinema operates with elements of the melodramatic genre, it can and should be enlisted in the cultural struggle. Gramsci pragmatically calls for, as Brecht never tired of doing, the critical appropriation of new cultural technologies for the political emancipatory struggle, the critical appropriation of those new cultural experiences which had, by virtue of their own appropriation of the 'structures of feeling', familiar to the audience, attested to an impeccable ideological functionality.[48] What will make the cinematic apparatus functional for the emancipatory struggle is a specific structure that it integrated into its apparatus: the structure of the popular novel, not only inordinately dear to the Italian reading public but also for this reason inordinately suitable for assimilating and disseminating an ideological content.[49] Moreover, Gramsci detects that the technologies of the cinematic apparatus are capable of incorporating a rhetoric of the sensory that far transcends the persuasive effectiveness of the spoken word. What Gramsci refers to are sensory semiotics, a language of gestures, signs and varying tonality known and utilized by the old rhetorical tradition. These sensory technologies have become extraordinarily functional in the cinema. He writes, and I translate:

> In oratory, it is not just the word that plays a role. There is the gesture, the sound of the tone, etc., a musical element, that is, which communicates the leitmotif of the predominant sentiment, of the major passion, and an orchestral element, the gesture in the grand sense, which disseminates and articulates the sentimental and passionate energies.[50]

And Gramsci reasons that cultural politics would do well if it learned from those technologies that assured cinema's unprecedented success. For a politics of mass culture, he adds laconically, observations of this kind are foundational.[51]

If in prison Gramsci's attitude towards the cinematic apparatus had changed from that of the Turin years, in that he had become more sensitive to the political potential inscribed in its technology, and its possible function in the emancipatory business, it is still not comparable to that of Benjamin as it emerges from his pioneering studies on the impact of new technologies on ways of seeing, judging, indeed on being itself. Gramsci tends to operate or make analogies with techniques that are known already when attempting to understand new technologies, as he does when analogizing the semiotics of the cinema with the good old rhetorical tradition. A constant in his account is thus a notion of the subject that has remained the same in spite of the far-reaching economic, social and technological trans-formations which have been taking place. What Benjamin envisages are not only changes in aesthetic or moral taste, in sensibilities and feelings, but also changes in perception, which, accompanying the ways of being of rationalized modernity, come close to a notion of the very structuration of being. Rationalization creates its own subject, and Benjamin, at least the Benjamin of the mid-1930s, does not consider that creation, next to Brecht, as a threat, as Adorno had when he critiqued Benjamin.[52] Processes of rationalization have, in Benjamin's account, created a new consciousness that, while adjust-ing to new experiential modes, apparently escapes commodification. Gramsci's relationship with new technologies, their conditions and their effects, is not always as firmly grounded as Benjamin's in that he does not reflect on the possible radical effects of new technologies on the structure of consciousness. Yet there is no doubt that he, like Benjamin, reflects not only on what that technology can do to or with a subject, but also on what needs to be done with that new technology. When Benjamin notes that the point is not to offer ideas of use to an existing apparatus of production, but rather to interrogate it in terms of what possibilities it has to offer to a producer intent upon changing the status quo, then Gramsci could certainly have given this argu-ment his wholehearted approbation.[53] And when Benjamin calls for the abolition of received literary genres and aesthetic norms, new ways for conceiving and evaluating the realm of art in the age of its reproducibility, then Gramsci, who has spent many of his prison years in reflecting on marginal cultural and literary practices, could easily have joined the Benjaminian camp.[54] Not the theatre critic of 1917 but the cultural critic in prison, let us say from 1929 to 1933, when Gramsci wrote, is arguably a fellow-traveller of Benjamin as well as Brecht. The examination of Gramsci's prison notes on Piran-dello, next on my agenda here, will I hope make these connections yet more evident.

4

Gramsci's theory of consciousness: between alienation, reification and Bloch's 'principle of hope'

OBJECTIVITY, SUBJECTIVITY AND GRAMSCI'S PIRANDELLO

Gramsci's notes on Pirandello in the *Prison Notebooks* suggest that Pirandello was not exactly one of Gramsci's privileged subjects of inquiry. He had not intended, as was the case with Manzoni, to dedicate part of his well-planned research programme to this Italian modernist playwright. Yet the Pirandello notes follow precisely the same organizational pattern as Gramsci's critical practice when applied in his treatment of Manzoni: Pirandello is viewed in relation to a set of wider issues, such that the discourse does not centre on or privilege information concerning Pirandello the playwright, but rather makes reference to a wide range of associated historical, social and cultural issues.[1] Gramsci's practice, which I have previously called his 'relational pragmatics', looks in connection with Pirandello something like this: production aspects of the Pirandellian plays are related to the predominant mode of theatrical production at the time, engaged in maintaining the preferred melodramatic taste of the period; the reception of Pirandello's plays by Catholic critics, who rejected his predilection for a pagan naturalism or for a fragmented subject; Pirandello's values and norms in relation to Catholicism; futurism with its techniques and aspirations in relation to Pirandello's cultural values; futurism and Pirandello in their relation to early twentieth-century Italian culture; Pirandello's philosophical assumptions, his modernity, his 'dialectic' in relation to popular culture; and so forth. What differentiates these notes from Gramsci's earlier Turin reviews of Pirandello plays is first and foremost Gramsci's new and much more benevolent attitude towards Pirandello. In the Turin years, Gramsci showed some enthusiasm for the explosively negative logic informing Pirandello's conceptual framework, the modern problematization of the concept of truth, which Pirandello seemed to introduce into his plays both on the level of form and content, yet Gramsci's language is distinctly critical of Pirandello on the whole.[2] In the Pirandellian play as well as in the theatre of the grotesque Gramsci had disliked the psychological one-dimensionality of the characters, their non-motivated psychological flatness, characters that are simple constructions without deep inner intuitions and feelings. As figures devoid of passion, motivation and will, they are deprived of those qualities which are necessary for struggle and confrontation, which alone enable the unravelling of dramatic motion and action. The aesthetic norms Gramsci lived by as a critic in Turin were, in spite of his marked interest in modern philosophical problems, essentially those of the traditional drama. That Pirandello calls into question received notions of reason, truth and meaning is to his credit, yet Gramsci would have preferred such content in a well-designed Aristotelian character. And he would have preferred the possibility of adjusting the Pirandellian play to some aspects of traditional idealist and perhaps Crocean aesthetic, where the presence of an intrinsic poeticity and not political or ideological rhetoricity defined the authentic work of art. In his prison notes on Pirandello Gramsci has undoubtedly moved further though not totally away from received aesthetics with its content/form problematic. While he as ever finds attractive Pirandello's problematization of received norms of seeing, he now shows greater appreciation for the innovative ways in which this problematization is enacted. In short, he has discovered some aspects of the complexity of Pirandello's theatrical apparatus. This leads him to what I would like to call a 'Benjaminian' understanding of the function of Pirandello, as author, as producer, and to a 'Brechtian' understanding of the dialectics obtaining between audience, staging, acting, directing and producing. It also leads him to a greater though still limited recognition of the radicality of these theatrical practices, of the negative dialectic, that is, inscribed in Pirandello's art.

Gramsci's investigation of his object of study, in which he grounds Pirandello's modernity and significance, looks something like this. By calling into question received notions of authority, truth values and meaning, by a sophisticated questioning of the precariousness of '*Sein und Schein*', of being and appearance, Pirandello, as Italian intellectual, has participated in one of the most advanced modern philosophical discourses. In so doing, he put Italy on the European theoretical map, even more so than the futurists, who in their non-negotiable rejection of traditional taste and values ultimately grounded themselves in a destructive radical negativity. This precluded much dialectical problematization.[3] Moreover, by offering his epistemological scepticism and his relativization of truth, empiricism and realism to a large theatre public, Pirandello has contributed to the process of radical modernization of Italian culture rooted in traditional and unexamined notions of objectivity, value, truth and common sense. Pirandello crafted the juxtaposition of 'common sense' with 'good sense', or 'critical sense' in a romantic form, in a paradoxical struggle between the two. His enacting of critique in a paradox solicited a positive response from the audience. In addition, by offering his sceptical view of common sense in the context of a theatrical apparatus attentive to changes in its very structure, Pirandello had also contributed to the transformation of the Italian theatre and its audience which for long periods had privileged the melodramatic over critical investigations. With Pirandello, reality was no longer displaced in a melodramatic presentation, but became the object of critical interrogation. This problematic was not only enacted by actors. In that Pirandello actively takes part in the production of this problematic as a producer who directs and organizes the material apparatus of stage design, lighting, colours, the semiotic makeup of the play, and in that he relates the spoken language of the actors to the multiple languages of the stage, Pirandello inaugurates a new theatrical genre: theatre as production. The author is no longer a playwright whose text is simply handed over to the leading actor of the theatre company, who then manages its interpretation by him/herself and by the various actors. Rather, the leading actor, being displaced by the operations of the producer, becomes one of many characters. The importance of a major exemplary character begins to disappear in this gradual democratization of the stage. As producer, Pirandello has initiated a dialectic between the language of the actors and the material apparatus of the stage. Yet there is a second dialectic he initiates as well: that of the 'philosophical dialogue' between the stage and the audience.

What Gramsci detects in the Pirandellian play are those aspects of Pirandello's art which have become part of theatre criticism and are valued by the regular Pirandello scholars in the later twentieth century. It is to Gramsci's credit that he picked out relatively early, and contrary to many of his contemporary critics, the modern, modernist and modernizing tendencies in Pirandello's work, in terms of both its theoretical content and its theatrical innovations. Surely, Gramsci is still somewhat undecided, in the early 1930s, as to how to validate the Pirandellian play from a traditional aesthetic point of view. 'His importance', Gramsci reasons, 'seems to be more of an intellectual and moral, i.e. cultural, than an artistic kind.'[4] Yet Gramsci appreciates the modernity of Pirandello's attitude in creating a theatre that does not intellectually lull the public with a monotonous repetition of set-ups, conflicts and mediations, whose melodramatic range is emotionally predictable by and familiar to the audience. Pirandello's plays rupture and explode the audience's anticipations by introducing an unsettling paradox between 'normalcy' and 'non-normalcy' which resists emotional identification while simultaneously requiring active intellectual intervention. A modern audience is capable of such speculative reflections. In this Pirandello's theatre is adequate to and perhaps even ahead of its time, and Gramsci welcomes its contemporaneity in the way in which Brecht welcomed the technical, theoretical and theatrical contemporaneity of Piscator and conceived of his own epic theatre, in which a passively consuming audience had been replaced by speculative and critical observers.[5] Yet perhaps what Gramsci values most in Pirandello is the critique of his contemporary philosophical culture, a critique which both demystifies received notions of objectivity and radicalizes the Kantian dualism of knowable phenomena and always unknowable noumena. Indeed, Gramsci tends to view the Pirandellian problematic primarily as an epistemological problem, as a critique of received notions of rationality, factuality and scientificity. And Gramsci seems to understand Pirandello's positing of a multiplicity of realities in the subjective as well as the objective world, a multiplicity from which multiple ways of approaching and validating facts and experiences emerge. Yet it should be pointed out that Gramsci reveals a problematic of his own when dealing with Pirandello. For there is some evidence that Gramsci's view of Pirandello's problematization of subjectivity and objectivity is marked by a profound undecidability on Gramsci's part. While Gramsci seems to value Pirandello's calling into question the unity of object and subject, he seems to attribute to Pirandello a critique not of a philosophical tradition, but of bourgeois culture. Gramsci does not present Pirandello's problematic as an intersubjectively valid epistemological problem. It seems to be a bourgeois epistemological problem, a problem that concerns a disappearing social class and not an ascending class. In other words, while Gramsci appreciates Pirandello's calling into question the unity of the object, as well as the precariousness of the unity of the subject in processes of cognition, whereby Pirandello unsettles a tradition, he is less inclined to apply this critique to all forms of cognition, to raise it to a general theoretical problem. The class origin of the cognizing subject seems to matter. So Pirandello's sensibility to a theoretical problem of modernity which parallels on stage and in a popularized form the findings of the Heisenberg principle of uncertainty, and their concomitant critique of scientific rationality, is apparently a theoretical position which Gramsci recognizes, but which he does not ascribe to the cognitive processes of all subjects, to modern rationality in general. The marginal groups, the proletariat, the common people, 'the popular creative spirit', all seem to be exempt from such prerogatives of being, perhaps living according to their very own structures of a rational, social and cognitive life-world.

While Gramsci makes the point of noting the fragmented consciousness of the Pirandellian subject, and of relating it to a bourgeois structure of consciousness, he also makes the point of not relating that fragmentation, and its possible social causes, to a non-bourgeois structure of consciousness. In the structures of the life-world of Gramsci's non-bourgeois subject, fragmentation and alienation do not seem to exist. What is there to be inferred but that its identity is, compared to bourgeois consciousness, intact? This assessment of Gramsci's position on the subject and consciousness seems to contradict an earlier version of this problematic. In his reviews of *Liolà* and of Ibsen's *Doll's House*, the audience knows how to react to these respective plays, thereby displaying the consciousness of a subject that knows what it wants and what it does not want. The bourgeoisie disliked the former and the working class liked the latter. In the Pirandello notes from the prison years, Gramsci does not confront us only with a view of consciousness as predicated on class, as he did in his Turin years. There is now also a qualitative difference. One social class guarantees the identity of the subject, and thus the possibility of self-determined human agency, whereas other classes do not. Pirandello's subjects reveal the structure of consciousness of the descending bourgeoisie. Their subjects are no longer in control of who they are or what they want. This is all very interesting particularly in light of the fact that Gramsci calls attention in the context of his discussion of Pirandello to a problematization of that position which detects and posits structures of being that seem to inform all experience quite independent from class. He addresses, for instance, Pirandello's notion of 'ideology' which he relates to the principle of 'theatricality' or 'performance' as a basic aspect of all experience. 'One should see', he interestedly recommends, 'how much of Pirandello's "ideology" is, so to speak, of the same origin as that which seems to form the nucleus of the "theatrical" writings of Nikolai Evreinov.'[6] For Evreinov theatricality is not only a particular form of artistic activity, that which is technically expressed in theatre in the literal sense. For him 'theatricality' is present in life itself, it is an attitude peculiar to the human being in that he/she tends to believe and to make others believe that he/she is different from what he/she is.[7]

Gramsci seems to understand what is at stake here when he, after relating Pirandello's 'ideology' to a principle of theatricality, which he correctly intuits in Pirandello's theatre, raises an ontological question. What is the 'meaning of one's real nature', he provocatively asks. If life is performance, theatre for others, then the true essence of human being, the subject of will, self-determination and intentional action, is on the verge of disappearing, losing its identity in always performing for others. Gramsci is quick to intercept that inexorable logic which would efface the identity of the subject – and which would catapult him into the ranks of late twentieth-century theory – when he dialogizes:

> Now what is the meaning of 'one's real nature', from which one tries to appear 'different'? First answer: 'One's real nature' can be taken to be the sum of one's animal impulses and instincts, and what one tries to appear as is the social-cultural 'model' of a certain historical epoch that one seeks to become. Second answer: It seems to me that 'one's real nature' is determined by the struggle to become what one wants to become.[8]

Essence and meaning collapse into one. And it is the second answer which appeals to Gramsci, who on the issue of the identity of the non-bourgeois subject, on the unified structure of non-bourgeois consciousness, will not budge. In fact, one has the feeling that faced with the possibility that the loss of the identity of the subject could turn into a general modern problem, even transgress and contaminate the non-bourgeois camp, he is more than willing to return to the bourgeois subject whose loss of identity he had first applauded on the Pirandellian stage. So when he addresses the issue of the unity of the subject in his comments on a negative review of Pirandello by the Italian theatre critic d'Amico, he vehemently disagrees with that critic on what Pirandello's intention might have been. D'Amico, as a Catholic critic, is dependent on a unified consciousness, which can be held accountable, for better or for worse, for human vice and virtue. So d'Amico is not thrilled about Pirandello's positing of multiple consciousnesses in one of his plays, *Six Characters in Search of an Author*. Gramsci argues against d'Amico. Pirandello is not out to posit the presence of multiple consciousnesses in the structure of one. He is out to amuse himself 'by raising certain "philosophical" doubts, by unsettling the unphilosophical and narrow minds. He is out to make fun of subjectivism and philosophical solipsism.'[9] Perhaps. Does Gramsci intuit, perhaps, that the very structure of the subject, which Benjamin related to processes of rationalization without ascribing to it a structure of commodification, is in itself structured by certain forces? Is the Pirandellian subject emerging not as a structure, or as part of a structure, but perhaps as the effect of structures? Has the structuration and structurability of the subject, which Gramsci makes out with his understanding of hegemony, begun? Is it not the presence of structures, of layers of consciousness, that enables resistance to domination? Yet Gramsci refutes d'Amico's fears. Other critics of Pirandello have surmised, against Gramsci, that d'Amico's fears were not unfounded. Pirandello's modernity is in his calling into question the unity of the subject, the crisis of ethicality that it entails, and his pointing to increasing fragmentation and alienation in human experience perhaps related to processes of rationalization and technologization.[10] For Pirandello probably intuited what the highly educated European bourgeois intelligentsia had intuited all along: the complete fragmentation and alienation of late bourgeois culture, which Lukács, for instance, addressed in one of his earliest works, *Soul and Form*, which he addressed again in his *History and Class Consciousness* in the form of reification, and which in its form of reification would inform much of the concept and critique of culture industry by the Frankfurt School.[11]

According to Gramsci, Pirandello is too much of a Cartesian thinker, too deeply rooted in the empirical tradition, to call into question the authority of the subject. There are epithets such as 'intellectualistic' which he applies to him. Is Gramsci determined to keep to a minimum a discussion of the structure of consciousness which potentially could engage all subjects, all social classes? When Gramsci detects in Pirandello's personality a tension between various ways of being, feeling and seeing, a tension between that which is Sicilian, Italian and European, he explains it like this:

> Pirandello is critically a Sicilian 'villager' who has acquired certain national and European traits, but who feels these three

elements of civilization to be juxtaposed and contradictory within himself. From this experience has come his attitude of observing the contradictions in other people's personalities and then of actually seeing the drama of life as the drama of these contradictions.[12]

Also here, where Gramsci has the opportunity to reflect on the possibility of a multiplicity of layers informing a subject's consciousness, he bypasses the issue. Appropriately, the next paragraph begins with a notation that abruptly intervenes in the trajectory of a logic differentiable from his: the paragraph begins with 'besides'. The interplay of the Sicilian, the Italian and the European elements in Pirandello's plays is not considered as the possibility of multiple forms of consciousness residing in a person's being; rather the tension between the Sicilian and Italian is explained by an old practice, that of

describing, satirizing and caricaturing the provincial who wants to appear 'transformed' into a 'national' or European-cosmopolitan character as an element not only of the Sicilian dialect theatre [*Aria del continente*], but of all Italian dialect theatre and also of the popular novel.[13] It is nothing other than a reflection of the fact that a national-cultural unity of the Italian people does not exist, that 'provincialism' and particularism are deeply rooted in the customs and in the way they think and act.[14]

And with this the possibility of Gramsci's discourse here on the structure of consciousness in its relation to the increasing domination of economic relations over social and cultural life seems to end before it has commenced.

It is one of the commonplaces in Gramsci scholarship to presume that 'Gramsci, like Croce and Lukács, lacked any appreciation of psychology in general'.[15] On the basis of Gramsci's prison notes on Pirandello, one is tempted to follow the lead. Yet such a position would ignore one of the great contributions of Gramsci to twentieth-century theory: his notion of hegemony. For this reason I rather conclude here that Gramsci reveals a complicated relationship with issues related to the structure of consciousness, to the unconscious, to psychology and even psychoanalysis. So one of the statements reproduced above decidedly points to Gramsci's understanding of a tripartite conscious structure not unlike the one we have been treated to by Freud. Without the psychoanalytical terminology Gramsci possesses its conceptuality. When Gramsci, in his attempt to define 'human nature', speaks of instincts and of a will that struggles to become 'what one wants to become', then Gramsci graphs the contours of a desiring Freudian id and ego that are not unencumbered by a co-ercing social super-ego against which they struggle. Surely, in this definition, Gramsci accords considerable space to will and critics have often been fond of pointing to Gramsci's indebtedness to volun-tarism, which is occasionally related, in Marxist and non-Marxist frameworks alike, to Gramsci's presumed subjectivism and idealism. I am not interested in settling such matters. What I find suggestive is Gramsci's apparent resistance to the Pirandellian countdown of the western subject. While Gramsci in his notes as a theatre critic in Turin had rejected on moral grounds the one-dimensional psychic structure of Pirandello's character in search of identity, in search of an author, in his prison notes Gramsci seems to overlook the psychic plight of the Pirandellian characters in his rejection of the universal validity claim Pirandello proposes on philosophical grounds. The fragmentary nature of Pirandello's characters, the alienation and isolation they address in their petty-bourgeois existence, seems none of Gramsci's business.

So while Gramsci can validate Pirandello as the deconstructor of an inordinately provincial Italy, he is reluctant to draw connections between Pirandello's pessimistic view of modernity and the processes of economic, social and cultural life from which the 'structure of feeling' of the Pirandellian character emerges. The life-world Piran-dello evokes, with experiences of alienation and fragmentation, of reification and commodification of the subject, does not seem to match the 'structures of experiencing' that emerge from Gramsci's society. While Gramsci in prison, thus at the time of his Pirandello notations, reflects on Taylorization, rationalization and moderniz-ation of industry, thus evidencing his awareness and, as we will see, his positive evaluation of rationalization, he seems to overlook the effects of the industrialization of culture and the life-world on con-sciousness in general. In this sense, and compared to Adorno, Mar-cuse and Horkheimer, his notion of modernity is benign. He does not see, as they did, or does not want to see, the underside of the dialectic. However, with this attitude he is not dissimilar to most of the Benja-min we know before his theses on history, and of the Brecht before or after Benjamin. Like both of these theorists, Gramsci too set out to produce a new culture under modern conditions of production, with new instruments, new techniques. That the future would not necessarily unravel but perhaps stop the dialectic, condemn it to a long and perhaps eternal phase of critical negativity, was not part of his design in his very last days in prison. The Pirandello notes of 1933–4 stem from these days.

SUBJECTS OF POPULAR CULTURE

I have already had the opportunity to point to what has been called Gramsci's 'realist' approach to a set of problems. As an intellectual committed not to preserving but changing the status quo he uses as his immediate point of departure, in contradistinction to much radical strategy, not what should be, or could be, but what is. In this he differs substantially from Lukács, who would have liked to impose his notion of what kind of authentic literature should be written, should be read, should be emulated by politically correct strategies: the realist literary canon within high culture. Yet Gramsci differs also from Marcuse and Adorno, who too, though for different reasons, had decided what kind of literature and art was best equipped to counter dialectically what they conceived as the all-pervasive reifications and commodifications of mass culture: highly esoteric modern art. Gramsci is closer to Benjamin (the Benjamin of the mid-1930s, that is) and Brecht in that all three of these theorists have primarily a positive rather than a negative attitude towards the new and transformatory cultural practices which are taking place against the background of and in relation to changing processes of production. The immense changes in the processes of production effect a new culture, new forms of literary production, of reception, new needs and expectations in the practices of everyday life. In this Gramsci acknowledges 'what is'. *Qua* 'realist' he has turned 'modernist', a modernist, however, who looks at his reality not from above but from below: from the point of view of the people involved in work and production, without whom the capitalist apparatus would perhaps cease to function, and their popular culture. More qualifications are necessary when speaking of these terms 'realist' and 'modernist', with respect to the place of 'popular culture' in Gramsci's cultural politics as he worked it out in his *Prison Notebooks*. This will allow me to speak of the extraordinary originality of Gramsci's cultural practice, often evoked by scholars, and of the areas in which he does not show the same ability to be extraordinarily original.[16] This involves his concept of hegemony, connected to his anticipation of a theory of need, and, as in my discussion of Pirandello, the unresolved issue of Gramsci's theory of the subject.

In designing the strategies for his cultural politics, Gramsci takes many clues from what we could call existing 'orders of knowledge'. So he takes some clues from modern architecture, others from modern economic management planning, and still others from his own production of Marxist theory. The framework of his strategy in matters of cultural politics looks then something like this. In some of the most celebrated passages in the *Prison Notebooks*, Gramsci addresses the problem of the Marxist dialectic in relation to both the Russian revolution and to countries where the revolution had, against all predictions, not taken place. This leads him to a problematization of the Marxist model of the dialectic, which posits a base dialectically related to various spheres of the superstructure. These spheres usually run under a set of categories including politics, culture, law, ideology, all those social practices which are not directly involved in the production of material goods but indirectly involved in the legitimation of the ways by which these goods are produced: extraction of surplus value. In his attempt to understand the mechanisms that lead either to the loss of or the maintenance of state power, Gramsci interrogates the ways in which the predominant class in power operates. What he finds is that the powers of the state, or rather the powers of the predominant class operating a specific state, extend far beyond the proper realm of the state with its major institutions: the army, police and law. The powers of a predominant class transcend the limits of what he calls the state or political society by extending to society at large, to civil society with its institutions such as schools, churches and the press, with its cultural organizations directing collective events and practices such as sports, theatre, leisure time and so forth. A predominant class produces and maintains power or, as Gramsci calls it, hegemony, via civil society, where a set of ideological practices guarantees the status quo anchored in political society, ultimately legitimating certain economic practices. There is much debate among scholars as to how to understand Gramsci's notion of civil and political society, whether these two spheres are ultimately identical or ultimately substantively different.[17] And there is not so much debate when it comes to the major concept related to civil and political society, namely hegemony. Most accounts appear to regard hegemony as predominant power that manages to assure 'spontaneous' consent to its dominant operations precisely because domination consists not only of institutions, traditions, coerced ideas, beliefs and ideologies, but of practices that involve the most minute operations and expectations of everyday life. A simple experience, and its signification via common sense, can be constitutive and constituting of the operations of hegemony. Raymond Williams has, in my opinion, written some of the most beautiful pages on hegemony. I paraphrase him like this: 'Hegemony is a lived system of meanings and values, not simply an ideology, a sense of reality beyond which it is, for most people, difficult to move, a lived dominance and subordination, internalized.'[18] Gramsci sets out to understand the operations of hegemony, the operations of predominant ideologies and languages, as well as the operations of counter-hegemony, in multiple forms of political, social and cultural practices on the macrological, yet above all on the micrological level. In referring to a national language as site of power, he puts it like this:

> Since the process of formation, spread and development of a unified national language occurs through a whole complex of molecular processes, it helps to be aware of the entire process as a whole in order to be able to intervene actively in it with the best possible results.[19]

The entire process of cultural production saturated by hegemony requires then not only or even primarily an analysis of the function of the major cultural institutions – high culture, the theatre, literary and artistic traditions of the past, literary movements – but also an analysis of cultural and social practices from all strata of society. These practices include readings of detective novels, serial novels, popular novels, and much more. And these practices also include a cultural production: a directed cultural production in the form of newspapers, journals, almanacs, periodicals, parish bulletins and so forth which in part enable these practices. Gramsci thus interrogates cultural practices not simply in terms of consumption or reception, but in terms of production or directed production for a specific consumption. The press (and here Gramsci agrees with Benjamin) is one of the most dynamic parts of the ideological structure, but not the only one.[20] Everything which influences or is able to influence public opinion, directly or indirectly, belongs to it: libraries, schools, associations, clubs, even architecture, and the layout and names of streets.[21]

Given then the inordinate mass of cultural and social experiences and practices in which hegemony operates, Gramsci suggests proceeding with some rational order. Just as in modern architecture the principle of rationality, of functionality, determines the layout, the whole edifice of cultural politics 'should be constructed according to "rational", functional principles, in that one has definite premises and wants to arrive at definite results'.[22] Yet Gramsci's rationality underlying his cultural programme, his critique of predominant culture as well as his design of a new culture, is not closed and static but typically open-ended and dynamic, it allows for dialogue, innovation, changes in strategy, adjustments, new perspectives. In this Gramsci attempts to combine a purposive-rational action with a value-rational action, a molecular form, so to speak, on the level of cultural politics and strategy, of the Habermassian project of universal pragmatics. Thus Gramsci writes: 'Just as in modern planned management the results often modify the premises, so in cultural planned management the premises are necessarily changed and transformed during the actual elaboration of a given activity.'[23] What Gramsci proposes is rationally planned political and cultural intervention, rationally planned in the interest of the best possible results.

The plan follows a tripartite order: first, Gramsci looks at the molecular processes of hegemonic cultural practices, in particular the reading practices, of many social strata, which allows him to research the differences of cultural production; he then asks what these reading practices reveal in terms of inner drives and needs, what the cultural production responds to or satisfies; and finally he draws up a balance sheet as to what needs to be done for a counter-hegemonic culture. What Gramsci finds is an inordinate number of journals, almanacs, papers, magazines, books, all of which differ in quality, in terms of their content, as well as in terms of the layout or the manner of presentation. They also differ in quantity. Certain journals have a larger circulation than others. What is Gramsci to deduce from his initial market research on 'the material organization of the ideological structure aimed at maintaining, defending and developing the theoretical or ideological "front"', which he conducts on behalf of his private 'Institute for Public Relations' run from and in his prison cell?[24] 'The truth of the matter is', he writes somewhere else, 'that everything which exists is "rational", it has had or has a useful function.'[25] What does it mean, then, when there is one group of people who primarily read books, another who read magazines, and even a third who read newspapers?[26] For one thing, it means that the reading public consists of many diverse groups which are differentiable from each other. It also means that one of these groups, those reading the newspapers, responds to an inherent structure of the newspaper: the style of journalism, let us say, which comes close to oratory and conversation, a style which is hurried, improvised, similar to speeches at public meetings, with rapidity of conception and construction. In that the newspapers are close to spoken communication, they are an efficient means of ideological diffusion, although the theatre, the cinema, and the radio produce with greater rapidity and more emotional force an ideological field of operation.[27] Newspapers, more than books, respond to the rhetorical taste of large masses of people.[28] This rhetorical taste is closely related to a sensibility to the operatic, to oratory, which marks Italian culture, compared with other cultures, to a large extent and to an inordinate degree.[29] The popular novel is perhaps the literary form best suited for the production of that operatic mode of experiencing the world. In the form of the serial novel, it is suited to integration into the daily newspapers. For this reason Gramsci recommends statistical research on the different types of serial which various newspapers print.[30] The serial novel thus plays a role according to Gramsci in the circulation figures of the papers.

Gramsci's analysis of reading practices and hegemonic cultural production reveals that the material organization of the hegemonic structure concedes, in fact guarantees and makes available, a large place to popular culture. If everything there is in some form rational or functional, there must be some reason for this state of affairs. How is one to explain the fact that many people read popular novels, although these novels are often translations from the French or English; that Italian culture produces readers but not its own writers of popular literature, which Gramsci relates to the lack of a national-popular culture in Italy.[31] How is one to explain that there is no lack of a popular culture without specifically Italian nationalist overtones; that the market offers translations of detective novels, many types of popular novels, serial novels, all of which 'simultaneously enjoy some degree of success and popularity'.[32] What are the reasons for the success and popularity of the popular novel? What Gramsci detects is that one form of popular novel predominates. And he deduces:

> From this predominance one can identify a change in fundamental tastes, just as from the simultaneous success of the various types one can prove that there exist among the people various cultural levels, different 'masses of feelings', prevalent on one or the other level, various popular 'hero-models'.[33]

Different 'structures of feeling' or 'structures of experiencing' tend to adhere to different 'hero-models', yet what they all have in common in popular literature is that the heroes are more important than their authors. 'The writer's name or personality does not matter, but the personality of the protagonist does.'[34] These heroes come alive, and whatever concerns their lives from birth to death becomes a matter of interest. This is the key to the success of sequels, writes Gramsci, even if these sequels are spurious.[35] Exemplary models of popular literature are on the one hand the *Guerin Meschino*, and on the other hand *The Count of Monte Cristo*, who represents most perfectly the preferred hero-model of many people: the superman.

What is fascinating about Gramsci's market research are the differences in the 'structures of feeling' he detects in his study of the readers of popular literature. We are here far from a simplistic dualistic model that pits bourgeois taste against mass culture. We are also apparently here far from a psychoanalytical model that proposes a universal intersubjectively valid psychic structure. So in his discussion of *Guerin Meschino*, one of the most elementary and primitive kinds of popular literature circulating among the most backward and 'isolated' strata of the people in the south and the mountains, Gramsci speaks of a specific popular psychology contained in that book and of a specific popular psychology apparent in the attitude of its readers. A determinate folklore, and a determinate common sense of that book, corresponds to a specific psychic structure of its readers, to the way in which these readers experience life on a conscious and unconscious level. Those who read the *Guerin Meschino* do not read the *The Count of Monte Cristo*, let alone detective stories. Gramsci suggests using such a book as an encyclopaedia 'to obtain information about the mental primitiveness and cultural indifference of the vast stratum of people who still feed on it'.[36] While Gramsci introduces a differentiation between the 'structures of feeling' of the readers of the *Guerin Meschino* and a more 'advanced' readership, those who read *The Count of Monte Cristo*, or those who read detective novels, he also examines those structures which might explain the great popularity of a specific hero, such as the superman. Readers approach the popular novel because of certain 'interests' which are being met in the reading process, fantasies which are enacted and lived. The superman is a preferred fantasy particularly of the petty bourgeoisie and the petty intellectuals. They are influenced by the novelistic images of the superman, which become 'their "opium"', their "artificial paradise"', in contrast to the narrowness and pinched circumstances of their real and immediate life'.[37] The interest which is being met is the desire to be 'an implacable "executioner" just for one day, to feel and enact, on the level of fantasy and imagination, the powers of the superman'. With the superman, readers in their powerlessness fantasize their own powers, as occurs in day-dreaming according to Freud and to which Gramsci makes a reference here.[38] Readers with a social inferiority complex dream with the superman for hours about revenge and about punishing those responsible for the evils they have endured. 'In *The Count of Monte Cristo*', writes Gramsci, 'there are all the ingredients for encouraging these reveries and thus for administering a narcotic that will deaden the sense of evil.'[39] Readers say yes to the way things are, to the status quo. As in Marcuse's, Adorno's and Horkheimer's account of the culture industry, the consumers of popular culture consent, by fantasizing otherwise, to their powerlessness or lack of control over their way of life. They themselves have become a commodity of reduced ego and will in the cultural and political business. The success of popular literature is thus due not only to its structure that responds to socio-psychic needs; its success is also contingent on creating that specific structure and not a different one in its mode of cultural production. Producers and consumers both get what they want, but what they both need, only one gets.

The material organization of the predominant culture reveals a structure of the life-world where cultural production is both constituted by and constitutive of the various fantasies and desires of different social groups. It seems as if in Gramsci's account the cultural apparatus creates its non-material needs. Thereby Gramsci produces a notion of art or hegemonic cultural production which takes into account the social and psychological makeup of its consumers. Indeed, it is the relation of consumer to product, the specificity of that relation, which seems more important than the relation of producer to product. The author has become irrelevant. While Gramsci does not discuss it in detail he does present an image of this phenomenon which is similar to an account Lukács gave as early as 1908–9. Lukács detected in his sociological study of modern drama the increasing domination of the economy and economic relations over social and spiritual life, where social and cultural forms are shaped by the fact that the main economic tendency of capitalism is the objectification of production, its separation from the personality of the producers. Through the capitalist economy an objective-abstract force, capital, becomes the real producer and capital has no organic relation to those who happen to own it; indeed it is often utterly irrelevant whether or not the owners are personalities at all (e.g. joint stock companies).[40] The relation of consumer to product is of primary importance to Gramsci. Analysing that relation in some detail will offer additional insight into the functioning of the hegemonic apparatus. For one thing, the consumers are not a homogeneous, uniform mass, subject to the effects of cultural manipulation and domination, but a contingent of various groups of people whose psychic structures, drives and needs are differentiable from each other. The various cultural products satisfy the needs of these various social groups. By using the term 'primitive' in the context of his discussion of *Guerin Meschino*, Gramsci seems not to look at these structures from a horizontal and quantitative point of view, where each structure represents the same value, but rather to present a vertical and qualitative image. Some structures are 'less primitive' or 'more primitive' than others. There are the peasants from backward areas of the south and the mountains, there is the petty bourgeoisie, the petty intellectuals, there is a '*classe media*', a middle class, and there is also the 'Taylorized worker' of the French novel during high capitalism.[41] The complexity which Gramsci evokes here in the *Prison Notebooks* on the structure of society contrasts with an earlier assessment of the readers of serial novels, written in 1918, where it is simply an amorphous mass of 'millions of women and young people' reading these fables, falling prey to a mentality and morality imposed on them.[42] Gramsci also criticizes in that context the disappearance of an old and well-established order: the author. Serials are written by ghost writers now.[43] The readers of popular literature cited by Gramsci in the *Prison Notebooks* are not amorphous but as diverse as the new cultural forms and genres that reveal, in the consumers' 'chemical' reactions to their substance, as Benjamin put it, the agreeable nature of this product for consumption by these diverse social groups.[44] It is the producers who have become amorphous. What Gramsci points to then is not the producer, but the way in which producers use the existence of people's drives, and the different expression of these drives in different people. By looking for unusual cultural products, instead of merely examining 'high culture', by not insisting on a qualitative separation of 'high and low culture', Gramsci validates effacing, as Benjamin did, the difference between high and low. Benjamin's discussion of '*Dienstmädchenromane*' and Gramsci's discussion of the serials are done in that spirit.[45] Both understand the far-reaching psychological and ideological functions of these genres, due to the values they incorporate in ordinary people's lives. For both it is not a matter of condemning such

109

literature as trash, but of understanding its function in ordinary people's lives and of pragmatically utilizing that understanding in the construction of a new and more democratic culture, adequate to the economic and social needs of all people. It is interesting in this context to note how similarly Gramsci and Benjamin pay attention to detail: they think about the ways in which these products were distributed among their consumers, and the itinerant bookseller appears on their theoretical stage. If a product was to reach the lowest social strata, the commercial book business was dependent on the itinerant bookseller, who knew how to bring stories of heroes and ghosts to the servants' world in the cellar and the attic.[46] Gramsci pragmatically reflects on the usefulness of such an institution for his counter-hegemonic business: perhaps this old-fashioned technology could be 'imitated', enlarged, controlled and stocked with less stupid books. In this way, ideas could be brought to the most backward strata of society.[47]

So in Gramsci's study of the cultural operations of the hegemonic class, he has paid attention to popular culture, to the relation of consumer to product in the context of that culture that cements, via subliminal operations, not opposition but consent to the status quo. And Gramsci reflects, as does Benjamin, on the enormous importance of the press in a society in shaping or countering the status quo. Gramsci would like to utilize this technical apparatus and structure it in such a way that it responds to the complexity, to the various groups of the social structure.[48] The object of his cultural programme is not, however, to work for a public opinion that legitimates economic, social and political inequities. Its object is to understand the needs of the readers and consumers, and then to 'transform them and homogenize them through a process of organic development that can lead it from simple common sense to coherent and systematic thought'.[49] Gramsci has no doubts about the difficulty of his project: 'A very common error is that of thinking that every social stratum elaborates its consciousness and its culture in the same way, with the same methods, namely the methods of professional intellectuals.'[50] And he continues: 'It is childish to think that a "clear concept" suitably circulated, is inserted in various consciousnesses with the same "organizing" effects of diffused clarity: this is an "enlightenment" error.'[51] Intellectuals have different ways of intellectually responding to an idea due to their long and intensive apprenticeship in the deductive and inductive business. Their minds have been Taylorized just as the body of the working class has been Taylorized in industrial production. Planned intervention in cultural production will have to redress the multiplicity of cultural consumption, intervene from the centre as well as margins, and include a heterogeneity of critical positions. One should look, he suggests, at centres and movements, take into account the local innovative pressures, which may not always germinate, i.e. develop into anything, but which must not for this reason be any the less followed and monitored. It

> is not always the most coherent and intellectually rich movements which triumph. Indeed, a movement often triumphs precisely because of its mediocrity and logical elasticity: anything goes, the most blatant compromises are possible, and may well themselves be the cause of the triumph.[52]

So in designing his cultural politics, in reflecting on cultural practices as counter-hegemony to bourgeois culture and ideology, Gramsci operates on several levels. On one level he views reality as a rational and functional order, perhaps better called a process, where everything possesses, in its multiplicity, an inherent yet perhaps not always visible functionality. We are here close again to traces of Gramsci's Spinozism, which seem to be connected though to his understanding of the simultaneous presence and functionality of different social groups. On another level, Gramsci operates from many points of departure in order to make out a given rationality, such as the rationality of bourgeois hegemony, which also operates in multiple ways and functions. Precisely because the hegemonic process is complex, penetrating sometimes even the simplest phenomena and actions, Gramsci suggests in his analysis of popular culture the validation of even the most trivial expression of that culture. 'It is a serious error to adopt a "single" progressive strategy according to which each new gain accumulates and becomes the premiss of further gain.'[53] Yet while there is much to be looked for and many positions from which to begin an analysis, Gramsci is not suggesting a *laissez-faire* critical practice. What he wants is, like Benjamin and Brecht, a new social operator, an engineer, an organic intellectual who designs plans and instruments for implementing a new culture, perhaps in the same way as he is trying to from his prison cell on the basis of his 'relational pragmatics'. With this he posits the possibility of directing and producing a rational – because universally functional – and rationalized culture.

Gramsci's analysis of popular culture is fascinating for a variety of reasons. While he recognizes, with the theorists of the culture industry, that new technologies, such as the commercialization of literature, enable producers of cultural products to manipulate the needs of people, he also believes, alongside Benjamin and Brecht, that these needs in themselves, which new technologies help to create and make possible, are not *ipso facto* to be invalidated. In this sense he comes close, in the early 1930s, to a theory of need, which, as a critique of the cultural pessimism of the Frankfurt School, had been worked out particularly in the 1970s in Italy.[54] Yet there is another major theorist who should now be mentioned in relation to Gramsci and his understanding of the industrialization of culture. When Gramsci argues against a contemporary critic in the context of a discussion of the reasons for the popularity of the detective novel and popular literature, and when he states his position on the effects of Taylorization on structures of experiencing, then he reveals crucial aspects of his way of philosophizing which bring him close to those principles we associate with Ernst Bloch: the encounter, in the Gramscian text, of the reality principle with the pleasure principle, leading to a Gramscian version of Bloch's principle of hope.

A critic had apparently argued that there are psychological reasons which account for the success of detective novels. People read them to 'revolt against the mechanical quality and standardization of modern existence, a way of escaping from the pettiness of daily life'.[55] Gramsci is quick to contend that this explanation is not adequate. 'But this explanation', he writes, 'can be applied to all forms of literature, whether popular or artistic, from the chivalric poem (does not Don Quixote also try to escape, even in a practical sense, from the pettiness and standardization of daily life in a Spanish village?) to the various kinds of serial novels. Is all poetry and literature therefore a narcotic against the banality of everyday life?'[56] Taylorization, standardization, rationalization are surely processes which Gramsci does recognize. Yet he would like to qualify the term Taylorization, dehistoricizing it, as it were, by talking about different effects of Taylorization on different people and at different times. People do not read popular literature to escape modern Taylorization, the rationalization of processes of production and the practices of everyday life. Taylorization is not merely an effect of modernity, of modern ways of organizing production and distribution. One has to take into account, writes Gramsci, the fact that the activity of a large part of humanity has always been Taylorized and rigidly disciplined and that these people have always sought to escape through fantasy and dreams from the narrow limits of the organization that was crushing them.

Coercion and consent, crucial terms in Gramsci's understanding of hegemony, are thus not only applicable to the capitalist mode of rationalized production. Oppressed people have always, writes Gramsci, sought to escape their oppression through fantasy and dreams. Is not religion, the greatest collective adventure and the greatest 'utopia' collectively created by humanity, a way of escaping from the 'terrestrial world'?[57] This is a crucial passage which attests, contrary to accounts that see no notion of the psyche in the Gramscian text, Gramsci's sophisticated notion of the psychic structure of the individual, of drives, of a consciousness that anticipates, in the rich experiences of day-dreaming, of fantasizing, Bloch's principle of hope, of better worlds in this world to come. The fantasies which are activated in the readings of popular culture are thus not mere answers to oppression, internal reproductions of consent to economic, political and cultural coercion, imaginary adventure at a time which in its tendencies towards total rationalization excludes adventure altogether. There has always been, then, in Gramsci's account, the search for adventure, in that there has always been a search for hope. Yet Gramsci is careful to differentiate again. While Don Quixote is, by transgressing principles of reality, the anticipating consciousness of utopia and hope, there is also in the same novel a figure that does not transgress that reality principle. 'What is most significant', writes Gramsci, 'is that alongside Don Quixote there is Sancho Panza, who does not want "adventures but security in life".'[58] A large number of people are obsessed precisely by the 'unpredictability of tomorrow; by the precariousness of their lives'. It is that obsession which produces consent, yet not everyone produces that obsession.

The image of Weber's iron cage of modernity as Taylorism, which emerges from the paragraphs Gramsci has copied from a contemporary critic, is thus an image which Gramsci can apply to oppressed social groups of the past. While Gramsci admits that in the modern world 'the coercive rationalization of existence is increasingly striking the middle and intellectual classes to an unprecedented degree', he simultaneously argues that existence in general has not become more monotonous, one-dimensional and less adventurous. In the everyday life of rationalized modernity, on the contrary, 'life has become too adventurous, too precarious, along with the conviction that there is no single way to contain such precariousness'.[59] And with the optimism of the will typical of Gramsci he concludes:

Thus people aspire to the adventure which is 'beautiful' and interesting because it is the result of their own free initiative, in

113

the face of the adventure which is 'ugly' and revolting, because due to conditions which are not proposed but imposed by others.[60]

It is this principle of hope which moves, as in Bloch's scheme, the dialectic, a subjective factor yet almost a natural force, present in some but not in all people. Don Quixote has it, but Sancho Panza not. It is an anticipatory consciousness, which Gramsci had made out in the 'popular creative spirit' despised by Manzoni, and which Gramsci was unable to detect in Pirandello's characters.[61] These, so it now turns out, were Sancho Panzas. As such, they were unable to defend themselves against the encroachments of rationalization and Taylorization on their consciousness, not because they were members of the petty bourgeoisie, so it seems, by following Gramsci's logic, but because there have always been those with and those without an internal drive for adventure, those with and those without a principle of hope.

While Gramsci realizes that new means of cultural production and distribution play a role in the immense educational processes of many cultures, he seems to distance himself from a position which reflects on the immense impact of new means of industrial production on the structure of consciousness. Reification, as it has been worked out by Lukács, and as it has been incorporated in the Frankfurt School notion of the culture industry, is not totally absent from his discourse. In his notes on 'Americanism and Fordism', in which he discusses the application of technology and processes of rationalization in American industry, he does address the enormous diffusion of psychoanalysis since World War I due to an increase in moral coercion exercised by the apparatus of state and society on single individuals. The form of coercion or restricting of human drives typical of highly rationalized processes of labour and work has led, so Gramsci acknowledges, to a pathological crisis. Thus, Gramsci explains:

> American industrialists are concerned to maintain the continuity of the physical and muscular-nervous efficiency of the worker. It is in their interest to have a stable, skilled labour force, a permanently well-adjusted complex, because the human complex (the collective worker) of an enterprise is also a machine which cannot, without considerable loss, be taken to pieces too often and renewed with single new parts.[62]

Yet Gramsci has also to concede that this maintenance of the worker leads to the mechanization of the worker, and to a gap between the manual labour and the human content of work. The Taylorized person can still think. That, Gramsci says, was also remedied. Ford educated its workers.

What is interesting in this context is that the differentiation which Gramsci establishes in place, the simultaneity of different psychic structures of a society on a horizontal level, is simultaneously a differentiation which he establishes in its verticality or in time. That is to say, he seems to emphasize the various degrees of consciousness when he uses terms such as 'more primitive' or 'less primitive', thereby opening up the possibility for ever more degrees of differentiation. In that sense the various levels have quantitatively speaking an equal value, but not qualitatively. While some levels of consciousness, let us say the 'more primitive', Gramsci hopes to elevate to 'less primitive' levels via his cultural and political reform, he seems to freeze the mobility of the 'most advanced' level in that the most advanced form of consciousness is not subject to time. In other words, while certain groups within the society are mobile in terms of their structures of consciousness and feeling, other groups are less mobile, or perhaps not mobile at all, even though foundational changes in processes of production could change the cognitive and psychic make-up of the 'most advanced' groups as well. What seems to matter then to Gramsci is not so much the ultimate trajectory of modern or even postmodern consciousness, subject to reification, alienation, commodification. Pirandello's characters and their plight are of secondary importance to Gramsci. What matters first and foremost is not that modernity might move in a certain direction with unforeseen consequences for the volitional possibilities of the subject. Rather, what matters is that the most disadvantaged consciousness can change to a higher form of consciousness, that mobility is possible, that the subject can change in terms of its cognitive, emotional and psychic structures. So for Gramsci, as for Bloch, an intrinsic principle of hope, a desire for change, whether on the conscious or unconscious level, is an important condition for effecting social change. Yet where Gramsci differs from Bloch, and ultimately from many of the members of the Frankfurt School, is not in his interest in the relation of consciousness to desire. Rather, where Gramsci differs from the Frankfurt School is in his interest in the micrological patterns that inform the relation of consciousness and desire. By this I am referring to Gramsci's interest in language. For while Gramsci understands the desire for freedom, with Bloch, as an intrinsic principle inscribed in the human condition, the ontological *quid pro quo* for any liberatory and emancipatory struggle, he simultaneously understands language, or communicative practices, as a territory which both enables and delimits possibilities of freedom. Language, in its form as a structure of values, and mediated by agents of the hegemonic class, can keep the subaltern social classes in check. Yet subaltern classes can invent new structures of value designed to subvert the hegemonic design. This invention is not only enabled by an inherent will to freedom, or, in the Blochian sense, by a principle of hope. For Gramsci, this invention of counter-hegemonies is in part contingent on the very structure of language itself. The materiality of language thus figures in Gramsci's understanding of consciousness and its relation to the production of hegemony and counter-hegemony. In this sense he surpasses the modernism of the Frankfurt School and aligns himself with or anticipates theoretical concerns which should become prominent in the second half of the twentieth century.

5

Phenomenology, linguistics, hegemony

BETWEEN PERCEPTION AND RECEPTION: GRAMSCI'S DANTE AND HIS READERS

In January of 1929, Gramsci writes from his prison cell in Turi to Tatiana Schucht, expressing great satisfaction about the fact that he would finally be able to 'write' in prison, to do scholarly work, that is. 'With this my greatest aspirations as a prisoner will be satisfied', he comments.[1] At this point, he had been in various prisons for over two years. He had been intermittently able to get reading material, often trivial literature and popular novels, but also an entire range of magazines and journals. He had been able to study some and keep up with major Italian cultural affairs. His writing, however, had been limited to the writing of letters, bi-monthly, to family members only. So he had been far from being in a position to do significant intellectual work the way he used to in his pre-prison years. When he was finally permitted to settle down to a writing routine, by early February of 1929, he outlines in the first Prison Notebook something that looks like a research programme he intends to pursue in prison. In a letter he considers this outline as a way to begin to order his thoughts and ideas.[2] In this outline, sixteen areas are of interest to him, one of which is entitled 'Cavalcante Cavalcanti: his position in the structure and the art of the *Divine Comedy*'.[3] So some research on Dante, the most prominent of Italian poets, was included in his programme. What Gramsci actually put down on the topic does not seem to be very much, however, compared to other issues he included in his outline and which he subsequently managed to research, study and do some writing on in prison. There is some speculation that after a period in which his health deteriorated and after a very serious physical and psychological crisis in the summer of 1931, Gramsci

117

shortened his research programme, perhaps in fear of not being able to complete any of his projects, whereby Dante was eliminated from the list.[4] Yet there is also evidence that it was precisely during the time of what is presumed to be his major crisis that he writes these notes on Dante, particularly in the summer and early autumn of 1931.[5] Frank Rosengarten has made several attempts, and quite convincing ones, to underscore, in spite of their brevity, the significance of these notes by linking the Cavalcante episode and the immense family tragedy it contains according to Gramsci's interpretation, to Gramsci's own existence in prison, which, as the letters from prison, particularly those to his young sons and his wife Giulia Schucht, reveal, bespeaks an immense tragedy of its own.[6] What strikes me about Gramsci's notes on Dante is not so much their small number, which is on some level explicable by Gramsci's undoubtedly limited express interest in the topic. Judging from the way he pursued other topics in prison, his persistence in ordering books and articles from Tatiana Schucht for his study of the history of Italian intellectuals, or of the problem of a theory of history and historiography, he surely seems not to be inordinately interested in a literary topic such as Dante. And at one point he says something to that effect. The entire Dante business is, he writes, 'of small importance, because I have never aspired to become a dantista and make great hermeneutical discoveries in that field'.[7] And he adds that this little study of Dante 'has been useful to me, as a check on my own memory'.[8] So what strikes me is not the possible insignificance of these notes in Gramsci's express overall research programme, but rather their possible significance. Their brevity, that is, should not keep us from interrogating them as to what their possible critical and theoretical value might be. Indeed, brief as they are, these notes are unusually dense. And it is their extraordinary density that makes them unusually suggestive to me. I think that they show many of the characteristics of Gramsci's research programme: not only some of his ways of seeing, of thinking, of feeling an object, but also possibly the relation of his ways of seeing to the structure of his life-world which is, at the time of his notes on Dante, not the structure of a life-world in general, of a social, intercommunicative world, but of a life-world in prison. There are, as we shall see, some elements in his reading of Dante that lend themselves, due to their semiological and structuralist components, to reconstructing a version of Gramsci's theory of the subject which brings him into the vicinity of other major twentieth-century critics. And there are, in addition, elements in his

way of pursuing a project which lend themselves, due to their phenomenological components, to reconstructing a version of a theory of
consciousness in relation to knowledge which brings him into the
vicinity of other major twentieth-century theorists. What I see emerging from the phenomenology of Gramsci's life-world in prison and its
relation to his 'insignificant' Dante scholarship are the contours, as I
shall argue in the following pages, of a critical theory of the subject
where a theory of the sign and a theory of perception interlock. In this
respect Gramsci moves in the orbit of phenomenology as we know it
from Merleau-Ponty, and of sociological linguistics also, as we know
it from Vološinov. Moreover, Gramsci seems to experiment here with
a theory of representation that is reminiscent of Roland Barthes. In
Gramsci's notes on Dante, designed perhaps as literary criticism to
challenge the dreadful timelessness of prison, there potentially resides
a theory of the conditions of possibility of the operations of consciousness which, by profitably combining a Marxist version of structural
linguistics and phenomenology, moves in the direction of a theory of
signification or communication, urgently needed for a study of the
micrological, material, linguistic operations of ideology and domination. That such a linguistically oriented theory of the subject is
useful not only for the study of the effects of hegemony, but also, and
by inference, for the study of the possible operations of a counter-
hegemony as well, is surely something Gramsci had in mind. To what
extent the critical practices which can be retrieved from Gramsci's
account have relevance for our own times is a different question which
I will address in my last two chapters.

With my analysis of Gramsci's notes on Dante I do not mean to
suggest they represent the hallowed ground on which he builds his
entire critical theory, in particular his notion of the subject in relation
to hegemony. There are many profitable ways of approaching an
extraordinarily unsystematic text, such as Gramsci's. Nor do I mean
to insist on the notion of 'two Gramscis', the one of the prison
notebooks and the one of the pre-prison years, in which perspective –
presumably – the former would be viewed as more authentic than the
latter, so that the Gramsci of the *Prison Notebooks* is the only one who
counts. Many of the motifs of the *Prison Notebooks*, of Gramsci's ways of
doing and seeing, are to some degree already apparent in his early
writings. As an example I would like to point to his interest in
linguistics and philology, as well as in literary problems, which dates
back to his university years in Turin, and, more so, and perhaps
related to his training, or his character, his way of paying

meticulous attention to 'philological' detail and differentiation. Or perhaps his obsession with differentials rather than universals, with minute details which at times powerfully unsettle received modes of orders and knowledge, is related not only to his training as a philologist or linguist, but also to his background, his childhood, his youth: Gramsci, a marginal member of a marginalized social group of a marginal geographical space, a deformed, younger and hungry child of an impoverished family from the economically backward and exploited island of Sardinia; Gramsci, whose distinct experiences, whose experiential knowledge, has long included differences and differentiations. I am not interested, though, in looking in the older Gramsci for the younger one, or vice versa. What I would like to suggest is rather that some of his earlier critical traits, whether always visible or not, often seem to retreat, remain with the past, such as his penchant for up-front polemics, while others, such as his will for phenomenological detail, surface in and with his *Prison Notebooks*, assuming there an unprecedented and significant presence. This I see as related in some ways to the structure of his life-world, of being and writing in prison, and not in freedom. The limitations of that structure are apparent in these few notes on Dante: poor material conditions, minimal research facilities, failing health and concentration, limited hours of writing, in a prison cell. What is not so apparent are the possibilities inscribed in the limitations of that structure. So the theory of consciousness, which I see related to Gramsci's concept of hegemony that springs forth from his 'insignificant' literary scholarship on Dante, may bespeak some of these possibilities. And it is to these that I will now turn.

As in his study of Manzoni, Gramsci will investigate his object of study, Dante's Canto X, from multiple and varied angles. Moreover, Gramsci works on the Dante notes, as he did with Manzoni as well as most other topics in the *Prison Notebooks*, necessarily intermittently, over a period of two to three years, depending on the research material he was able to obtain via Tatiana Schucht. Yet the initial entry on the tenth canto of the 'Inferno' of Dante's *Divine Comedy* seems to have been written in one specific time period, since that initial entry constitutes paragraph 78 in Gramsci's Prison Notebook 4. What he outlines here are some aids to memory, or what look like pieces of information which he apparently intends to incorporate into his research on Cavalcante. Thus he registers the following information in that first paragraph on the topic in a form that resembles fragments of sentences. They look, in my enumeration, something like this:

1 The question of 'structure and poetry' in the *Divine Comedy* according to Benedetto Croce and Luigi Russo.

2 Vincenzo Morello's reading as *corpus vile*.

3 Fedele Romani's reading of Farinata.

4 De Sanctis.

5 Question of 'indirect representation' and of stage directions in drama: do the latter have artistic value?

6 Do they [the stage directions] contribute to the representation of the characters? In as much as they limit the actor's freedom of choice and lead to a more concrete description of the given character, certainly.

7 See Shaw's *Man and Superman* with John Tanner's handbook as an appendix: an intelligent actor can and must use the appendix as a guide for his own interpretation.

8 The picture at Pompeii of Medea killing the children she had by Jason: Medea is depicted with her face blindfolded. The painter is not able to or does not want to depict that face. (There is, however, the case of Niobe, but in sculpture: to cover her face would have meant to take away the specific content of the work.)

9 Cavalcante and Farinata; father and father-in-law of Guido.

10 Cavalcante is the one punished in the circle.

11 No one has observed that if the drama of Cavalcante is not taken into consideration, one does not see the torment of the damned in that circle being *enacted*.

12 The *structure* ought to have led to a more exact aesthetic evaluation of the canto, since every punishment is represented in act.

13 De Sanctis noticed the harshness contained in the canto by the fact that all at once Farinata changes character.

14 After having been *poetry*, he becomes *structure*, de Sanctis explains; he acts as Dante's guide.

15 The poetic depiction of Farinata has been admirably re-created by Romani: Farinata *is a series of statues*.

16 Then Farinata acts out a *stage direction*.

17 Isidoro del Lungo's book on Dino Compagni's *Cronica*: the date of Guido's death is established in it.

18 It is strange that scholars did not think first of using Canto X for approximating this date (or has someone done so?).

19 But not even del Lungo's reckoning served to interpret the figure of Cavalcante or to explain the function that Dante makes Farinata fulfil.[9]

These nineteen entries, initiating his study of Dante's Canto X, are followed by three more paragraphs in which Gramsci no longer offers a varying number of sentence fragments, but rather settles down to outline his major argument. That is, what Gramsci appears to have done in and with the first paragraph is to have a private session of brainstorming, a rigorous interrogation of his memory, after which he puts down on paper all the information he can gather in his mind at that particular moment on the topic of Dante's Canto X. This information includes the following:

1 Previous scholarship on Dante: Croce, Russo, Morello, Romani, de Sanctis.
2 The question of stage directions and its relation to actors and audience, with reference to George Bernard Shaw.
3 The concept of blindness or concealedness as Gramsci remembers the picture at Pompeii of Medea killing her children.
4 The question of structure and poetry in the tenth canto.
5 The relation of historiography to poetry.

We could reduce this body of information to the following schema. By introducing a new notion of interpretation, one that pays attention to the relevance of stage direction to interpretation and the concept of blindness or concealedness in relation to understanding, Gramsci criticizes and corrects previous scholarship (Croce, Russo, Morello, Romani, de Sanctis) on the issue of Dante's Canto X, particularly with respect to the question of the unity or disunity of structure and poetry in that canto. And this is indeed what Gramsci thought he had accomplished, judging from a letter to Tatiana Schucht dated 20 September 1931, in which he registers the propositions and the conclusion of his argument. 'It seems to me', he writes, 'that this interpretation should completely undermine Croce's thesis on the poetry and structure of the *Divine Comedy*. Without structure there would be no poetry, thus also structure has a poetic value of its own.'[10] Yet is this all that is happening here? Is Gramsci merely correcting Dante scholars, and in particular Croce, on the Cavalcantean front? Had he indeed studied the items on this list and knowledgeably incorporated them into his interpretation or are these mere items of information which he cites not because he perceives their content but simply because he happens to know of them? Which sources and documents does he have at his disposal, and how does he proceed in prison? In order to answer some of these questions, let us first look at how Gramsci thought he had corrected Croce on this Dantean issue, and then, at how he works.

In Canto X, Dante meets in the sixth circle among the heretics, who are punished there, two Florentines: Farinata degli Uberti and Cavalcante dei Cavalcanti. The first is the father-in-law and the second the father of Guido Cavalcanti, one of Dante's close friends. Dante and Farinata get involved in a political discussion on Florentine affairs; and Cavalcante inquires as to why his son Guido does not accompany Dante on his journey through hell. Dante answers ambiguously something like this: actually I am not really here by my own design, it is that person over there (Vergil) who leads me here, that person whom your son Guido, if I am not mistaken, was not all that fond of (held in disdain). By using the past tense, was, was not all that fond of, or held in disdain – the Italian reads 'ebbe in disdegno' – Dante intimates that Guido was a phenomenon of the past, gone for ever, and not alive in the present. So Guido's father, Cavalcante, at hearing this, and not being further briefed on the matter, collapses in grief. In the second part of the canto, Farinata and Dante discuss the problem of the Epicureans and the way they are punished in the sixth circle. Since, as materialists, their emphasis in life is on the materiality of the present, and not on the immateriality or eternal ideality of the future or the past, their punishment reverses the powers of their intellectual desires: they are allowed to know the past and the future, yet not allowed to know anything about the present.

Previous interpretations of this canto had privileged the masterful figure of Farinata. The tenth canto was, by definition, so to speak, Farinata's canto. So 'Guido's disdain' led to speculations concerning such matters as what the relation of Guido Cavalcanti's poetry to imperial poetry, Vergil's, might be, or what Farinata's political and historical clairvoyance, or his predictions with respect to Florence, were all about. These interpretive efforts encouraged a fragmentary view of this canto in that such interpretations could not meet the requirements of romantic (and in particular of Crocean) aesthetics. Attentive to incorporating the aesthetic or the poetic with the historical, ideological and political, the poetry or form with what they called structure or content, de Sanctis and Croce felt ill at ease when it came to Canto X. So their solution was to consider only the first part of the canto representative of Dante at his best. The second, 'non-poetic', more prosaic part was, as they read it, mere 'structure'. In short, they set out to stress the disunity of this text. Now it was Gramsci's opinion that driving a wedge into the text was ill-advised. He attempted to

show how the second part of the canto was important, indeed necessary, for interpreting the first part. 'It is curious', he writes, 'that Dante
criticism, old-fashioned and pedantically detailed as it is, has never
called to our attention the fact that Cavalcante is the person truly
punished among the Epicureans in their burning sarcophagi.'[11] What
is really going on, Gramsci claims, is not only that two dramas are
actually taking place here, of Farinata and Cavalcante respectively,
but also that these two dramas are organically related to each other.
Farinata's discourse in the second part of the canto, hitherto considered a non-poetic, intellectual, dogmatic and prosaic lecture on the
predicament of the heretics in hell, that lecture, Gramsci argues,
functions as a 'stage direction', which reveals the full drama of
Cavalcante to the reader who can properly interpret these directions.
They give the reader the essential elements necessary for the productive construction of the whole picture. The full drama of Cavalcante is
not the ambiguous message that his son might be dead, but that the
reader knows that Cavalcante, being punished as a heretic by the law
of retaliation, cannot see and know that which he presumed to see and
know while alive: the materiality of the present, that his son is alive.
And since Dante the pilgrim, as is his style, hesitates little when it
comes to bestowing on the wretched of hell select punitive measures in
addition to their already inexorable pains, he hesitates little when it
comes to offering startling ambiguities rather than certainties to
Guido's imploring father. Left to his own limited devices as citizen of
Dis in the sixth circle of the heretics in hell, the fact that his son is dead
is the only message that Cavalcante, necessarily blind to the present,
can receive and interpret. In this lies the immense ineffability of his
drama, which only the reader, thoroughly briefed not by the denotative narrative provided by Dante, the author of the text, but by the
'stage directions' provided by Farinata, an agent internal to the text,
is able to make out creatively. Cavalcante's punishment, as it is being
acted out on the narrative stage, his ineluctable unawareness of his
blindness, as object of desire of the reader's gaze, ineffably multiplies
Cavalcante's pain next to the reader's pleasure. In this act of interpretation, the unity of the canto, the amalgamation of poetry and
structure, has been obtained. The active participation of the reader in
that hermeneutic process, by creatively combining the visible and
invisible bytes of information offered by the text, established the
immense impotence inscribed in Cavalcante's fate. The reader fills in
the gaps – that which is invisible, or absent, in the text – thereby
guaranteeing, against de Sanctis, Croce, or other critics, the aesthetic

unity of Dante's Canto X. Poetry and structure metaphorize into one in this act of interpretation.

There are many apparently heterogeneous elements in Gramsci's interpretation of Dante that lend themselves, profitably I think, to further theoretical discussions. On some level, these elements can be distinguished from each other as pertaining to specific disciplines or theoretical inquiries. One concerns, for instance, elements for a theory of representation which Gramsci assembles on the basis of the representation of suffering in the history of painting and the plastic arts. The epistemic blindness of Cavalcante, unknown to himself but known to the reader, heightens the character's suffering while simultaneously eliciting more powerful dramatic effects. Close to this there resides in Gramsci's reading a version of a theory of the unexpressed, of silence, of the invisible, the inaural and the sensorily concealed which posits, not the presence, but the absence of explicit visual and verbal languages as a condition for the production of meaning. In addition, there are elements for a theory of the sign in that the shifting of signifier to signified produces more than one reading of a text. Furthermore, there are elements for a theory of reading or interpretation, as well as the material conditions of communication and the production of signification which speaks both of the possibilities and of the limits inscribed in a productive reading of a text. There are, in addition, elements for a theory that links narratology, and the communicative structures individuated in a narrative, to theatrical communication. Again, this theoretical direction borders on a theory of reading and processes of the production of meaning and knowledge. And finally, there is again Gramsci's tendency to approach a problem from multiple points of view, as if he worked from phenomenological premises, within which the object to be studied is infinitely more complex than the concepts, terms and individual approaches designed to grasp that object.[12] For this reason it is difficult to say what Gramsci's precise intentions were when he set up the heterogeneity of his theoretical discourse. Since some of Gramsci's elements accommodate, in their heterogeneity, a problematization of subject to object in relation to the conditions of possibility in the production of meaning, I have chosen to comment on two of them. For working purposes I will call them 'discourse I' and 'discourse II'. 'Discourse I' experiments with a subject-text-object relation which tends to point to the conditions on the basis of which an object or addressee of a message or text responds to the structures inherent in that text. The focus is on the reader as receiving subject. 'Discourse II' also experiments with a subject-text-object relation. It tends to point to the conditions on the basis of which a subject produces a text and meaning in the interaction with the object. The focus is on the reader as perceiving subject. Let me begin with 'discourse I'.

In Gramsci's reading of Dante's Canto X, there exists not only the author and the text, or the reader and the text, a subject-object relation, as Gramsci described it in his analysis of Manzoni, for instance – not only a subject who produces an object (author/text) or a subject who looks at or encounters an object (reader/text) – but also another factor. What Gramsci introduces in his reading of Dante is a structure, a formal structure, that is, of many interdependent levels and functions. Due to this interrelatedness Dante's reader has, in Gramsci's account, as one of the elements of that structure, a specific function to fulfil, and a specific position to assume in relation to the producer of this text and so, ultimately, in the reading and interpretation of it. What is highly interesting, then, is that Gramsci operates, in the context of 'discourse I', conceptually with a series of assumptions that are reminiscent of theories of signification and communication as they have been worked out in recent narratology and semiotics. They are also reminiscent of linguistic theories as they have been worked out by the Soviet linguist Vološinov and his circle.[13] Gramsci certainly does not use the current terminology of phenomenology, semiology, narratology and semiotics. There is, none the less, little doubt that he is conceptually probing similar terrain when he interrogates the structural similarities of theatrical (mimetic) and narrative (diegetic) forms of communication in his reading of Dante.[14] For Gramsci sets up a structural model that not only accommodates the multilinearity of the narrative; it also accommodates the multiplicity of structurally interdependent discourses such as the mimetic and diegetic forms of communication in his reading of Dante's *Divine Comedy*. Readers of Dante's epic poem recall that Dante, the author, has Dante, the pilgrim, narrate a series of events pertaining to the pilgrim's journey, the pilgrim's private life (interaction with fellow travellers), the pilgrim's public life (interaction with the figures he meets), the pilgrim's inner life, and so on. The trajectory that seems to obtain most prominence is the one that graphs the pilgrim's encounter with various historical, religious and intellectual figures. What Gramsci underscores in his presentation of Canto X, then, is that Dante, the pilgrim, does not report, in indirect speech, on his encounter with Cavalcante. Rather, this encounter is reported on in direct speech, in the citation of dialogic exchanges taking place between the pilgrim and the characters he encounters here and at other stations during his journey. This not only allows Dante to move the action from a mostly 'plusquamperfect' past into an 'plusquam-imperfect', still open-ended, present. It also becomes the condition of possibility for acting out the present in a dynamic form, in a dialogic performance between the characters, which has a diegetic as well as dramatic function. So narrative and drama seem to be contingent on each other in the structure of the *Divine Comedy*.

Recent studies in narratology carried out against the background of Soviet linguistics and Czech structuralism differentiate between those communicative models that pertain to narrative and those that pertain to drama.[15] Gramsci seems to condense these two models into one. While the readers of the narrative receive the messages emitted by the author's interaction with the characters, they do not only function as receivers of that emission. By comparing the readers of this epic poem to spectators of a play or drama, Gramsci transgresses the received borderlines between the literary genres. What Gramsci also does is to underscore the participatory function of the reader in this drama, and thus in the reading of Dante's text. Next to the dialogic performance between Dante the pilgrim and the various characters he meets, there is an additional performative act taking place. What I am referring to are the performative acts of the readers, who activate, with their performance, a process that sorts, combines, condenses and eliminates sensory data in the reading of the text. The transposing of the reader of Dante's text into a spectator means that other functions usually associated with dramatic productions begin to emerge: the actors, the directors, stage design, script, semiotic devices, codes and so forth. And indeed, all of these functions are part of the structure of Cavalcante's drama and it is due to their dynamic interaction that the drama, and possibly also the narrative, continues to evolve. What Gramsci seems to emphasize, then, is not so much who the characters are and what they do, but rather – similar to narratological and communicative models – how they function, how their actions or their performance affect other actions and performances in the structure of this dramatic model. While the reader/spectator represents, in the totality of this artistic structure, but one of the many functions that operate within the structure, Gramsci is sure to assign a privileged position to the reader/spectator in the reading of Canto X. The reader, like Brecht's critical spectator of the epic drama, has to intervene in the process of reading and interpreting the text. Identificatory processes between spectator and characters, integral parts of classical drama, are surely ruled out in this modern reading of a medieval text. A functional reader becomes the *raison d'être* of a functional text.

In a paragraph entitled '"Structure" and "Poetry"', Gramsci comments that Dante does not provide a set of statements, a verbal description, of what is going on.[16] As in theatrical productions, the playwright does not communicate verbatim to the reader, as in narrative, the sequence of events that have taken place in the past. Dante does not account diegetically for Cavalcante's ineffable suffering. He suggests that ineffable suffering by taking recourse to many levels of differentiable semiological codes. These semiological codes do not, however, amount to the total picture either. By inserting gaps into the narrative drama, by leaving some information semiologically, visually, verbally, aurally, unexpressed, veiled, so to speak, the readers are called upon, in their deciphering of the semiotic codes, not to represent or reproduce the narrative, the action as it is taking place. Rather, they are called upon to present themselves to the action, to take a place in it, to participate in it, to intervene in it. When Gramsci takes the visual and verbal gaps in the text as the basis that allows for movement in the narrative, he intuits a process which has been described by Roland Barthes in his *The Pleasure of the Text*. The insertion of gaps increases pleasure and the desire for knowledge when reading a text. Indeed, Barthes takes this phenomenon to be the basis of all knowledge-producing processes.[17] Gramsci does not only focus ön reading or interpretation, on a subject that reads an object, but he also seems to point to, or at least tends towards looking at, the interaction between the subject and the object. He assigns Dante's reader/spectator a performative, communicative function in the reading of the text. The problem here is that while Gramsci does assign that dialogic or communicative function to the reader, which potentially empowers the reader to intervene autonomously in the course of a structure, he is simultaneously also quick to point out that performance, while necessary, is an intervention that takes place within certain limits. Dante's readers, while they must intervene, none the less cannot freely intervene when or how or from which position they like. Dante has rigorously programmed positionalities into text.

The readers of this programme are invited to decipher a set of heterogeneous semiological devices scattered throughout the text. These include the posture of Cavalcante, 'not upright and manly like Farinata, but humble, downcast, perhaps on his knees', a posture which, in speaking a body-language of pain and defeat, visually anticipates the tragedy of a father learning of the death of his son.[18] In contradistinction to Farinata, who, statue-like, and in the face of adverse destiny, does not budge, there is Cavalcante, with his face distorted, his head sinking and his back bending. In addition, there is a contrapuntal tonality governing the dialogic rhythms between Dante the pilgrim and Cavalcante, bytes of information of varied volume and intonation which enhance the gradual unfolding of Cavalcante's inexorable drama. The slow, circumspect and grave rhythm by which Dante the pilgrim, positioned in power, chooses to respond to the anxiety that rapidly propels the questions of Cavalcante's powerlessness, not only adds Cavalcante's ineffable sense of uncertainty concerning the life of his son, but also condenses the intensity of the drama. While Dante the poet does not describe Cavalcante's drama, he offers enough semiological information which, in addition to the verbal explication or the so-called 'stage directions' of Farinata, concerning the vicissitudes of the heretics in hell, enables the reader to produce a chain of signification in spite of the invisible and the unexpressed. In this sense, every element of the text relates to other elements, they together constitute a linguistic and semiological structure that yields a large yet not indefinite number of combinations. As in linguistic structuralism, each of the elements in that structure or system affects other elements in that system, indeed it is defined by the relation one element entertains with another in binary combinations. Farinata's pride, for instance, functions to underscore Cavalcante's misery, as the misery of the one highlights the pride of the other. It seems that one could hardly exist without the other in the economy of that drama.

That Gramsci would look at the Cavalcante episode in Canto X from a relational point of view should by now not be surprising to anyone. I have pointed to Gramsci's tendency to examine a phenomenon from a relational point of view throughout this study. Yet it should also be remarked that the elements in the structure as Gramsci makes them out do not possess equivalent quantitative and qualitative values. Just as the reader is a privileged quantity in the process of reading, indicating a differential with respect to, let us say, Dante, the pilgrim, as element in the drama, Gramsci also introduces differentiations when it comes to the positions the characters assume in the dramatic economy. By placing Farinata as an element or a function into a system of relations, which prepares the importance of

Cavalcante's drama in the process of Canto X, he simultaneously deprives Farinata of the importance he has held in previous scholarship. On the other hand, by emphasizing Farinata's function in that system of relations, culminating in the drama of Cavalcante, he does not simultaneously relate Cavalcante, as an element or a function, to other elements in the structure. The semiological and structural system of Canto X becomes subservient to the production of one specific meaning, which, assembled on the basis of apparently quantitative equivalences of bytes of present and absent information, culminates in the misery of Cavalcante. That misery is both constitutive of and constituted by the differentials that govern the structurations of Dante's text. What emerges, then, from Gramsci's reading of Canto X, is not only that internal structural relations are the key for assembling visible and invisible elements of the text, the unexpressed and the expressed contained in the ineffable drama of Cavalcante. Nor is it only that external structural relations, between the reader, the characters and the author, enable a productive reading of the text. The reader's productive combinatory force, crucially necessary for activating the interpretive assembly-line where elements are moulded into the re-production of Dante's designs, that reader becomes unintentionally inactive, fixed and positioned in accordance with Dante's intentions. There is no unlimited interpretive pleasure of the text. Reader and text amalgamate into one in the closed structure of Dante's ultimate intentionality.

What is interesting in Gramsci's discussion of Dante is, on the one hand, his view of the importance of the reception rather the production of a work of art, which already marks his aesthetics and which brings him into the vicinity of the critical theory of the Frankfurt School, as I have argued in previous chapters. In his notes on Dante, there are at least two additional elements. Reception of a work of art or a text moves in the direction of a theory which I think we can call a theory of reading or a theory of interpretation. Similar to Barthes' reader, Gramsci's reader of Dante, by creatively filling the sensory gaps, the silenced, the unexpressed, finds pleasure in the text. So the reader is no longer a positioned and fixed consumer of a work of art, who passively reacts to the text, but rather one who actively participates in the production of a text or meaning. Without the reader, there would be no text. And similar to the critical spectator of Brecht's epic drama, Gramsci's reader of Dante functions as a critical spectator, who actively intervenes in the production of meaning by dialectically assembling the semiological elements, as well as the stage directions. As for Barthes and Brecht, Gramsci's reader is no longer simply a passive consumer of a text. Dante's readers actively approach the drama, intervene in it, fill the gaps and produce meaning. And, most importantly, as readers who consciously pursue the assimilation of sensory data, they are perceiving subjects who mediate between what there is and what they have to offer, between their epistemic ability to assemble the visible with the invisible, the unexpressed with the expressed, in a process that produces meaning somewhere in a space between the subject and the object, between the reader and the text, similar to epistemological processes as they have been worked out by post-Husserlian phenomenology. What I find fascinating here is that Gramsci's reader appears as a perceiving, communicating and receiving subject. As a perceiving subject Dante's reader is, in Gramsci's account, similar to a phenomenological subject, empowered to create his/her own version of an object. As a communicating subject, Dante's reader intervenes in the production of meaning. And what about the receiving subject? In the context of Canto X, once the perceiving subject has fulfilled its function, it promptly changes into a receiving subject. As such, it no longer perceives or communicates with the text at all, but mechanically reacts to programmed stimuli. So the reader changes from a position of active perception to passive reception. Dante's readers react to a system of signs which, in their heterogeneity, ultimately produce that which the author intended them to produce: a homogeneous meaning. The readers, as addressees of the writer or of an enunciation, do not produce an individual response or an utterance that functions as an action in the way J. L. Austin describes it in his speech-act theory.[19] The dialogicity of language, that which is inherent, according to many linguistic accounts, in all language activities and which allows, in the very act of enunciation, for the introduction of new ways of seeing that normally transcend the rigour and formality of the linguistic structure, that dialogicity evaporates in the mechanical reproduction of finite combinations contingent on the enunciations of the author.[20] That reader has little individuality or autonomy in intercommunicative processes. Indeed, that reader does not communicate at all, but reacts to subliminal and express signals alike of Dante's expert programme, 'spontaneously' reproducing consent to the linguistic powers inscribed in the text.

TOWARDS A CRITICAL THEORY OF ACTIVE
COMMUNICATION: GRAMSCI AND VOLOŠINOV

From the many theoretical insights Gramsci offers with his brief study of Dante, I have chosen to comment on just two which significantly problematize the conditions of possibility for the production of meaning in communication. For working purposes I have called them 'discourse I' and 'discourse II'. 'Discourse I', as I have argued in the previous pages, seems to posit, as in structural linguistics, that readers or speakers are caught in the prison-house of formal linguistic-semiotic systems that prescribe and limit the production of meaning. As is the case with Dante's Canto X, even the invisible and unexpressed elements ultimately fulfil precise functions in a determinate circumscribed space. The reader is the object of desire of a rigorous formal system, a subject who does not construct but who is constructed for the representations produced by that system. That reader is devoid of will, intentionality and an inner life, always already constructed and managed by an external and mechanistic system of signs the motions of which function unencumbered by individual speech acts and enunciations. It is also a reader who is not socially organized, who belongs to no social, historical, or ideological context. It is a powerless organism outside place and time, reacting to stimuli and only capable of producing that which is always already there. Is this a notion of the subject Gramsci pursues in 'discourse I'?

I should point out here that it is precisely when Gramsci extends his reading of Canto X to all of the *Divine Comedy*, when he draws up a structural model or a grammar of reading on the basis of one specific Dantean canto, and when he intends to apply that grammar – as with the morphological work pioneered by Vladimir Propp in the area of fables – to all of the 100 cantos of the *Divine Comedy*, when he possibly begins to reflect on homologizing his logic to other, non-literary communicative activities, when the reader of Dante's text is at the verge of being transformed into a reader of social and cultural texts, it is at that very moment that Gramsci balks.[21] In the already mentioned letter to Tatiana Schucht of September 1931 in which he discusses his Dante notes, he focuses on the relationship of the 'stage directions', provided by the author of the text, to the reader, that relationship which produces the meaning of the text. Here Gramsci not only focuses on Dante's Canto X. He also claims that all 'the structure of the *Divine Comedy* has this enormous function', to elicit the productive yet programmed reading of the text by the reader.[22] Did it

132

occur to Gramsci at this point that this structuralist model could be applied not only to literary texts but perhaps to social and cultural texts alike? Surely, positing the structural and poetic unity of Canto X against Croce's dogmatism on the matter was one thing Gramsci intended, and that intention he executed well. Indeed, Croce's aesthetics in general are no match for Gramsci's theoretical insights related to his interests in complex linguistic and communicative processes and in any event more in tune with the theoretical avant-gardisms of his time, scrutinizing received notions of subject-object relations in the production of knowledge. That Gramsci's reader of Dante possesses, in contradistinction to Croce's, an epistemic disposition for deciphering the multiplicity of languages and semiotic codes that inhabit the text is then an advance over Croce's idealist orthodoxy. Gramsci operates here with a tendentially phenomenological model within which a perceiving subject is able to make out and assemble a multiplicity of semiotic codes. Simultaneously, however, in that Gramsci's perceiving subject is a reader of Dante, not living outside space and time but operating within the spatial and temporal structures of Dante's text, Gramsci's reader is both a perceiving subject and a receiving object. I find it difficult to assume that for Gramsci, theorizing the conditions of possibility of reading and the production of meaning of one canto of Dante's poem, and even extending that theory to all of the cantos, would lead *ipso facto* to extending that theoretical element to all reading and meaning-producing processes in general. Yet is reading a literary text, for Gramsci, as precisely as that mode can be made out by a specific grammar, different from reading, understanding, interacting with other texts?[23] In the letter to Tatiana Schucht referred to above, Gramsci remains within the framework of a literary text, within the framework of Dante's writing, when he touches on this point. It seems as if he is almost apologizing for experimenting with a theory of reading that potentially has far-reaching implications for a theory of the production of meaning, norms, ideals and values. He comments on his theory, in parenthesis, like this: 'I have written this in a hurry, and all I have is Hoepli's Dante.'[24] Besides, all of this, he continues, 'ought to be examined very carefully, and one item at a time',[25] one canto at a time, that is. So in the very same letter and at the very moment that Gramsci positively states that his reading of Canto X undermines Croce's interpretation – a statement he had every reason to pronounce with confidence – he seems to intuit, perhaps, in his subsequent discussion of the relation of stage directions to interpretation, of the relation of semiotic emission and subjective reception, that his reading of Dante is not inconsequential for a theory of the production of meaning in social interaction. In any event, he does not pursue here either this radical departure from received notions of the production of knowledge, or the radical implications for a theory of meaning. He does not comment further on the powers he ascribes to the subject/reader in creating his/her own object in the context of the epistemological/phenomenological model he experiments with, nor does he comment on the powerlessness he ascribes to Dante's reader when it comes to creating individual and autonomous responses to the programmed signs in the context of the semiological and communicative model he is experimenting with. Instead, perhaps surprisingly, he calls the entire effort into question. Who knows, he writes to Tatiana Schucht, if I am really after something here with my Dante research. There are all kinds of material I have on Dante, and I really should check it out, but either I have not seen it for a long time, or I can not get to it because it is packed away. 'Professor Cosmo would be in the position to tell me whether I have discovered something indeed, or whether there is something in my argument that could be further developed in a little article, in order to pass some time.'[26] And for the record: Gramsci's former and old Professor Cosmo, a Dante scholar and a dedicated anti-fascist, did not find in Gramsci's Dante fragment all that many interesting ideas to share. What he did share with his former pupil was bad health, poverty (he had been put out of office due to his anti-fascist sentiments) and a melancholic temperament: 'I am also,' he writes, 'as you are, in a state of mind and in that age in which all one has left are memories.'[27]

I do not think that it is very profitable to speculate as to why Gramsci intercepts his logic at this point, why he abandons, that is, with Dante his 'discourse I'. That discourse contains, next to elements of structural linguistics, elements of a linguistic and communicative theory that intransigently seeks relationalities between subjects and objects while simultaneously opting for definitive differences in position and power in these relations. Dante needs readers, yet only to impose on to them his programmed system of signs that mechanically elicits their pre-programmed responses. What I would like to propose here, to put it simply, is this: while Gramsci no doubt evokes the image of a reader who is caught in a rigorous system that inexorably imposes meaning and truth, it is unlikely that he subscribed to such an explanation of the conditions of the production of meaning. While he can agree to parts of 'discourse I', that individuals are caught in structures and contexts, it is more difficult, if not outright impossible, for him to agree with the second part: that nothing can be done about it. As I will discuss in the remainder of this chapter, it is that part of 'discourse I', that something can be done about it, which is linkable to 'discourse II', that subjects often produce, in their interaction with the other, something new. From his scattered notes on linguistic matters to his notes on philosophical and political issues there is little doubt that Gramsci prefers a theoretical communicative model where the subject is not caught in inexorably determinate linguistic structures. What Gramsci tends to prefer is a theoretical communicative model where the subject is in a position to interact with an object and with other subjects, and it is in the very interaction with the object and other subjects that the subject can create his or her own object of knowledge according to the circumstances or the goals the subject intends to achieve. Dante's reader in part fulfils the requirements of this model. The reader, as we recall, creatively assembles the sensory data, whether visible or invisible, unexpressed or expressed, in the act of creating his/her own object in this act of interpretation. It is that aspect of 'discourse I', containing both an ontological and epistemological element, which is more congenial to 'discourse II'. That discourse is concerned with a phenomenological and social philosophy of freedom, with the conditions of possibility for autonomous human intervention because and in spite of given conditions and structures. In order to back up some of my proposition, I will turn to Gramsci's writings on linguistics.

Gramsci's studies of linguistic and communicative processes, which he began as a young student at the University of Turin and to which he dedicated his last research efforts in prison, known as Prison Notebook 29, encouraged, I think, a view of social interaction, social relations and relations of power that tend to comprehend the inherent linguisticality constituting these relations. In this, Gramsci, more than many other critical theorists of his epoch – and I am thinking here primarily of the Frankfurt School – intuits the importance of language, of linguistic processes in the production of ideologies and relations of power. On the other hand, Gramsci shows affinities with the linguistic-structuralist work carried out in the Soviet Union in the 1920s. The theorist who comes most readily to mind is Vološinov. While it is important to state this point, it is equally important not to overstate it. The bulk of the *Prison Notebooks* do not deal with linguistics, but with power relations, in particular the way in which hegemonic classes produce and maintain ways of seeing that do not challenge the status quo but somehow elicit the 'spontaneous' consent of subordinate classes, questions of ideology in the broadest sense. Yet to the extent to which values, norms and forms of seeing and understanding are not merely abstractly imposed by one social class or culture on to another, but are introduced, maintained and reproduced in the practices of language-using subjects, Gramsci comes close to an understanding of the materiality of language in the practices of everyday life. Indeed, it has been argued, by an outstanding reader of the Gramscian text, Franco Lo Piparo, that crucial cultural and political concepts usually ascribed to Gramsci, such as 'hegemony', which attempt to grasp the multiplicitous nature of the practices that inform and maintain power relations, have been derived from Gramsci's linguistic studies.[28] I find this a compelling proposition. No doubt, under the direction of one of the foremost Italian linguists of the time, Matteo Bartoli, Gramsci familiarized himself with problems relative to normative and historical grammars, comparative linguistics, the dissemination of dialects and the prestige and power, and with it, forms and norms of seeing, one language exercises over other languages. Gramsci was up to date with the philosophical and theoretical implications of the battle between the linguistic faculties, between the so-called neo-grammarians and the neo-linguists of the time, taking place in the first few decades of the twentieth century in Italy against the backdrop of international linguistics. The former, the neo-grammarians, had proposed, in the name of greater scientificity of linguistics, the need for a normative grammar which would explain linguistic laws and changes from within a determinate structure. They subscribed to a monogenetic view of language development and change. The latter, the neo-linguists, had proposed the study of normative grammars in space and time, such that linguistic laws and changes were tied not only to internal structural operations of the language but also to language users who live in specific places at specific times. In short, the former had proposed a model that would severely undercut the possibility of individual and intentional speech acts capable of effecting linguistic change, and the latter had proposed a model which would assign a transformatory function to individual speech acts. From Gramsci's notes on linguistics in his last notebook it is apparent that he both emphasizes the individual component in linguistic production, which he sees as historically and culturally determined, and a collective component, from within which and against which the individual component traces its course and possibilities.[29] That component is historically, culturally and biographically determined as well. To keep to linguistic terminology, *langue* and *parole*, formal linguistic structure, synchrony, and individual utterance, diachrony, are caught, according to Gramsci, in the contextualities of what we call history, time and place, that is.

Whether linguistics was merely a determinate point of departure for Gramsci's conceptual framework, as Lo Piparo will have it, or whether it is a constant in his way of doing and seeing things throughout his writings, is not easy to make out. There is no systematic treatise on linguistics written by Gramsci, such as we have, for instance, from the Soviet linguist Vološinov.[30] Yet there are many insights which show that Gramsci was close to Soviet linguistics of the 1920s and 1930s, in particular Vološinov's, and a few scattered sentences, both in his Dante notes and in his notes on linguistics, suggest that much. In a note entitled 'Criticism of the "Unexpressed"', Gramsci wonders whether Dante's procedure of silencing information which is ultimately crucial for understanding the drama of Cavalcante could serve as an example of a poetics or a theory of the 'unexpressed', a theory that ontologizes the unexpressible. This problematization, which would bring him close to a theory that postulates the inability of language to grasp the true being, to call it, in Heideggerian parlance, the impotence of language to get hold of the essence of '*Sein*', is something Gramsci seems to reject. One cannot speak or write, he says, but in a language that is historically produced.[31] 'Can one reconstruct and criticize a poem other than in the world of concrete expression and historically produced language?'[32] Surely, Gramsci is out to silence romantic, aesthetic and philosophical voices postulating Dante's voluntary inclusions of ineffabilities. When Dante weaves into his text 'absences', when events remain invisible and feelings unexpressed, then, Gramsci argues, this is not due to Dante's intentionality. Rather, it was the best he could do. 'It was not a "voluntary" element', Gramsci writes, 'of a practical and intellective character', that *clipped* Dante's wings. He 'flew with the wings he had', so to speak, and 'he did not renounce anything voluntarily'.[33] The gaps in the Dantean texts are contextually and historically produced by the power and the powerlessness of the language of Dante's time.

Gramsci, then, has no intention of ousting from his theoretical model the historical component, the contextual nature of language. Nor does he intend to oust from his linguistic model the social component of language. And finally, he does not oust from his system

137

the individual component of language. For all of these reasons, Gramsci moves in the orbit of Vološinov. Like this Soviet linguist, Gramsci sets up a relationship between *langue* and *parole*, between the formal language and the individual utterance. That relationship between the 'collective' or 'historical' component of language (*langue*) and the 'individual' component (*parole*) is a dialectical one, where the context of *langue* intersects with the context of *parole*. Just as every cognitive thought belongs from the very start to an ideological system and is governed by a set of laws, it belongs at the same time to another system, the system of the psyche, writes Vološinov, a statement which could have been authored by Gramsci.[34] Experiential knowledge, inner experience, a world of inner signs and meanings, dialectically interplay with the outer signs.[35] That Dante's wings were clipped, as Gramsci expressed it, is a sign of the sociality of Dante's inner life-world, of the dialectical relationship that the inner life of memory, psychology and system of meaning obtains with the outer life, a world of politics, culture, ideologies and economics. And when Gramsci understands Dante's efforts not as a monologic expression, but as a way to enter a dialogue with a reader, to communicate with a reader, then he tends to posit, with Vološinov, that the 'real unit of language that is implemented in speech is not the individual, isolated, mono-logic utterance, but the interaction of at least two utterances, in a word, dialogue'.[36] In Gramsci's reading of Dante, the individual act of reading presupposes the interaction with the text, and Dante's text found its *raison d'être* in the interaction with the reader. Dialogics, as Vološinov postulated it, against Saussure, by insisting on a non-separation between system and utterance, between *langue* and *parole*, between writers and readers, is an essential component of Gramsci's version of communicative theory. Equally essential for Gramsci is Vološinov's insight which is crucial for maintaining the non-separation of diachrony and synchrony in historical and sociological linguistics: 'The primary target of linguistic investigation should be exactly that which reveals the creative aspect of human language', writes Vološinov in a sentence that echoes the Humboldtian empha-sis on the creative aspect of human language.[37] Indeed, it is this creative aspect of human language, the possibilities and the powers inscribed in it, the individual speech act with its dynamic layers of 'inner life', memories, experiences and symbolic representations in their relations to the 'outer life', the other, or the object, which Gramsci seems to treasure most. So when Vološinov states that 'the semiotic nature of human communication cannot be grasped, if the novelty of the speech act and its relevance are disregarded as super-ficial phenomena, as "merely fortuitous refractions and variations or plain and simple distortions of normatively identical forms"', then he is not only correcting Saussure on an important matter.[38] He also and inadvertently comments on Gramsci's alternating feelings for Dante. When the reader's interaction with the text reveals the mutual inter-dependency of reader and text in the production of meaning, and the possible production of new significations, Gramsci remains on that textual ground. Yet when the reader's interpretive act and its rele-vance appear not as creating or producing new meaning but as merely fortuitous refractions and variations of Dante's, the author's pro-grammed normativities, Gramsci abandons Dante.

The selective affinities between Gramsci and Soviet linguistics, in particular between Gramsci and Vološinov, deserve more consider-ation than I can give here. What I would like to emphasize, though, is this: while Gramsci's writings include many linguistic insights which the work of Vološinov discusses in more detail, Gramsci differs from Vološinov on one important count. Gramsci not only argues for the dialectical interaction of various contexts in a dialogic situation, where various systems, such as the 'collective', the 'social' and the 'individual' meet. Given Gramsci's predilection for what I have called earlier a 'relational pragmatics', a way of seeing that places a phenomenon in a multiplicitous relation with and to many other phenomena, it should come as no surprise that in his understanding of linguistic interaction many levels intersect with each other. What I would like to note here is that the relation between the 'collective' or 'historical' component of language and the 'individual' component is not merely one of dialectics. In contradistinction to Vološinov, Gram-sci does not only set up a relationship between the *langue* and *parole*, understood as a relation between the concept of system and the concept of individual utterance, of development or evolution, be-tween synchrony and diachrony, that is. Though Gramsci does, like Vološinov, opt for a position that counters the opposition between synchrony and diachrony in that he understands that every system necessarily exists as evolution, just as evolution is inescapably of a systematic nature, Gramsci also advances beyond Vološinov, I think, when he insists on differentiations both within system and individual utterance. So language is not merely *langue*, language of a specific class or, as Vološinov would say, a context, that speaks the language of an ideological system of a specific economic, social, or political class. In Gramsci's linguistic theory, language is not only class-related but also space-related, the language of a specific region in its relation to the language of other regions.[39] Language is situated in specific locations in a geographic space which contributes to its hegemony, a space from which its power disseminates, its prestige radiates, to various degrees and intensities over and above other social classes, spaces and regions. This position, the hegemonic position of a language or a dialect, determines the adaptation of that language by other people who speak different languages, different dialects, and hold different systems of belief. It is the positionality of one language with respect to other languages which effects the dissemination of words and grammatical forms, of values, norms and ways of seeing and judging.[40] So it is not only the context, the social, cultural, economic context within which an individual utterance takes place that is important. Equally important is the speaker's position in relation to his/her context as well as in relation to other contexts, be they apparent or not so apparent, at the moment in which the utterance takes place.[41] Gramsci's theory of linguistics, incomplete and fragmented as it might be, is for this reason an advance over Vološinov's. It anticipates a theoretical model that is potentially capable of dealing with issues as far-ranging as gender, race and geography rather than merely with class in the context of a communicative theory. I will discuss some of these issues in the next chapter. What I would like to offer here is that the active component in Gramsci's linguistics is no doubt linked to his overall conceptual scheme, to his practical philosophy, his liberatory and emancipatory philosophy of praxis.

THE PHENOMENOLOGY OF THE PRISON WORLD: GRAMSCI AND MERLEAU-PONTY

It has rarely gone unnoticed in studies of Gramsci's work that his philosophy of praxis requires an active and creative component which can account, or be held accountable, for processes of stasis and processes of change. In general, this active and creative component of Gramsci's philosophy runs under the terms of 'voluntarism', 'subjectivism', 'idealism' and so forth. It has also been considered a residue of Gramsci's indebtedness to Croce. What I would like to point to instead is the connectedness of this active and creative component, where action becomes action not simply by putting individual will into motion, but rather by creating something new. And conversely, motion takes place within a structure, where the 'I' meets the 'you' or 'other', where the subject meets the object, and it is the creative aspect of motion or action which is capable of transcending that structure, which is capable of effecting the non-identity of subject and object. In Gramsci's reading, Dante, the subject, needs the reader, or the object, to produce meaning. Meaning resides in that interrelation, it is contingent on it. Similarly, the reader/subject needs the text/object to produce new information or knowledge. As in Merleau-Ponty's phenomenological project, the production of knowledge resides in that interrelation between a perceiving subject and a perceivable object. In what we might call Gramsci's theory of the subject, creativity, or the production of something new, is always related to, connected and interacting with the other or the object. Without these processes of interaction between subject and other subjects or objects, there is neither object nor subject. And there is no production of meaning. What Gramsci seems to suggest is that the study of the operations of ideology, of the production of value and meaning, does well to take into account the micrological operations of consciousness which produce and maintain the ideologies of specific relations of power, and which can produce, due to the non-identical relation of subject to object, counter-ideologies to specific relations of power. If power, its effects, its possibilities are to be examined, then the conditions of the operations of consciousness, the inherent connectedness of the individual act to structures that lie within and without, to structures that are both perceivable and imperceivable, even in their most minute material linguisticality, need to be taken into rigorous consideration. Power, as meaning and effect, feeds not only on the visible, but also on the micrology of the often hardly visible or audible. In this sense, hegemony is of many designs.

What emerge from Gramsci's 'insignificant' notes on Dante are then the contours of a theory of the sign that points to the interrelationality of the micrological with the macrological. What also emerges is a theory of perception, a phenomenological theory, that points to the existential interdependency or interrelationality of subject and object. As in Merleau-Ponty's description of consciousness, forms of knowing are embedded in that interrelationality, rather than merely either in the subject (subjectivism) or in the object (objectivism).[42] By the same token, in that Gramsci's Dante functions within a pre-reflective structure of given values and ways of seeing that inform his representational strategies in the *Divine Comedy*, Gramsci points to the notion of pre-reflective structures within which consciousness is embedded. This notion parallels Schutz' study of the phenomenology of the social world, where the structures of the life-world, a being with the other, that is, plays a role in action, motivation and representation.[43] Simultaneously, however, Gramsci had suggested, with his reading of Dante, that it is the subject's (reader's) ability to decode the complexity of the object (text), to read the visible and invisible signs, that leads to the production of meaning. So in this version of a phenomenological theory of knowledge, the subject functions as a *tabula rasa*, rearranging the sensory data without addressing the complexity of the subject. That subject functions outside the structures of a life-world, and as that it is reminiscent of Husserl's subject in his early phenomenological theory. The major phenomenological processes emerging from Gramsci's reading of Dante, written under the difficult circumstances of a life-world in prison, invoke a subject that rigorously constitutes a world of meaning in the interrelationships with objects, while simultaneously displaying the restraints a structure of a life-world imposes on consciousness and perception. That subject, I would like to propose here, is reminiscent of the imprisoned Gramsci himself. In my concluding pages, I would like briefly to address the contours of Gramsci's phenomenological project in prison and provide some evidence for my contentions on the basis of Gramsci's letters.

What emerges from my examination is, on the one hand, a Gramsci or a subject who, at the beginning of his prison term, confidently offers his sensory perceptions, or his body, to the stimuli of the objective world, as if his body and his mind seemed impervious to the constraining structures of his life-world in prison. Yet it can also be seen as Gramsci's unconscious desire to reproduce the conditions of the production of meaning by phenomenologically interacting with the other or the object, by indeed rigorously seeking this interaction in phenomenological detail as a condition for his survival. This interaction with the other is both external, an active engagement with the objective world around him, minimally stimulating as that world is, and internal, with his world of memory and experiential knowledge. And indeed, it is this rigorous interaction with the objects of his inner world, his memory and his experiential knowledge, which in part produces the many insights we find in his *Prison Notebooks*. On the other hand, there emerges a Gramsci or a subject, in the course of his long prison term, who resists activating his perceptive abilities in the context of his prison world, who withdraws his body from the stimuli surrounding him, and who withdraws his emotions from his inner world. In this he seems to struggle against the strictures imposed on him, withdrawing from the world of the other, while simultaneously strengthening the position of the 'I'. This struggle becomes particularly poignant when he both insists on the primacy of the 'I', the primacy of consciousness, the primacy of his subjective understanding of his situation, when he insists on his subjectivity in determining meaning, while simultaneously recognizing that the structures of the life-world in prison, which he attempted to transcend by interacting with it over a period of eleven years, ultimately constrain his abilities to produce the kind of meaning that could be meaningful to him: his freedom. In this sense, the structures of his life-world in prison, which enabled him to value theoretically the interaction of the I with the Other in most minute detail, is not only a condition of possibility to see the new and to invent new insights. In his case, as a prisoner, the structures of his life-world become insurmountable strictures, the potentials of which are effectively effaced by the enormous impotence and paralysis they have imposed on Gramsci.

As an anti-fascist intellectual, Gramsci shared the fate of many anti-fascists in the 1920s: Mussolini's henchmen could strike at any time. As one of the leaders of the Italian working-class movement, though, Gramsci was more vulnerable than many other anti-fascist political activists. Mussolini's henchmen would pursue him with particular rigour. So when Gramsci was arrested, in spite of the immunity that was his due as a member of the Italian parliament, in November 1926, he displays the disposition of a person who knew all along that his arrest was more than likely to take place. The letters which he was allowed to write in his initial prison phase, to his wife Giulia, to his mother and to his landlady, bespeak a prisoner who stands up to his fate. 'I am quiet and peaceful', he writes to his mother.[44] 'Morally I was prepared for everything. Also physically I will try to overcome the difficulties I might have to face and to stay in some kind of an equilibrium. You know me, deep down I am always ultimately good-humoured: this will help me to survive.'[45] What Gramsci was also prepared for was that his imprisonment would extend over a long period of time. He thus organizes, from the very start, some kind of intellectual activity for himself. In one of the first letters from prison, perhaps even the first letter he wrote, he asks his landlady to send him some of his books. He requests a German grammar, a handbook of linguistics authored by Bertoni and Bartoli and a copy of the *Divine Comedy*.[46] Since it took over two years before Gramsci was allowed to pursue in prison intellectual work that resembles a research programme, the eagerness with which he begins his research reflects the intensity of his desires: to exercise some kind of control over the structure of his new life-world in prison that condemns the prisoners' bodies to the monotony of a restricted array of sensory stimulation, their minds to the vagaries of their inner lives, and both body and mind to the peculiar laws of causality governing the prison world. Gramsci evokes the immense difficulty of that structure in an angry letter from November 1929 directed to Tatiana Schucht:

> What precisely do you know, concretely, about my daily life in prison? Nothing or practically nothing. Tell me, how should you be able to assess the effects of your activities which you initiate on my behalf, no matter how banal and insubstantial these initiatives might seem to you? There is no way you can know these things, there is absolutely nothing you can know. The entire process of causation, of cause and effect, in prison, is fundamentally different from causation in everyday life, because all actions, feelings and reactions lack one basic element – the freedom of ordinary existence, no matter how relative that freedom might be. Given these circumstances should not I be the one who decides what ought or what ought not to be done, should not I alone make these decisions, since I am the one who is in prison, I am the one who is deprived of freedom, I am the one who suffers the consequences of any initiative, endangering the conditions of my everyday life in prison?[47]

And further along in the letter he reiterates the differences between the structures of ordinary and prison life, differences, he insists, that are known not to the ones living in freedom, but to prisoners alone. 'It is objectively impossible for you, as an outsider, to understand the harrowing conditions of my life over the last few years.'[48]

Survival in this atmosphere meant, for Gramsci, from the beginning, a rigorous constitution of a private world of meaning based on an intensive and complex interaction not only with inner objects (the world of memory), but also with outer objects (the phenomenal world, texts, studies, interaction with others via correspondence). While there is no doubt that Gramsci's training in philology conditioned his aptitude for seeing detail and variation, as is commonly remarked, I would also like to propose that it is in the context of his life-world in prison, in his resistance to the timeless monotony of sensory stimulation, that he heightens his awareness of phenomenological processes. Representative of this awareness is his attention to and desire for detail in many letters from prison. In one of the early

letters, addressed to Tatiana Schucht, he writes about his transfer
from one prison to another:

> I arrived at Ustica on the seventh. On the eighth I received your
> letter of the third. . . . The most difficult part was the crossing
> from Palermo to Ustica. We tried to cross four times and three
> times had to return to Palermo harbour because the ferryboat
> was driven back by a storm. . . . The island has an area of three
> square miles and contains a population of about thirteen
> hundred, of whom six hundred are ordinary convicts, i.e. hard-
> ened criminals. The people here are extremely hospitable.
> We're not all settled yet. For two nights I slept in a large room
> together with friends of mine. . . . The wind, which blew through
> every crack, past balcony, window and door, sibilant or sound-
> ing trumpets, kept irritating me.[49]

From a political and social theorist and activist used both to dealing
with difficult conceptual schemes and traditions, and acting on the
grand political stage of the 1920s in Italy, and, so far as I can tell,
uninterested in the more modest practices of everyday life, Gramsci
has turned into a human being attentive to every motion his body
experiences in the practices of everyday prison life. This detailed
attention to the body is equalled by his detailed attention to memory.
About a year into his prison sentence he writes as follows, again to
Tatiana Schucht:

> I forgot, at our last meeting, to thank you for the handkerchief
> and to congratulate you as you deserve. The little geese seem to
> have come out beautifully. I don't remember whether I've ever
> told you the story of the handkerchiefs embroidered by Genia. I
> used to love to make fun of her, insisting that the swallows or the
> other embroidered ornaments were always lizards. And, in fact,
> both the ornaments and the monograms of those handkerchiefs
> showed a distinct tendency to take on saurian characteristics.[50]

Two years later, again to Tatiana Schucht, he writes:

> I received the parcels of medicine together with the other things
> that you sent me. The oversocks are fine, but I'm afraid that my
> shoes will get the better of them. In any case, I won't wear out
> more than a pair of socks a week. There is no point in sending
> me tonics such as 'Benzofosfan' or tranquillizers like the ones
> you sent last time: I'm sure that they have no effect on me. . . . I
> reminded Carlo that when I was in prison in Rome, I received,

either from him or from you, a package of Turkish tobacco that I appreciated very much, since it resembled Italian Macedonian tobacco before they started mixing it with American tobacco.[51]

Four years later he writes, this time to his son Delio:

> I was very glad to get the parrot feathers and the flowers. But I can't imagine what the bird is like and why he is losing such large feathers. Maybe the artificial heat is bad for his skin. . . . I once saw a sparrow, who was in a bad way because he ate only the soft part of bad bread, recover with the addition of a little green salad to his menu.[52]

From the beginning of his imprisonment to one of the last letters written to his sons, Gramsci produces a maximum of descriptive information based both on his minimal sensory life-world, his outer life, and on the richness of his memories, his inner life. Surely some of the detailed and precise information he includes in his letters has a practical function: he must specify with care to others, usually Tatiana Schucht, what he wants and how he wants it, given the restrictions of his daily prison life. Imprecise information will get him what he does not need or want. 'I've had to develop a style to suit the circumstances', he writes to his wife Giulia Schucht, 'because of the many times that I have been subjected to censorship during the events of these past years.'[53] The style he is referring to is his tendency towards the concrete, which can also be viewed as pedantry. Yet it is not only for practical reasons that he tends towards detail. In one of his moments of crisis, three years into his prison sentence, the writing of letters, with their attention to detail, is equivalent to an essential will for life.

> This month you've hardly written to me at all: a card on November twenty-eighth and then a note on the twenty-ninth along with Giulia's letter. But I also have very little desire to write now. All my links with the outside world seem to be breaking, one by one. When I was in prison in Milan, two letters a week were never enough: I had a mania for being chatty by letter. Do you remember how crammed my letters were? During the week, all my thoughts were aimed towards Monday: what would I be able to write? How could I phrase something in such a way that the letter got through? Now I no longer know what to write or how to begin.[54]

As long as Gramsci maintained contact with the outside world, and with his inner life, his will to survive, in his own account, was intact. His rigorous interaction with objects, whether with the objective world of prison or with the world of knowledge and ideas, archived in his memory, has a similar function. This rigour is above all an attention to detail. Surely, one could argue that it is not only his will to live which shapes his inordinate attention to detail and his archaeology of memory. The conditions of writing in prison themselves, the absence of research material and possibilities, the absence of any interaction with imprisoned comrades who shared his intellectual passion, all of that might have heightened Gramsci's attention to phenomenological detail with respect to material he did have at his disposal, and with respect to the arsenal of memory the fascists had been unable to take away from him. What Gramsci had at his disposal when working in prison was his experience, his experiential knowledge and his memory. His relentless search for details in his memory is possibly linked to an immense intellectual desire to look for relations between that which he had materially and concretely at his disposal and that which was available to him only in his memory, relations between that which seems not to be, and that which is, relations between presences and apparent absences, passionate excursions of a mind condemned to silent thinking. Yet I think that his attention to phenomenological detail is also and perhaps above all linked to an existential desire, to keep producing meaning, to live, to remain a subject, long after Mussolini had successfully executed his plan to make one of the greatest political and theoretical activists of his time into an impotent object.[55]

Part III

BEYOND THE MODERN, BEYOND THE POSTMODERN

6

Gramsci's intellectual and the age of information technology

THE ADVENTURES OF A CONCEPT IN GRAMSCI'S TEXTS

There is little doubt that one of the major interests Gramsci pursued in his *Prison Notebooks* is the notion of the intellectual, the study of the intellectual as a sociological category, and reflections on the intellectual as a cultural and ideological producer. There is also some evidence that this topic has an extraordinary status in Gramsci's intellectual and emotional economy. This is at least the message one gets when reading the correspondence of two of Gramsci's closest friends during his prison years, Piero Sraffa and Tatiana Schucht.[1] So when Sraffa, always intent on encouraging Gramsci's will for survival, senses the possibility of the prisoner's physical and psychological countdown, he suggests engaging Gramsci in an intellectual discussion on the topic of the intellectual.[2] Since Gramsci's correspondence had been limited by the prison authorities to bi-monthly letters exclusively to family members, Sraffa himself could not directly engage in such an epistolary exchange with Gramsci. He outlined, however, a rhetorical strategy for Tatiana Schucht, Gramsci's sister-in-law, which, consisting in socratically eliciting responses to a set of interested inquiries on the topic, he hoped would renew or at least stabilize the dying prisoner's will to live. The ploy seems to have worked, at least for a while. The notes Gramsci wrote on the question of the intellectual are for this reason perhaps not only the most compelling but also of extraordinary importance for his philosophy of praxis in general. Next to and linked with the notions of political and cultural hegemony, of civil and political society, and of coercion and consent, there squarely resides one of Gramsci's major contributions to the problematic of the twentieth-century intellectual. And without the intellectual, I would like to add, there is perhaps no Gramscian critical theory.

My intention in this chapter is not to offer a detailed treatment of Gramsci's notion of the intellectual in relation to other seminal Gramscian theorems, such as hegemony or the distinction between civil and political society. There already exists a sizeable body of work in this area, not least because studies of Gramsci's theory that claim adequacy would find it difficult to circumvent such crucial issues. I see no reason to duplicate these efforts. Rather, what interests me is to ask whether the sphere Gramsci ascribes to intellectuals and intellectual activities and the way in which he understands this category historically and sociologically is of relevance for delineating a theory of the intellectual and of intellectual functions in and for our era today. More specifically, if one understands the theory of the intellectuals Gramsci develops as the result of an analysis that is in the last instance related to his place and his time, as a way to assess the contributions or the lack of them to significant democratic change by the various intellectual strata of his epoch, then one might be able to develop the contours of a critical theory of the intellectual commensurate with our own place and time. The social and cultural organization of the contemporary USA (and to some extent other western industrialized and technologized nation-states as well as Japan) seems to be increasingly constituted by processes of informatization and technologization which radically transform the nature of our societies. These transformations, which affect the production and dissemination of information and knowledge, are sometimes marked by the term 'postmodern'. Mark Poster has recently argued that the predominant mode of being of late twentieth-century western nation-states seems to have exchanged its previous 'mode of production' for a current 'mode of information', thereby extending the argument to economic matters as well.[3] The critical question I would like to raise in my discussion of Gramsci's theory of the intellectual is this: to what extent does Gramsci's theory of the intellectual, which contains as a minimum four analytical models of intellectuality, remain a valid one for our reality and which if any social, political, or cultural function can we ascribe to the category of the intellectual in an age of information technology? I will argue that many of Gramsci's notes on the intellectual are at the very least useful points of departure for dealing with that same problematic in our own time. I will then outline a series of analytical models on the basis of various Gramscian texts.

These models represent for Gramsci intellectual activities and functions as they operated to further or to resist democratic change in Italy in the first few decades of our century. In general economic and political terms, Italy moved towards a gradual adaptation of Fordism in the industrial sector, particularly in the north, and towards state interventionism in economic and political affairs. In social and cultural terms, Italy at that moment moved in the orbit of what we call rationalism and modernism. In this sense, Gramsci's theory of the intellectual is deeply rooted in what we call the 'modern' paradigm. Its usefulness for the 'postmodern' remains the issue to be explored in the second part of this chapter.

Model 1: The traditional intellectual: artist, philosopher, poet

Gramsci's notion, or rather notions, of the intellectual evolved over a lengthy period of time. Judging from Gramsci's earlier writings, those before 1920, his concept of the intellectual seems at that time to be mostly limited on the one hand to the category of cultural writers, of disseminators of ideas and values via written texts. On the other hand, as an accomplished journalist, Gramsci was surely well aware of the communicative, the cultural and ideological function that not only philosophers/poets but also writers in general assume.[4] He was aware of the crucial ideological importance of institutions such as publishing houses and presses at a time when print rather than radio and tv was the primary means of communication between the state apparatuses and the public. These publishing houses and cultural journals somehow functioned as private institutions for the formation of public opinion. They were extraordinarily significant for commenting, whether critically or not, on the communicative processes and relations between the state apparatuses and the public, for designing cultural and philosophical agendas. Individual intellectuals who had the means to produce and distribute their own journals – such as Croce, for instance, who published his *Critica* – often represented such institutions and the power inscribed in them, thereby assuming a public leadership role.[5] In this sense Gramsci's understanding of this type of intellectual is closely linked to the ideological and communicative function of that category. In the formation of a new and more democratic culture, as Gramsci envisioned it, intellectuals, *qua* thinkers, philosophers, writers and journalists, would consequently also play a major leadership role. Just as in the ideological legitimation

processes of the bourgeois and the nascent capitalist culture intellectuals had once been paramount, the production of a new and
socialist culture would not succeed unless it had its own intellectuals
working on its behalf. So in articles written by the young Gramsci
before his active engagement as one of the leaders of the Italian
working-class movement, he emphasizes this ideologically educative
function of the writer/intellectual. Yet he also hoped that these writing intellectuals would participate in the launching of cultural organizations designed to involve the economically and socially less
advantaged groups of people in a cultural literacy programme. Gramsci himself worked in such a context. He took part in the 'cultural
literacy programme' both as a critical reader of classical narrative
and philosophical texts, which he hoped to make available to the
culturally disadvantaged social groups, and as someone who presented talks and led discussions in cultural centres and adult education programmes expressly set up for the dissemination of cultural
literacy and progressive thought among the working class.[6] Up to
1920 or so, Gramsci thus adhered to an understanding of the role of
intellectuals not dissimilar to what one might call an 'idealist' or
'traditional' notion of the intellectual, reminiscent of the liberal assumptions that inform the question of the intellectual in eighteenth-
and nineteenth-century Europe: in a society divided into an educated
few and an illiterate many, as was still the case in Italy even in the
early decades of this century, the educated few have a significant
moral and cultural function to assume in the education of the masses.
Among their tasks was working to reduce cultural illiteracy by introducing the classical canons of western philosophy and Italian
culture, as well as familiarizing large masses of people with more
modern and international writers and artists who embraced the
progressive cause. In both areas, it should be pointed out, Gramsci
aimed, from the very start, at expressive and conceptual quality. 'A
concept which is difficult in itself cannot be made easy when it is
expressed without becoming vulgarized', he writes sometime in 1918,
advocating a demanding, stimulating and provocative style of presentation which, rather than adjusting the level of conceptual difficulty to
a theoretically illiterate or underdeveloped audience or reader, would
purposively activate dynamics of reflection and critical exchange.[7]
'The tone of the articles ... must always be just above this average
level, so that there is a stimulus to intellectual progress', Gramsci
writes further.[8]

Model 2: The 'Structure of Feeling' and 'Intellectual Community'

By 1920 or so, when Gramsci was deeply involved in the political struggle and had gained valuable experience alongside the industrial workers of the Italian north, there is a slight shift in his understanding of the intellectual. Or rather, what Gramsci now adds to his received notion of the intellectual as arbiter of progressive philosophical and literary taste and educator of the masses is a more differentiated perspective as to how and to what extent intellectuals might operate in cultural struggles for democratic change. In the articles stemming from the early to the mid-1920s, Gramsci's own way of writing, of doing cultural work as an intellectual, changes, and with it apparently his notion of the intellectual. Gramsci's new intellectual no longer simply spells the gospel hierarchically from above, albeit the Marxist one, authoritatively disseminating ideas and values, ideologically desirable as these ideas might be in the demystification of the existing power structures and in the construction of a revolutionary consciousness. Nor does this intellectual merely assume a negative function by critiquing or polemicizing against the predominant ideas of 'bourgeois' or liberal intellectuality. If Gramsci's intellectual, and Gramsci *qua* intellectual, would still launch, by 1917, with youthful revolutionary fervour a fierce attack against bourgeois liberals and politically passive individuals alike, polemicizing simultaneously against the cowardice of those who claim political impartiality, the hypocrisy of proclaimed innocence, and the monstrosity of parasites who pretend indifference, culminating in his 'I hate those who are indifferent', the Gramsci of the early and mid-1920s changes rhetorical modes.[9] Alienating confrontation appears to make room for politically productive negotiation. Gramsci's new intellectual is now called upon not to reduce his/her field of influence by rhetorically restrictive methods but to expand the sphere of cultural literacy. This includes the identification of already existing cultural, moral, philosophical and artistic potentials of the proletariat, the mobilization of the latent intellectual power of the people. It also includes the identification of those forces or figures among the liberal intelligentsia whose collaboration even at its most minimal could only further the anti-fascist and working-class cause. Yet Gramsci's change in rhetoric should not be viewed only as an expedient political manoeuvre, the tactics of a pragmatic strategist. There is some reason to believe that Gramsci's evolving way of doing and seeing things, quite possibly linked to his own historical and political experiences, affected his assessment of what intellectuals are and might do. From a position which would place progressive intellectuality above the masses of the people and urge its distinct separation from other political forms of intellectuality, Gramsci now assumes a position which examines and validates the activities of the intellectuals from what we might call both a horizontal and a vertical point of view. The left intelligentsia will engage in dialogues and even forge alliances with individual bourgeois intellectuals, particularly with anti-fascist intellectuals of the liberal bourgeoisie when politically expedient and appropriate, while it will simultaneously participate in cultural processes that both engage and further the intellectual potential among the working class. Gramsci himself lives up to this agenda of cultural politics: he invites one of the most influential liberal and anti-fascist intellectuals of the epoch, Piero Gobetti, to write and direct the literary and theatrical columns of the major journal of the Italian left of the time, the *Ordine Nuovo*.[10]

So Gramsci's intellectual was, by the early 1920s, not only a 'traditional' intellectual who educates the masses from above, or a critical journalist who purposively engages in progressive cultural literacy agendas. He/she was also and simultaneously a cultural politician who would align him/herself with other progressive forces of the Italian community, and who would take into account the intellectual powers inherent in popular epistemology and culture by eliciting and challenging them. In 1926, shortly before his arrest, and five years into a most intense phase of political activism, Gramsci writes his piece 'On the Southern Question'.[11] In spite of its incomplete and somewhat fragmentary character, this essay represents one of the most suggestive and seminal pieces written by Gramsci. The notion of the intellectual represented here constitutes an additional phase in the complex evolution of this Gramscian concept. This new phase is perhaps best characterized by what I would like to call Gramsci's 'grammatological turn'. In previous years, Gramsci had mostly elaborated on the activities of progressive intellectuals, on a definition of where and how progressive intellectuals intervene in the struggle for a democratic culture and change. This led him to examining the functionality of progressive intellectuals relative to the classes which have been traditionally considered non-intellectual, as well as relative to those social classes which have traditionally monopolized 'high' culture, the bourgeoisie, that is. By the early 1920s Gramsci began to experiment with a notion of intellectuality that would extend that concept to the proletariat as well, as we have seen in the discussion above. In order to grasp the similarity in mental activity between some intellectuals and some members of the proletariat, Gramsci seems to have abandoned the semantic predominance of the noun 'intellectual', as in the unit 'progressive intellectual', when he introduced the adjective 'intellectual', as in 'intellectual proletarian'. This move allowed him to continue to differentiate sociologically between two economic categories, the intelligentsia and the proletariat, while simultaneously identifying some of the activities which they sometimes share: an intellectual function, that is. By the time Gramsci writes his essay 'On the Southern Question', he seems to abandon this semantic unit of adjective and noun, as in 'progressive intellectual', or 'intellectual proletarian'. Instead, 'intellectual' *qua* noun and 'intellectual' *qua* adjective now appear as independent and autonomous semantic units, which allows Gramsci freely to attach them, and the functions they embody, to more than simply two sociological groups. It is difficult to say whether Gramsci's grammatological manoeuvres were the result of empirical and experiential observation, or whether he imposed a preconceived conceptual or theoretical scheme on his empirical data. What we can say is that his new and unorthodox way of handling language and its possibilities broadened his perspectives on the functions and the sites of intellectual work, in that it enabled him to conceptually grasp the multiplicity and heterogeneity of intellectual voices in Italian society.

If Gramsci's 'original' intellectual was predominantly an educated disseminator of ideas, of traditional and revolutionary ideas alike, the 'intellectual' we encounter in 'On the Southern Question' is the product of and a function in many social sites. To be sure, this essay was not written as a general treatise on the problematic of the intellectual. It was written by Gramsci expressly to deal with the problematic of the relatively industrialized Italian north and the mostly agrarian Italian south, two geographic areas utterly separated from and hierarchically related to each other on the basis of the relative economic prosperity enjoyed in the north and the economic destitution suffered by many in the south. Yet the analysis Gramsci provides in this context, the way in which he conceptually and terminologically differentiates between intellectual functions and possibilities, is apposite to my theme in this chapter. The agricultural south, writes Gramsci, has been systematically exploited by the industrialized north.[12] In addition, the industrialists of the north have forged an alliance with the big landowners of the south in order to keep things the way they are. This alliance is what Gramsci calls an 'agrarian bloc', a consensus, a communicative action, that is, between the owners of the means of production in the north and the land-owners in the south. This consensus depends on a nationwide ideo-logical reproduction of that state of affairs, a reproduction that occurs on many social levels and in many forms of legitimation. In the north, received images of a south 'as a lead weight', writes Gramsci, predom-inate.[13] This lead weight supposedly

> impedes a more rapid development of Italy; the southerners are biologically inferior beings, semi-barbarians or complete bar-barians by natural destiny; if the south is backward, the fault is not to be found in the capitalist system or in any other historical cause, but is the fault of nature which has made the southerner lazy, incapable, criminal, barbarous, moderating his step-mother's fate by the purely individual outburst of great geniuses, who are like solitary palms in an arid and sterile desert.[14]

And in the south, the reproduction of this consensus takes place in a variety of spheres. There are, on the one hand, exceptional minds in the south, who, in spite of the lack of cultural institutions and enlight-ened communities, have managed to reach a high level of cultural formation.[15] As intellectuals, they understand themselves as auton-omous, politically unattached but linked to the great cultures of the western tradition. Notwithstanding their self-assessment, these exceptional intellectuals often ideologically support the big land-owners of the area. Indeed, the social stratum of the landowners produces its own intellectuals for this very purpose. On a secondary or perhaps another level, consensus is produced and circulated by the intellectuals of the rural petty bourgeoisie: the pharmacist, the lawyer, the priest, the local newspaper editor, the schoolteacher, and so forth who express, with a few exceptions, a set of values which have a specific function: emotionally, ideally and materially to tie the exploited masses of the peasants to the landed property owners. As mediators between the peasant masses and the big landowners, this group of rural petty-bourgeois intellectuals is extremely important for the survival of the agrarian bloc. Without their multifaceted and ubiquitous ideological mediation in the many interstices of what Gramsci will later call civil society, consent to the status quo could not be maintained. The peasants of the south themselves do not produce intellectuals of their own, an intellectual group, that would critically reflect on and represent the interests of the peasant class. As such, the peasants are without a voice. Although most peasant families aspire to produce an intellectual, in particular a priest, this aspiration is not coupled with the desire to give an autonomous voice to the peasant class. Rather, this intellectual born on peasant soil will facilitate some peasant access to the rural petty bourgeoisie, ideologically forging the mediation between the big landowners and the peasants, and, by implication, the consensus between the owners of the means of production in the north and the landed property owners in the south. What complicates matters in Italy, writes Gramsci, is that the south furnishes the Italian state with many of its administrators and bureaucrats. The military, the police, the legal institutions, that sphere of society which Gramsci will later call political society, the repressive apparatuses of the state, are primarily staffed by southerners. Gramsci writes: 'The southern intellectuals are among the most interesting and important strata of Italian national life. It is sufficient to remember that three-fifths of the state bureaucracy is composed of southerners to be convinced of this.'[16] That intellectual stratum, Gramsci claims further, is marked by a specific psychology: 'Democratic in its peasant face, reactionary when its face is turned towards the big property owner and the government, much given to political intrigue, corrupt, disloyal.'[17] In contradistinction to these various intellectual strata in the south, there is the new intellectual of the north, a product of capitalist processes and industrial change, who has become a 'technical organizer, a specialist in applied sciences'. Yet in as much as Italy as a country was not, at Gramsci's time, industrially as advanced as other countries, the intellectual Gramsci suspects will prevail in Italy is not the new intellectual of rationalization and technologization, but the traditional one, who continues to carry out intermediary functions between the masses and the various state apparatuses. These in turn mediate between the masses and the owners of the means of production by legitimating the consensual status quo.

Gramsci's differentiated analysis of intellectual functions in 'On the Southern Question' is directly linked to the events of a historical moment in which it was written: the defeat of the left in Italy, of the northern industrial workers, that is, the rise of fascism and its consolidation by 1924, the support it had received from the rural petty bourgeoisie in the south, from its intellectual functionaries on many levels and in the interstices of the state apparatuses. As an historical document, unfinished and somewhat fragmented as it might be, this

Gramscian essay is surely one of the most valuable. Yet this essay also transcends its historical contingencies. For one thing, it is a text which contains many if not most of the elements of Gramsci's complex theory of the intellectual as he develops it in his *Prison Notebooks*. For another, it contains elements which allow us to circumscribe some of Gramsci's methodological aporias that carry his critical theory. It indicates how his analytical processes on the one hand operate with received conceptual and terminological apparatuses, and how on the other hand he experiments with, mobilizes and freely but not arbitrarily invents others in order to grasp the cultural forces and dynamics of his time and to strategize agendas for social, political and economic change. By the time Gramsci writes on the topic of the intellectual in his *Prison Notebooks*, he integrates the complex system of functions and relations as he has worked it out in 'On the Southern Question'. When dealing with this topic, he now writes, one should reflect on the 'maximum' limits of acceptance of the term 'intellectual'.[18] And he continues:

> Can one find a unitary criterion to characterize equally all the diverse and disparate activities of intellectuals and to distinguish these at the same time and in an essential way from the activities of other social groupings? The most widespread error of method seems to me that of having looked for this criterion of distinction in the intrinsic nature of intellectual activities, rather than in the ensemble of the system of relations in which these activities (and therefore the intellectual groups who personify them) have their place within the general complex of social relations.[19]

It should be pointed out that it is precisely because of Gramsci's endeavour to see phenomena in relation to one another, as he expresses it here, that the various notions of 'intellectuals' he presents in his texts do not cancel each other out. In this sense, in the evolutionary trajectory of this Gramscian concept, one notion does not replace, substitute, supplement, or marginalize another. Rather, in Gramsci's critical theory, a plurality of equitable notions squarely exist next to each other, possibly because, as Anne Showstack Sassoon suggests, these various concepts attempt to grasp the many diverse levels and functions of what I would like to call here 'intellectual realities'.[20] Various intellectual functions and relations as Gramsci makes them out in his reality intersect in the Gramscian text.

On the one hand, Italian society produces the traditional intellectual, the rhetorician, who creates and disseminates 'high' culture. Croce stands as an example of that. In that this intellectual, whether consciously or unconsciously, either legitimates or challenges the values of the predominant culture, he/she is also a propagator of ideology. Gramsci's approach to this type of intellectual function is thus to begin with a traditional Marxist one, but also one that has in the Italian tradition affinities with the cultural agendas of eminent idealist cultural critics, such as the Spaventa brothers and de Sanctis.[21] As part of the superstructure, that intellectual function supports or resists progressive historical and cultural forces and it is on the basis of his/her partiality for the democratic cause that he/she will be judged. However, when Gramsci engages in a deliberate dialogue with Piero Gobetti, and when he encourages dialogic interaction of left intellectuals with the liberal anti-fascist intelligentsia in general, then he begins to transcend this traditional Marxist model. For what he is evoking in the context of his politics of alliance with the liberal intelligentsia is a nascent and powerful understanding of what we might call, in the conceptual traces of Kuhn, an 'intellectual or cultural or critical community' working not for the status quo but for significant democratic change. So what Gramsci seems to begin to graph is not only a master narrative of the ideological function of the intellectual as part of the superstructure, understood in Marxist terms, but also a microhistory of the category of intellectuals that points to a system of intellectual communities. This graph includes interestingly and significantly an attempt to design a psychogram of these various communities. An understanding of the collective psychological traits of a specific group or community, of its 'structure of feeling' in its various manifestations and complexities, coupled with familiarization with its members' unacknowledged assumptions, their imagery, their experiences, their practices and, above all, the cultural mission they ascribe to themselves, will enhance the study of the role the intellectuals fulfil in Italian society. When Gramsci chooses the formulation '*esprit de corps*' in that context in order to circumscribe the notion of 'intellectual community', then he does not refer simply to the class character of the bourgeoisie and its intellectuals. It is precisely the point of his discussion of the '*esprit de corps*' to describe relations that seem to go beyond class. By choosing a formulation such as '*esprit de corps*', he points, whether inadvertently or not, to the conditions of possibility of intellectual production, conditions which do not preclude the existence of a body but to the contrary insist on the placement of the body in a specific environment. As such, and more specifically in terms of the production of an intellectuality, of a set of ideas, and of the choices one makes in producing a specific set of ideas and the values attached to them, the activity is not only or primarily contingent on class, or on the will to produce ideas that might transcend the interests of an economic and social class. Rather, and equally often, if not more often, the production of intellectuality is contingent on a very basic reality, namely the body. That body lives within the 'structure of feeling' of a specific community, the socio-psychic language of which informs a person's imagistic and symbolic referentiality. What differentiates one 'intellectual community' from another are the respective languages that are spoken in each, their forms of communication, which contain the emotional, psychological and evaluative registers of their specific 'structure of feeling' or community. The 'structure of feeling' of one community, and the experiences, assumptions and exclusions underlying it, are not identical with but different from the 'structures of feeling' of other communities.

From Gramsci's discussion of Gobetti it is apparent though that one is not necessarily caught in the emotional and evaluative net of one specific 'structure of feelings'. Indeed, one can take part in more than one 'intellectual community' and consequently speak perhaps not the language but a 'dialect' that approximates a specific 'structure of feeling'. Some dialogue, in the sense of the Habermassian communicative action, can occur in spite of the difference in the background 'structure of feeling'. So what enables the cultural dialogue between Gramsci and Gobetti is not primarily their political stance, which is in any event far from identical. Gobetti is a liberal and Gramsci is a Marxist. Nor is it a civilized desire to get along harmoniously with each other. Surely, both Gramsci and Gobetti are marked by an extraordinary open-mindedness coupled with intellectual integrity. What enables the communicative process between these two theorists is a warrant or a dialect they share, the 'dialect' of enlightenment principles from which to reason and from which to pursue an agenda of freedom for all. The ability to share that dialect is something like a condition for productive consensual discourse, for communicative action. Two differing heirs of the enlightenment, originating in two differing 'structures of feeling', can meet on the fragile ground of a gradually evolving new 'structure of feeling', a new intellectual community, a new moral and social paradigm.

It should be pointed out here that the condition of communicative action between Gramsci and Gobetti is not a universal language they share, but a 'dialect'. A dialect is in general a form of language which is peculiar to a particular group and may be viewed in relation to other languages. At times, a speaker can embody that relation, and Gobetti represents such a speaker. He is able to entertain a dialogue with Gramsci and to enact a communicative process because they both share the dialect of enlightenment principles and an emerging 'critical community', as Gramsci points out. Of crucial importance here is again Gramsci's effort to introduce plural and equally coexisting sectors on a horizontal level, while vertically differentiating within a given category in such a way that the various sectors do not cancel each other out. This formal model, which allows for differentials, is mobilized in this context of the 'structure of feeling' as it relates to Gobetti. While one of the dialects Gobetti speaks enables him to engage in communicative actions with Gramsci, he also speaks a number of other dialects the warrants of which irrevocably sever his links with Gramsci as they forge new communicative links with 'intellectual communities' that do not share Gramsci's political goals. Among these is an 'intellectual community' whose 'structure of feeling' informs the self-assessment of embodying the cultural tradition of an entire nation. It is the 'intellectual community' of the Italian cultural elite. Similar to the high priests of sacred institutions, they secure the continuity of the present with the past. A strong relation to the past, a reverence for received artistic, cultural and philosophical traditions coupled with an embracing of lofty values, plays thus a crucially significant role in their specific 'structure of feeling', and it is difficult, perhaps impossible, for them to make a complete break with the past. It is not Gramsci but Gobetti who can engage in communicative practices with that community, it is Gobetti and not Gramsci who shares the symbolic and imagistic warrants of that dialect. And more so, it is precisely because of this possibility of dialogic encounter with the mandarins of the Italian cultural establishment, which Gobetti entertains and which Gramsci cannot entertain, that Gramsci cannot afford to sever his relations with Gobetti. 'Not to understand this means not to understand the question of the intellectuals and the role which they play in the class struggle', is what Gramsci laconically has to say about the extraordinary theoretical and political importance of this issue.[22]

Model 3: The 'organic intellectual', the 'new intellectual', the 'critical specialist'

In the *Prison Notebooks* Gramsci's attention to the problem of the intellectual is framed, on the one hand, in a study of the history of the Italian intellectual. On the other hand, however, Gramsci also elaborates a series of concepts as we have encountered them in my examination of Gramscian texts above. Among these is the concept of *'esprit de corps'*, which we can render, as I have done above, as 'structure of feeling' or 'cultural, critical, intellectual community'. The emphasis here is not so much, however, on the complex way by which long-established 'intellectual communities', such as the mandarins, can be eventually enlisted, however marginally, in the agendas for democratic change. Rather, here Gramsci approaches the problem from a different angle, examining the resistance of some 'intellectual communities', indeed the historical resistance of the Italian intellectual, to democratic change. Gramsci also examines in the *Prison Notebooks* the conditions of possibility of an emerging new kind of 'intellectual community'. These two major arguments in the *Prison Notebooks*, on resistance to change as well as the creation of a 'new intellectual', can be described as a discussion of the 'traditional' intellectual and the 'organic' intellectual, a distinction which Gramsci also makes. Hereby, the 'traditional intellectual' would stand for the politically resistant intellectual in the world of feudalism or capitalism, and the 'organic intellectual' for the world of nascent socialism. In some instances Gramsci indeed understands these two concepts in such a way. To reduce Gramsci's problematization of the intellectual to this distinction is not, however, what I have in mind here. It would not serve my purpose, nor would it do justice to the text. In the *Prison Notebooks*, Gramsci's discussion of the intellectual in relation to resistance and in relation to the creation of a new intellectuality mobilizes an entire series of concepts which we have already encountered in my examination of other Gramscian texts. Among these are, to begin with, the concept of 'structure of feeling' in its relation to the conditions of enunciation of the 'traditional intellectual'. In addition, Gramsci activates the same concept of the mediatory and legitimatory function of the intellectual-ideological activities of professional and semi-professional strata and institutions in capitalist civil society as we saw in his essay 'On the Southern Question'. The intellectuals mediate between the owners of the means of production and those who do not own and organize the means of production, those who sell their labour power to these owners.[23] As pharmacists, lawyers, teachers, priests and doctors, as scientists, researchers, technicians and engineers, as military personnel, judges and members of the police, as agents of institutions, that is, they do not produce forms of knowledge, but disseminate information or withhold information in the service of disciplining the body and the mind for the powers that be. These types of intellectual exercise 'subaltern functions of social hegemony and political government'. As agents within cultural and social institutions they mediate between the interests of power (the owners and controllers of the means of production) and those social groups who serve the interests of the class in power. Just as the coercive state apparatuses of political society are mobilized when necessary to secure the status quo, the apparatuses of civil society elicit the 'spontaneous consent' of the masses of the people to the status quo, to the general direction imposed on social life by the dominant and fundamental economic group.[24] The prestige of these agents and institutions and the credibility they enjoy cement their position and function in the world of production. They guarantee hegemony. What Gramsci now also adds to these discourses on the intellectual are on the one hand tentative conceptualizations of what and how a 'new intellectual' might be; on the other hand he experiments with a new concept of 'intellectuality'.

The distinction between 'traditional' and 'organic' intellectual is, as is the case with most Gramscian distinctions, a complex one that expresses more than simply one function or relation. In his history of the Italian intellectual, Gramsci found that 'every social group, coming into existence on the original terrain of an essential function in the world of economic production, creates together with itself, organically, one or more strata of intellectuals which give it homogeneity and an awareness of its own function not only in the economic but also in the social and political fields'. In this sense, traditional intellectuals are also organic intellectuals. As such they propagate and legitimate, whether advertently or not, the world-views or the conceptions of the world of the social class in economic and political power.[25] Yet Gramsci is careful in emphasizing that while traditional Italian intellectuals have organic ties with the historical moment in which they arise – whereby the priest would represent the organic intellectual, the legitimator and ideologue of feudalism – they also have ties to their 'structure of feeling'. The logic underlying the imagistic and cultural experiences of a specific community, of a specific 'structure of feeling', relates or ties the traditional Italian intellectuals (the philosopher, the artist, the poet) often more closely to the world of Aristotle and Plato than to the political world of their own time, writes Gramsci.[26] It is for this reason and due to that logic that Italian intellectuals have often understood themselves politically as autonomous, independent from the predominant social groups and political formations of a particular historical moment. This is the case, for instance, with the 'intellectual community' of priests and the clergy, whose historical emergence and legitimatory activities might be mostly organically tied to feudalism but whose 'structure of feeling' survived the transformation from feudalism to capitalism. Next to the organic intellectual of capitalism, the technicians, the operators, the engineers, there still exists the intellectual community of the clergy: a traditional intellectual. And conversely, the great Italian intellectuals, perhaps with the exception of Machiavelli, have historically opted for cosmopolitan and international metaphors rather than for national ones, for selective affinities with classical and ancient authors and philosophers rather than with contemporary politicians, for a utopian imagery that celebrates the grandeur that was Rome rather than the coming into being of a unified and independent sovereign Italian nation.[27] As such, they have traditionally lived outside the parameters of political organicity, following a logic of their own that celebrated autonomy, self-determination and independence. This presumed autonomy of the traditional Italian intellectual, writes Gramsci, is nothing but a social utopia.[28]

It is difficult to make out in Gramsci's account whether the traditional Italian intellectual is organically more tied to a historic moment or to a 'structure of feeling'. In other words, it is difficult to make out the specificity of the organicity of the traditional intellectual. While in Gramsci's macrohistory every major mode of production produces its own intellectuals and legitimators, as in a Marxist account, Gramsci also narrates a microhistory of the intellectuals the linearity of which is not tied to a linear narrative of history. What seems significant to me is that Gramsci does not, however, introduce a conceptual framework of rupture, of discontinuities, when telling his many stories of the Italian intellectual. His method is in this sense a positive rather than a negative one, a method of critical thinking that extends boundaries rather than delimiting them, a method that is attentive to adding rather than subtracting, to extension rather than reduction, to wanting to see more rather than to see less. He does not follow a preconceived conceptual scheme.

Next to one account of what we might call a traditional intellectual, there coexists, however, in Gramsci's *Prison Notebooks*, another account which describes an intellectual community that seems to be both organic, traditional and new at once. This is the intellectual community of capitalism. That category is organic in that the capitalist entrepreneurs have organically created it alongside themselves. It is traditional in that this category embodies the predominant values and ways of seeing of the predominant economic class. This 'intellectual community', organically arising from the capitalist mode of production, contains, for instance, the industrial technician, the specialist in political economy, the organizers of a new culture, the manager of a new legal system.[29] As such they propagate the conceptions of the world proper to the capitalist mode of production. However, in that this group adheres to a 'structure of feeling' that propagates technological progress, a technocratically functionalist future, and an instrumentalist rationality, it is also differentiable from the groups of the traditional intellectuals, who celebrate the past. It should be noted here that Gramsci differentiates a series of organic 'intellectual communities' within the upper echelons of capitalism. While the capitalist entrepreneurs can create, from within, an intellectual managerial elite of economists, engineers, lawyers and cultural politicians to fulfil complex tasks of high-level organization, the entrepreneurs themselves represent something of an 'intellectual community' in that they organize the managing of these higher levels of social organizations. This presupposes on their part a combination of leadership qualities, knowledge of individual and collective behaviour and psychology, technical know-how and economic competence.

It should be pointed out that Gramsci's history of the intellectuals constitutes an interrogation as well as a critique of the 'traditional Italian intellectual' for not supporting democratic causes, for resisting political and social changes, that is. However, this critique does not extend to the organic intellectual emerging from the capitalist and tendentially Fordist order. While the 'new intellectual' of the capitalist order is surely ultimately not the model of what Gramsci has in mind, that 'new intellectual' of a capitalist denomination can get quite close to Gramsci's ideal model of a new form of intellectuality. 'In the modern world, technical education, closely bound to industrial labour even at the most primitive and unqualified level, must form the basis of the new type of intellectual', explains Gramsci.[30] And he writes further:

With our journal *Ordine Nuovo*, we worked to develop certain

167

forms of new intellectualisms and to determine their new concepts, and this was not the least of the reasons for its success, since such a conception corresponded to latent aspirations and conformed to the development of the real forms of life. The mode of being of the new intellectual can no longer consist in eloquence, which is an exterior and momentary mover of feelings and passions, but in active participation in practical life, as constructor, organizer, 'permanent persuader' and not just a simple orator.[31]

This description opportunely underlines the differences between Gramsci's vision of a future intellectual and that organic new intellectual he detected in the capitalism of advancing industrial nation-states such as Italy since the gradual implementation of Fordism. The new emerging intellectual functions of Gramsci's future intellectual are both specialized and 'non-specialized', non-specialized in the sense that the specialist knows of the overall directedness and relatedness of the mode of production, the place he or she inhabits in a system of relations, and who consciously participates, or refuses to participate, in the direction a particular mode of production chooses to adopt. This constitutes what I would like to call a 'critical specialist'. So Gramsci's celebrated new notion of an 'organic intellectual', which I have called here 'critical specialist', participates in specialized forms of production, distribution and exchange, while simultaneously purviewing the place of this form of production and distribution in a system of relations. That model of intellectuality is not a technocrat of advancing capitalism, but a 'critical community', which, tied to processes of rationalization and technologization in the sphere of material and cultural production, does not forfeit attempts to grasp conceptually the systems and subsystems within which rationalization and technologization take place. Rather, it critiques such processes should the democratic project become jeopardized.

Model 4: The 'universal intellectual'

An account of Gramsci's concepts of intellectuality would remain thoroughly incomplete if I did not point to one of the more suggestive paragraphs concerning intellectuality in the *Prison Notebooks*. These are taken from notes on theoretical and practical philosophy, or, conversely, from notes that discuss the problem as to who constitutes a philosopher and who a legislator.

In a famous paragraph, Gramsci writes:

It is essential to destroy the widespread prejudice that philosophy is a strange and difficult thing just because it is the specific intellectual activity of a particular category of specialists or of professional and systematic philosophers. It must first be shown that all men are 'philosophers', by defining the limits and characteristics of the 'spontaneous philosophy' which is proper to everybody.[32]

With this note, Gramsci begins to efface the difference between intellectuals and non-intellectuals, between intellectual and non-intellectual activities. As users of language, as agents in communicative processes, all people are ultimately philosophers and intellectuals. For language is not only grammar, but a 'totality of determined notions and concepts'.[33] Language contains conceptions of the world. Moreover, people are all ultimately philosophers in that they make sense of things, by comprehending and judging their experiences in terms of 'common sense'.[34] In addition to common sense, there are 'entire systems of beliefs, superstitions, opinions, ways of seeing things and of acting which are bundled together under the name of "folklore"'.[35] Furthermore, it is by being constituted in language, by engaging in communicative practices in the context of social institutions, that human beings are also political beings and legislators. So people are not only users of language within which they express their conception of the world. They are also implementers of rules and norms, of what is and what is not considered acceptable. 'A parent is a legislator for his/her children, but the parental authority will be more or less conscious.'[36]

By extending the notion of intellectuality to all human beings, speaking, thereby, of universal or universalizable intellectuality, Gramsci does not propose that there are no distinctions between the 'traditional intellectual' and the 'universal intellectual', or between the 'universal legislator', namely the parent, and the 'specific legislators', namely the personnel of the state of great legislative power. His universalizing of intellectuality, reminiscent in many ways of Marxist ontology but also of Aristotelian ethics, is designed in large part to address the problem of ideology, meaning and hegemony. If all people are thinking individuals, in that they are language-using individuals, they have conceptions of the world which guide them in their meaning production processes. Some of these conceptions support the status quo. It is by addressing the political content of conceptions of the world, by making people aware of the non-neutrality of their ways of thinking, by raising their consciousness, that all people can potentially become critical thinkers. So while all people are thinkers or universal intellectuals, it is one of the tasks of the 'intellectuals who are not only universal intellectuals but also critical intellectuals' to put forth the notion that all people are 'universal intellectuals'. With this notion Gramsci participates in a quite specifically Italian philosophical tradition, marked, among others, by the philosophy of Giambattista Vico, whose discussion of 'know thyself' invited human beings to be conscious of the fact that they are historical beings, as such not only constituted by history but also constituting history. Yet while Vico would ascribe only to intellectuals the possibility of a historicist consciousness, Gramsci ascribes this possibility to all human beings.[37]

'MODE OF PRODUCTION' AND 'MODE OF INFORMATION'

The above discussion is designed among other things to point to the complexity that informs Gramsci's notions of intellectuality. There is some feeling in the Gramsci community that the complexity of Gramsci's conceptual apparatus cannot be emphasized enough.[38] That is why the four general models I have discussed in the context of Gramsci's theory of intellectuals surely do not exhaust his approach to the subject. They are meant primarily to point to Gramsci's differentiated way of dealing with a reality, with his time and his place, within which he detected many intellectual activities and functions that furthered or hindered the democratic cause. I think it is important to restate that the analysis of the various kinds of intellectualities Gramsci provides is mostly tied to Italy in the first few decades of our century, to her foreign and domestic politics. What he pointed to were intellectual activities which contributed to democratic change, which resisted change, or which could be mobilized for democratic change in Italy at a specific historic moment and under specific economic, political, social and cultural conditions. While Gramsci's theory is suggestive and surely extraordinarily flexible, I do not think that all of the categories he develops in that context are profitably applicable to reality in the USA or that of other western nation-states as accelerating processes of informatization effect the production and dissemination of knowledge and ideology and, therefore, the conditions of intellectual functions and activities in relation to political practices. There is a possibility that perhaps not so much the cultural but the socio-political and economic constellations of some Central American or South American nations are at this point to some extent not dissimilar to those of Italy in the first few decades of this century, and that for this reason Gramsci's analysis of the category of the intellectual might find some useful and more extensive application there.[39] What we, living in a western nation-state at the end of the twentieth century, can adopt from Gramsci, I think, is not so much the results of his analysis, culminating in his particular theory of the intellectual. What we can examine are his ways of viewing and doing analysis, and amend or transform them for the political needs in our time. I have previously in this study attempted to describe Gramsci's critical theory as being based on certain kinds of analyses, on a certain kind of 'differentiating practice'. The project of examining Gramsci's critical analyses in terms of our needs, a critical adaptation and transformation of some of his views for our political realities, is what I would like to call the practice of 'differential pragmatics'. A first step then of practising 'differential pragmatics' is minimally to assess the various and differentiated intellectual functions and possibilities in our reality, to assess the many ways and places in which knowledge and information are produced and disseminated in relation to power. This presupposes a minimal assessment of the forces and transformations that shape our realities. A second step is a minimal interrogation of the differentiated conditions of the production of knowledge, of the conditions within which we produce knowledge and values, and an interrogation of how we can contribute to democratic transformations and change.

Yet my project of 'differential pragmatics' is more easily proposed than carried through. How are we to assess our realities, and the power relations inscribed in them, and from which angle do we propose to challenge these relations and work for change? It is a commonplace, for instance, to describe our reality by using the various grammatical registers of the word 'postmodern'. As substantive or adjective, postmodernity or postmodern indicates that it comes after and is not identical with modernity or the modern. Many areas of human activity in the western world, from architecture to the arts and philosophy and literature, indeed seem to function within the context of a paradigm which is different from the earlier twentieth century. The paradigm of the later twentieth century indeed seems to produce a multiplicity of forms, a plurality of tastes, pastiches, it speaks of the unfoundationality of belief systems, of the incapacity of rationality to grasp the whole, of the contingency of scientific data on

171

the position of the observer, of the positionality and indeterminacy of knowledge, and of the power inscribed in the arbitrariness of authority. Multiplicity, plurality, decentralization, unfoundationality, arbitrariness, non-accumulative structures of knowledge and so on are some of the supplemental terms which inform the discourse on and which describe the practices of postmodernity, thereby displacing more traditional descriptive ways, such as hierarchy, centralization, linearity, determinacy, causality and so on.[40] While many human activities, whether of a theoretical or a practical nature, can be described as postmodern particularly if and as long as we remain within the realm of culture and cultural practices, it becomes more problematical, so it seems to me, uncritically to apply the term postmodern with its almost endless array of supplemental terms when it comes to politics, international relations, financial and economic affairs, and the power relations in international politics. So while there are surely good reasons for understanding the earlier twentieth century as modern and the later as postmodern, particularly in the realm of cultural and artistic practices, I find it difficult to reduce the many aspects of human activities to cultural practices alone, or to house the multiplicity of human activities and relations, on a national and international level, in the terms 'modern' or 'postmodern'. What I have found immensely suggestive in Gramsci's analytical procedures throughout this project is his ability to be extensive rather than reductive in his attempts to grasp the multiplicity of reality. In that sense, the adjectival pair of 'modern' and 'postmodern' may simply serve as a way to enter the discussion, without ascribing to that pair inordinate substantiated referentiality or extensive descriptive power, however.

What seems to differentiate, to begin with, late twentieth-century realities in western nation-states from earlier twentieth-century realities is not so much the principle on which their economic structures rest. Western capitalism, whether in its phase of high capitalism, around World War I, or in its phase of what is sometimes called late capitalism, since World War II, is still solidly anchored in the profit principle, as it has been since its inception in Britain in the eighteenth century.[41] So what seems to differentiate later western realities from earlier ones, the 'modern' from the 'postmodern' paradigm, is apparently not the principle on which the economic structures and substructures rest, but rather a series of phenomena and practices which involve many sectors of society, ranging from the social and the political to the cultural, and from the technological to the economic sector. The transformation of western society in the twentieth century has been taking place on many structural and infrastructural levels, and it varies from nation-state to nation-state. However, the general tendency has been towards expanding the rationalization of production processes, exporting, as it were, Fordism to many parts of the world, particularly since the end of World War II, while simultaneously condensing the financial and managerial organization of these processes of production. A metaphor that aptly captures this phenomenon is expansion in production and contraction in control. These processes transforming the forces of production seem to have been accompanied by political and cultural processes, of relations of production, which are marked by state interventionism on the one hand, and by ideological processes of legitimation on the other. Both are functional in the easing of the tensions and contradictions that arise from an economy ultimately staunchly pursuing profitability for a few at the expense of many. Interventionism and legitimation play an important role in the effective political management of economic crisis situations, curtailing the emergence of acute economic, social and political crises. The system of the welfare state, or welfarestatism, is part of such political management. By providing a minimum basic subsistence for citizens who have succumbed to the necessities of rationalization in production, who have been laid off when production no longer yielded profits, the state seems to manage the effective control of its people. Simultaneously, the increasing rationalization of industrial processes has led to the gradual rise of a service sector which seems to replace, and continues to replace, ever larger parts of the industrial sector. This phenomenon is also known as increasing bureaucratization of the western nation-state. With the industrial working class, the blue-collar sector, diminishing and the white-collar service sector increasing, the class divisions, once typical of high capitalism, no longer seem to hold. And conversely, with the gradual disappearance of the traditional, unionized working class and the gradual appearance of a large service sector, traditional ways of measuring exploitation, of relating underpaid labour power to the production of profits, also apparently no longer hold. The working class, once, as material condition for the production of profit, the ideal body for liberatory and emancipatory agendas, no longer seems to constitute the backbone of the present nation-state, in particular as this state has begun to exchange large parts of its industrial sector not only for a service sector, but also, as of the last few decades, for an information-technological one. In this scenario, the working class is

173

no longer 'the standard-bearer of freedom', to use a formulation by Mark Poster.[42] Impulses for radical democratic politics will, therefore, no longer emanate from the working class, so it is presumed since the 1980s, but from the formation of new social and cultural groups that pursue various liberatory and emancipatory agendas.[43]

The transformation of twentieth-century reality towards ever increasing processes of rationalization and bureaucratization is marked by the evolution of a culture industry which, particularly since World War II, is engaged in the production and reproduction of a mass culture needed for mass consumption. The culture industry primarily functions in the production and direction of desires and values, channelling human needs for happiness and meaning in the direction of compulsive purchasing of goods and values offered by the commodity market. In that this culture industry engages in the ideal reproduction of consumers, it functions as a political and social institution designed to manipulate and control unconscious and conscious desires of the masses of the people. Aided by highly sophisticated technological advances in the visual and electronic media, the culture industry skilfully manipulates the symbolic and imaginary experiences and needs of the people. Needs and desires are opportunely combined into one under the dictatorship of the principle of profit embodied in the commodity form. The culture industry has become a form of domination. Theorists within the modernist paradigm, such as Adorno, Horkheimer and Marcuse, reckoned that culture industries, by manipulating the desires and needs of large masses of people, contributed to, or channelled energy towards, rendering one-dimensional the citizens of the modern western nation-state, pacifying millions into accepting the dullness of consumer society. Yet these theorists also formulated models of resistance to these forms of domination. One-dimensionalizations can be countered by the artistic avant-gardes, Adorno suggested, by means of formal innovation and experiment. For Marcuse, resistance originated in the political margins, in social alternatives, in the underground. Indeed, with the Frankfurt School theorists, with Adorno's understanding of the potential of negative dialectic, or Marcuse's optimistic and wholehearted support of liberatory and emancipatory agendas, resistance to mass culture, and the pivotal role intellectuals assumed in that dialectic of resistance, had not yet conceded defeat.[44] The story of the widespread youth and student movement in the 1960s is a solid testimony to the groundedness of their theory.

Yet perhaps the most crucial transformation of western society,

174

both on the level of the production of commodities, and in the way in which we produce knowledge and meaning, is linked to what we might call the information technology revolution. This transformation, linked to advances in cybernetics, electronic engineering and telecommunications, has been steadily evolving since the end of World War II. Yet it seems that only now can we begin to assess its impact on the way we live everyday life. A good many studies have examined the impact and the possibilities of information technology on and for the way our societies organize production and institutions, on and for the way they produce, process, collect, distribute, manipulate, transmit and control information, knowledge and values.[45] Four major assessments emerge, and I will briefly and rather schematically reproduce these below.

To put it simply: there are those theorists who believe that the rapid growth and rational application of information technology could eventually secure an easier life for all. In a highly computerized, informatized and automated society, a reduced need for human labour in production and distribution would result in an increase in leisure and creativity. According to Yoneji Masuda, one of the master architects of the notion of a benign information society, or Computopia, as he calls it, this is a distinct possibility.[46] This roughly constitutes assessment number one, which in some ways is an extension of the philosophical foundations of Fordism and Taylorism. Automation and freedom potentially collapse into one in a metaphor that postulates that machines will eventually replace human labour. Intellectuals or producers of information and knowledge are called upon in this scenario to help secure the path towards the benign potentials of Computopia, particularly since there are signs that Computopia could easily turn into its opposite: a Big Brother society of total surveillance and control made possible by the immense potential of information technology.

The Big Brother society of total surveillance is at issue in the second assessment. It goes something like this: while information technology informs processes of production and distribution, reducing the need for human labour, and increasing the possibilities for leisure and fun, it also informs processes of social and political control by bombarding its population with a ubiquitous yet well-directed production of multiple televised images and realities. In this vision, we move towards or already live in a self-regulating society of systemic surveillance and domination, from which there is hardly any escape. And further, there is little room to negotiate a different future in the

175

context of this vision.[47] State, culture, economy and finance all amalgamate into one unpurviewable complex system within which the practices of everyday life are inexorably constituted. With the accelerated introduction of information technology on many structural and infrastructural levels in western society, and, in particular, the introduction of increasingly sophisticated information technologies in an already highly functional media industry, the binding parameters of experience and values for large masses of people are non-negotiably produced and reproduced, contained, controlled, manipulated and even dominated by forces that seem to elude interrogation, much less confrontation. Conditions for significant resistance to mass domination on such a large scale continue to disappear. This condition, which Lyotard powerfully described in his *The Postmodern Condition*, apparently not only limits the autonomy and self-determination of the people in the western nation-states, but also limits the functions and possibilities of the purviewers, producers and disseminators of knowledge and values. Intellectuals have, for Lyotard, mostly lost their function.[48] Caught not in unified but heterogeneous processes that defy unitary experiences of cognitive, ethical and political discourses, the intellectual can turn avant-garde artist and revel in the insight that imagination and sensibility infinitely exceed any form of representation. Yet at the margins and concentrating on a micro- rather than a macro-picture, the intellectual somehow survives. Whether called 'specific intellectual', as Foucault chooses to do, or 'the subversive artist', to use Lyotard's term, the intellectuals of late capitalism, caught in a systemic web of dominating structures and substructures, locally operate in minimal ways. In this depiction of reality, functional alternatives are drastically reduced.

The third and the fourth assessments of the impact of immense processes of rationalization constituted by and constituting the age of information technology on our experiences and the production of values and knowledge in late twentieth-century culture stand somewhere between the two extreme positions of Computopia and Big Brother society. The emphasis is not so much on whether life in the age of information technology is either an opportunity or a threat, but rather on how or to what extent we can analyse the transformations taking place in the spheres of production and in the social and cultural relations of production, and make out the powers that direct or control these transformations. The notion of the unpurviewability of contemporary ways of organizing and controlling power and implementing domination has, in this account, not much of a chance.

So the predominant metaphors of these accounts include those of linearity and hierarchy when it comes to power structures. They also include those of decentralization and the ubiquity of power when addressing social and political domination. A linear narrative of power, whereby the powerful from above control the powerless below, seems to be crucially important for discourses on inequities and injustice and for resistance to such inequities. However, a horizontal narrative of power is equally powerful for describing inequities in power relations, in that one site of power can dislocate a site of power next to it, thereby rendering that site powerless. The complexities of the modern life-world, as they have emerged over the last few decades, make it difficult at times to delineate the boundaries of power and its operations. This perhaps accounts for the fact that we are presented with images which ascribe to a handful of intellectuals the possibility of grasping the enormity of the transformations and complexities taking place; others evoke self-propelling complex systems and subsystems of information and knowledge, thereby curtailing if not eradicating notions of social and individual comprehension and responsibility.[49] In the latter case, rationality, so it seems, at least of the traditional kind, is no longer capable of grasping these transformations.

There is by now enough data, however, to realize that the reduction in human labour power ushered in by information technology has not necessarily produced more leisure but rather an increase in unemployment.[50] The gradual disappearance of the traditional industrial working class under the impact of the rise of the service and now information sector has not led to the disappearance of what is a traditional by-product of working-class life: unemployment. Moreover, the introduction and spread of information technology in many spheres of production has led to underemployment of skilled labour, and to massive re-skillings in many sectors, often accompanied by massive relocating. There seems to have been, in the course of the last few decades, an 'apparent move away from regular employment towards increasing reliance upon part-time, temporary or subcontracted work arrangements'.[51] While this move is primarily related to the economic reorganization of some sectors of production, the reorganization itself has been made possible in large part by the rapid growth and application of information technology in the planning of the production and distribution sector. In addition, many western companies, both in the so-called hard and the soft sector, in industry and management, have been able to organize production processes in such a way that the production is subdivided into many partial processes which are relegated, for reasons of profitability, to cheaper labour forces and locations mostly in the developing world. This practice is surely not peculiar to the age of information. Multi-national western capital, particularly since the end of World War II, has in general allocated parts of its production processes to locations where the labour force is cheaper, as part of its global hegemonizing. This practice is known as out-sourcing of manufacturing to the Third World. What distinguishes the current practice, however, from the previous one, is that the growth in information technology enables those in command of this technology to organize and manage its various processes of production more flexibly, and, in conjunction with accelerated techniques of problem-solving made possible by information technology, to speculate and contract or dis-contract sites of exploitable labour more flexibly and profitably. The extent of geographic transferability of partial processes of production also adds to the profitability of this practice, as well as to the concentration in control of the 'global assembly-line'.[52] Furthermore, in that information and knowledge become increasingly integrated in the production of a product, the possession and flexible (speculative) use of 'high info tech' or the lack of it heightens the gap between the developed and the developing countries. Indeed, the possession of high info tech might be such an advantage that the developed world would leapfrog into the future, leaving the developing world inexorably behind.[53]

The age of information technology has, in this account, not done much to change the economic conditions of many social groups. This holds not only for the western world, but for the rest of the world as well. Indeed, the gap between the western world and the non-western world, the north-south axis, as it is sometimes referred to, seems to widen. It would surely come as no surprise that systems of relations of power, as much on the state as on the cultural level, are mobilized in the legitimation of these inequities. And it would also come as no surprise that those social groups affected most by the rapid transformation of our societies under the aegis of information technology would somehow find ways of analysing and theorizing resistance to this immense process of homogenization accompanied by intensified social and political iniquitous differentiations. Indeed, this position informs the fourth assessment of the information technology. How and in what way can we formulate alternative agendas that meet the challenges of the information age? 'Many developing countries have large pools of educated labour in areas most appropriate to current change, such as software', writes Juan Rada.[54] It thus remains a possibility, it seems to me, that intellectuals in developing countries can use and command information technology for social and political purposes more appropriate to those countries. And conversely, it remains a possibility that the use and command of information technology by underprivileged social groups in the western nation-states likewise can continue to further social and cultural projects commensurate with democratic and egalitarian practices. While the systemic nature of our realities surely defines to a large extent the boundaries of intellectual mobility, whether we inhabit a site in the western or the non-western world, such that intentionality and purposiveness or action contexts are absorbed by the rationality of self-regulating systems and subsystems, there still remain action contexts where meaning and values are produced in dialogic encounter. Indeed, while the systemic nature of our realities increasingly delimits the possibility of agency, responsibility and autonomous and self-determinative action, as Lyotard and many other theorists have maintained, it is the potential of information technology that opens up the possibilities of dialogic encounter with social groups and formations that continue to resist economic and cultural domination, whether in the western nation-states or in the non-western world. In other words, aspects of Habermas' model of action contexts, of a life-world that eludes the purposive rationality of system and subsystems, aspects of his notion of a 'universal pragmatics' practised in the life-world and capable of producing consensus on problematical social and political issues, are perhaps applicable to a critique of the western organization and management of the non-western global assembly-line. It is to a brief discussion of this possibility, in particular as it appears in the light of Gramsci's way of assessing intellectuality and differentiation, that I will now turn.

BETWEEN HABERMAS AND LYOTARD: GRAMSCI'S INTELLECTUAL AND 'DIFFERENTIAL PRAGMATICS'

I would like to refer again to Gramsci's remark on the problem of the intellectual:

Can one find a unitary criterion to characterize equally all the diverse and disparate activities of intellectuals and to distinguish these at the same time and in an essential way from the activities of other social groupings? The most widespread error of method seems to me that of having looked for this criterion of distinction in the intrinsic nature of intellectual activities, rather than in the ensemble of the system of relations in which these activities (and therefore the intellectual groups who personify them) have their place within the general complex of social relations.[55]

Gramsci's challenge to the notion of applying a unitary criterion to the study of intellectuals seems more pertinent than ever. The ensemble of the systems of relation has reached ever new heights of complexity in the postmodern world, such that they seem to exceed the utmost powers of analysis or critical accountability. This complexity of systems and subsystems of relations is particularly developed in the western nation-states. However, in that there is also a trend towards the transnationalization of capital unencumbered by its national origin, the financial power of the west contracts as it globalizes. And conversely, the trend towards globalization of the assembly-line, towards the transnationalization of production unencumbered by national boundaries, consolidates the managerial powers of the financial transnational complex. The managers or agents of these processes are often financial, political and economic specialists with prestigious academic ties, an intellectual elite which both represents and transcends national economic interests in its transnationalizing activities. It is important to note, however, that these activities are transnational when it comes to securing financial gain, yet not when it comes to making policy which would disseminate financial gain among the less advantaged cultures and societies in the world.[56] It is also important to note that these activities are constituted by intellectuals mostly originating in the USA, Canada, Japan and countries of the European Economic Community. So while developing countries take part in the expansion of systems and subsystems of relation, in the restructuring and transnationalizing of the forces of production immensely facilitated by information technology, I think that it is important to remember that these developing countries do not take part as autonomous and independent partners. Rather, developing countries become mostly objects of hegemonizing globalizations. The various think tanks and institutes, in particular the Trilateral Commission, that ideologically prepare the internationalization and transnationalization of the world economy, are mostly stocked by western intellectuals who, in spite of their tendentially cosmopolitan political identity, represent the western economic, financial and cultural point of view.[57] The economic and financial complexities that engulf the relations of systems and subsystems should not keep us from recognizing that power and domination are still intact. With this I want to evoke not only the metaphor of the ubiquity of power but also the equally powerful metaphor of a ubiquitous inequity of power. While in our western societies and cultures this metaphor of the ubiquitous inequity of power often engages discourses on social, cultural, economic and gender relations, expediently schematized by the problematic of gender, race and class, it now increasingly involves, particularly as technology information precociously catapults itself into coming of age, the developing non-western world as well. A theory that claims critical edge while neglecting the uneven relationality governing systems of relation between the developed and developing cultures, between late capitalism in the west and the manifold and complex hybrids of feudalism, capitalism and technology in non-western countries, has little claim to such critical force. This, I would like to contend, goes for a theory of the intellectual as well.

What 'differential pragmatics' can adopt from received critical theory, modern and postmodern alike, are ways of locating and analysing operations of sites of power and domination and their systems of relations. What it can adopt from critical theory of the Frankfurt School kind is an insistence on the differentials that separate those with more power and command from those with less. What it can adopt from critical theory of the Habermassian kind is to explore ways and situations conducive to bridging inequities and differentials, among these the dialogic situation, which is perhaps potentially designed to achieve consensus among two initially dissenting parties. What 'differential pragmatics' can adopt from Gramsci is his way of analysing the conditions for the possibility and impossibility of dialogic situation, which includes a recognition of the various 'structures of feeling' within which our bodies, situated in specific places and in specific times, contribute to shaping our will into producing and accepting some values while rejecting others. The production and dissemination of knowledge, of specific kinds of information and values, is not unrelated to the spaces within which our bodies move, and from the languages and dialects we can or cannot share due to the 'structures of feeling' that structure our consciousness and our unconscious. Finally, what 'differential pragmatics' can add to critical theory is not its insistence on resistance to power, which critical theory, whether in its modern or postmodern version, has ultimately, though sometimes there seemed to be some doubt, always done anyhow. The very writing of Lyotard's *The Postmodern Condition*, in spite of all declarations to the contrary, is a testimony to that. So what 'differential pragmatics' can add to critical theory is not so much an emphasis on resistance to power and domination, but insistence on the insight that our resistance to power, our critical thinking, must take into account our relation, as western intellectuals, to the non-western developing world, our position, that is, as producers and disseminators of knowledge, and meaning, in terms of its function with respect to the non-western developing world. More concretely, resistance to power will have to take into account the conditions of this relationality between western intellectuality and non-western developing cultures, in particular as these conditions are marked by processes of informatization and technologization in the age of the information technology revolution. By this I do not mean to maintain that analyses of relations of power as it affects western intellectuals within their society and institutions, or as it affects the various social strata in our societies, should be abandoned in favour of the western/non-western problematic. Recent studies in this area, in particular Andrew Ross's *No Respect: Intellectuals and Popular Power*, are distinct and welcome reminders of the fact that an interrogation of the protocols of knowledge on the US side of the ocean, in this part of the western world, is a non-negotiable exercise.[58] I fully agree with Ross when he writes that it is necessary to examine the institutional affiliations of professional intellectuals 'in order to understand and transform codes of power which are historically specific to their disciplinary discourses'.[59] And I agree with him that the 'critique of essentialist notions of sexuality and sexual identity on the part of feminists, gays and lesbians, and of race and ethnic identity on the part of minority intellectuals', which has been addressed primarily to discursive or representational categories, was also done 'in the full knowledge of the effects of these categories upon real, persecuted bodies'.[60] What I do mean to say, however, is that the problem of the function and the position of intellectuals in the west should not be insisted on without occasionally interrogating the subtexts of interests and concern often informing the choice of problems, of the relation that obtains between choice of and response to theoretical and practical problems and the specific function and position of intellectuals in this society. Or to put it more plainly: many problems western intellectuals tend to address bespeak, in the name of universality, particulars which are proper to western intellectuality. What I also would like to say, more importantly, is that the concern with sex, race and class, as imperious as these concerns are in the context of our societies, should not be carried out at the expense of not viewing our relatedness with the non-western developing world, of not examining our actual or potential complicity in relations which are mostly uneven and unequal. Both research programmes can surely coexist with each other. In the remainder of this chapter, I will outline a brief sketch of political and democratic possibilities between us and the non-western developing world, possibilities which I see informed by the new conditions of information technology.

Relating our activities as intellectuals to non-western problems is surely nothing new. In some ways, Noam Chomsky stands for someone who has done exactly that for a long time, and continues to do so. Many of his publications demand the responsibility of the intellectual in dismantling the manufacture of ideological consent to the hegemonizing desires of western nation-states, in particular the USA.[61] His way of proceeding is surely one recommendable and necessary way of doing critical work, and the way many intellectuals continue to choose to do it, in spite of Russell Jacoby's contention that in the age of academe, US intellectuals have forfeited social and political responsibility.[62] In Gramsci's classificatory system, Chomsky would stand as the 'traditional intellectual' of the right kind, a progressive member of an intellectual elite who uses skills and intellectual powers in the demystification of ideologies and legitimations of the predominant economic and political class. What Chomsky does not command, however, in contradistinction to Gramsci's 'traditional intellectual', such as Croce, for instance, is, all notoriety to the contrary, a significant profile or presence in the public sphere. His access to apparatuses for the production and dissemination of social, cultural and political meaning, which in Gramsci's time was represented by the owners of newspapers, journals and publishing houses and which in our time is represented by the mass media, has been effectively curtailed. While Chomsky's projects and public appearances help to undermine the public relations industry incorporated and endorsed by the media, the way in which he has been refused significant access to the predominant media brings home the fact that an increase in access by progressive intellectuals to the predominant media industry would undoubtedly further Chomsky's and other progressive causes. Chomsky does stand, none the less, as an important symbol of intransigent intellectual and moral challenge to

183

undemocratic and inegalitarian practices of the western nations with respect to the non-western developing world. He reminds us in no uncertain terms that 'the third world societies as a whole today are at a lower level of development than were the industrializing societies of Europe and the United States in the eighteenth century'.[63] And, moreover, that 'the industrializing societies of Europe and the United States were not faced with a hostile environment in which the major resources had already been preempted'.[64] As an intellectual who uses his or her capacities to see relations rather than simply specializations, Chomsky would also fit Gramsci's bill of the 'critical specialist'. As a highly skilled linguist he does not only engage himself in the production and applications of forms of knowledge relevant to his field of specialization, but critically relates his intellectual activities to other social practices and relations as well.

While the notion of critical intellectuality which I tentatively outline in the context of a 'differential pragmatics' easily affords the respect and the place that is due to Chomsky's practices, particularly in that he insists on the relations between western intellectuals and the non-western developing world, his practice represents but one possible model for a theory of intellectuals. What I would like to propose next to it is a critical practice that extends Chomsky's sphere of action. From Gramsci's classificatory system I borrow, for these purposes, the notion of the 'structure of feeling' or 'critical community'. I formulate this practice as something like this: the advent of information technology has accelerated processes of globalization in production and the organization of production in complex systems and subsystems. It has also contributed to increasingly excessive economic gaps between the western and the non-western worlds, which in turn are determinative in decreeing the quality of life or the lack of it. These processes of globalization or transnationalization have to be produced as well as reproduced not only in the material realm, but also in the symbolic realm, in the realm of production, exchange and marginalization of political, social and cultural values and meaning informed by processes of communication, by communicative actions. In both spheres, in the material as well as the symbolic realm, agents or human beings, and not only machines, telecommunicative apparatuses and apparatuses of cultural and institutional power, are taking part. There is good reason to believe, following Althusser, that the symbolic realm of values and ideologies of individual agents succumbs to the apparatuses within which agents fulfil specific functions and which produce these functions as effects of those apparatuses.[65] There is also good reason to believe, with Lyotard, that the symbolic realm, increasingly colonized by all-pervasive and powerful transpersonal communicative apparatuses, succumbs to the laws of the system itself, whereby all action, whether material or linguistic, cognitive or ethical, inexorably moves within the orbit of an informatized technological order directed by no one but the systemic nature, the self-regulative nature of the system itself.[66] Yet there is also reason to believe, not only with Habermas, but also on the basis of experiential knowledge tied to feminist practices, that the symbolic realm participates in the production of actions and practices, or participates in the suppression of actions and practices, neither of which is necessarily interlaced with the determinations of self-regulative systems.

Habermas distinguishes, in his *Theory of Communicative Action*, and in the context of a social theory of late capitalism, of western nation-states, that is, between the concept of system and the concept of life-world, containing system-integrated action contexts and socially integrated action contexts respectively.[67] In the system-integrated action context, at the place of work, agents do not purview the consequences of their actions in that their actions are co-ordinated and functionally interlaced in ways unintended by the agents. The agents themselves act in a rational-purposive way, in order to maximize personal gain, pleasure and profit. In the socially integrated action context, in the public sphere of citizenship, of acculturation and socialization, agents can interact and co-ordinate their actions in such a way that they negotiate problems on the basis of a norm or in reference to a norm. This can lead to a consensus. While personal profitability motivates agents in the system-integrated action context, consensuality can motivate the socially integrated action context. According to Habermas' notion of 'universal pragmatics', human beings (in the western world?) are morally mature and rational beings capable of fairly, equally and reciprocally negotiating a common good for the two parties involved, even though the resulting consensuality might in essence delimit the individual absolute freedom (negative freedom) of one or of both parties. Given this scenario, dialogic encounters, based on rational procedures and in reference to agreed-upon normativities, are, for purposes of pursuing or establishing justice or rationally justifiable situations for all, universalizable. A communicative ethic might facilitate the interpretation of needs and a reciprocal satisfaction of individual needs in processes of communicative action.

As intellectuals, as disseminators and producers of a set of know-ledge and values, and as suppressors of other sets of knowledge and values, we can, for one thing, examine the possibilities of dialogic exchange with values and forms of knowledge from non-western parts of the world. An examination of the conditions of possibility and impossibility for dialogic encounter in the Habermassian sense will probably take into account the dynamic structure of information technology. That structure appears to facilitate conditions for re-ciprocal exchange. Whereas in previous technological advances, such as in radio and tv, the technological potential of these apparatuses made their users always potentially not only receivers of messages but also producers of messages and possible counter-messages, as Brecht and many other theorists, including Enzensberger, have maintained, the forces controlling the production of radio and tv and their organiz-ation as political apparatuses seem to have made sure that democratic usage of radio and tv remained a theoretical possibility but not an actual practice, with few exceptions. The computerization of large segments of society opens up a terrain with new possibilities. Equipped with a computer (the costs of which have been steadily declining) and hooked up, via a modem, to a terminal, we are now in a position to communicate via electronic mail with anyone in the world who operates a computer under the same conditions. As a result, we no longer need to be present bodily in order to convene workshops and conferences, although most of us still are. As I understand it, the world of high finance and transcapitalization has quickly seized on these opportunities. It is not difficult to imagine the organization of global conferences for democratic purposes, which would begin to interrogate cultural, economic, moral and social issues relative to the effects of the transnationalizations of capital and production and the concentration of gain with respect to the rest of the developing world. The steadily decreasing cost of computers and the zeal with which they are promoted globally should make it possible not only for privileged intellectuals in the west but for many citizens of this world to operate a computer. The conditions for intellectual and moral exchange with users of computer terminals in other parts of the world have been met, so it seems to me, and in some areas they are already put into some use.

While communicative action that transcends the necessity of bodily presence in a circumscribed place is increasingly becoming a possibility, such that we, as western intellectuals, are enabled to exchange information and values with non-western producers and disseminators of information, there remains a theoretical issue which I would like briefly to address. Communicative action, in the Habermassian sense, strives for consensus with respect to controversial or problematical issues against the background of a set of norms agreeable to the negotiating parties involved. What norms will inform the background against which we engage in communicative action with producers of information and values from non-western worlds? Contemporary ethics of communicative action claims, in its universalistic dimensions, that our moral maturity should enable us to meet the demands and needs of both parties involved in a reciprocal fashion. Our sense of justice, constituting inherent and rational grounds, enables us to choose one solution over another not at the expense of the other party but in the mutual production of a consensus. The question I would like to raise is to what extent can we, as western intellectuals, meet non-western producers of information on the same ethical, moral and rational grounds? Can an ethics of communicative action stand the test of universality when confronted with communicative situations whereby the experiences, wishes and needs of one party are continuously jeopardized, imperilled and marginalized by the practices of the other party complicitously taking part, whether consciously or not, due to their privileges in lifestyle and their quality of life, in the reproduction of economic powers and political domination in the developing world? Will a universalistic ethics based on rationality, morality and a sense of justice do when negotiating with citizens of the developing world?

The work of feminist critics of the ethics of communicative action is useful, I think, for beginning to examine a response to this dilemma. Nancy Fraser and Seyla Benhabib have pointed out, for instance, that a critique of universalistic moral theory has no difficulties in dismantling the way in which the specific dimensions of women's experiences may again be bypassed by that theory. Fraser, for instance, explicates, among other things, how in Habermas' model of system and life-world the subtext of gender is obfuscated in that the woman's function in production and symbolic acculturation of children is relegated to the symbolic and socially integrated action context, and not related to the economic system which also or perhaps above all depends on the production and symbolic reproduction, on child-bearing and child-caring.[68] What Fraser also calls into question is a set of Habermassian categories, such as working agent, the citizen and the participant in a consumer society, in that in all three cases women's functions are qualitatively distinct from those of men.

Unequal working conditions, limited access to public political space, and women as preferred subjects of interpellation for the advertising industry point to the gender blindness of Habermas' categories and thus, by implication, to the unequal and genderized social, political, cultural and economic status informing the respective grounds in communicative actions. And Benhabib contends, on the other hand, by relying on Carol Gilligan's findings on the specificity of the moral instance in women, that the needs, emotions and affects of individual people, in particular women, which in part constitute the relational-interactive identities of women and are crucial for assessing the specificity of their moral maturity, have been bypassed by universalistic moral theorists attentive to defining rationality and justice on the basis of a sovereign self unencumbered by desires and needs.[69]

Fraser and Benhabib are useful for beginning to formulate the critical status of normativities when meeting up, as western intellectuals, with a world, such as the developing world, which does not and cannot meet us on equal ground. I tend to think that reference to universalistic moral norms and values would not easily be convincing in a dialogic situation in which the so-called moral maturity of western intellectuality and western rationality more often than not unfolds its layers of immense indifference to the unspeakably unjust global economic orders. With this I do not mean to propose that universal moral values, as they have been developing in particular since the Enlightenment and in so far as they are attentive to the dignity and humanity of every human being, are not useful and noble as ideals. Yet, I think that they perhaps should take a less pronounced place in the encounters we seek with the underprivileged world. The dedicated work of some contemporary critical intellectuals suggests that a 'critical community' of western intellectuals is gradually emerging that is making it its province to examine our position and function with respect to the effects and possibilities of global uneven relations. Gramsci, whose theorizing is not unrelated to his origins, to his position as member of an underprivileged community far away from the centres of power and domination, to his intellectual and emotional experiences as a Sardinian existing and thinking at the margins of Italy and the western European world, has, in a not insignificant way, an insight to contribute which might inspire us in the formulation and conceptualization of our own meeting with uneven global relations. I am referring, again, to his incomplete essay on the 'Southern Question'.

The impulses for change, so he writes, do not come from the intellectuals, although the various intellectual strata are functional, both in the producing, to various degrees and in various ways, of world-views and values conducive to the spontaneous consent of the masses to the status quo, as well as in the producing of counter-hegemonies to this status quo. The impulses for democratic change do not arise from privilege. They arise from the underprivileged, from the exploited masses, from the poor, from the politically, socially, culturally and economically marginalized. In Gramsci's account, lower-strata intellectuals interpreted these impulses, perhaps provided them with direction. And higher-strata intellectuals, often eminent public figures as well, balance the sheet, mostly in the form of justifications, between the interests of power and the lower strata of intellectuals. I am not prepared to translate Gramsci's sociological and psychological assessment of his reality into ours. Perhaps it is not translatable. What I consider useful is his insight, corroborated by my own experiences in the feminist struggle, that impulses for change do not arise from privilege, but from underprivilege. On this note, what I would like to propose is this: 'the structure of feeling' we move in, the tradition of progressive and liberal thought, is extraordinarily flexible and allows us to speak and perhaps even understand some dialects of the underdeveloped world. As intellectuals, we might be able to function as mediators between the needs and desires of developing cultures, and the mandarins of our establishments. Yet this 'structure of feeling', which allows us to communicate with global power and global powerlessness, is grounded on more than a dual activity. While it enables us to look critically at Eurocentrism, androcentrism, logocentricity and western systems of justice and rationality, it is also a structure which bespeaks our complicity in the exploitation of the underdeveloped and developing world. In spite of the various struggles we undertake against domination, our bodies move, none the less, in immense privilege, inordinately saturated with material and cultural goods, technology and consumer products on a scale incommensurable with that which governs the practices of everyday life for millions of people. While we do not choose the place where we are born, we can choose the places and ideas deserving of our energies. These places, I tend to think, increasingly amalgamate with cultures and societies of developing worlds, and perhaps it is proper for us, as critical intellectuals and arbiters of hope, and stationed in the intellectual power apparatuses of the west, to seek out these impulses for democratic change, to receive the messages that reach us from these worlds, and translate them, by way of our theoretical tools, for ours.

7

In lieu of a conclusion: Gramsci, feminism, Foucault

It would be difficult for me to conclude a project of this nature without making some reference to Gramsci's relation to feminist theory, to feminism, to women. I would like to point out right away that as far as the latter issue is concerned, Gramsci's relations to women, as they evolved in the context of his position as one of the major leaders of the Italian working-class movement, and as they were shaped by his unfortunate long imprisonment, deteriorating health and impending death, do not lend themselves to a happy interpretation. Indeed, the picture is, taken from a late twentieth-century point of view, not a rosy one. It carries the distinct mark of a pernicious historical rationality that exerted, and often still exerts, a destructive influence on the lives of women.

My research suggests that two women seem to have sacrificed their desires, their visions, their health and perhaps even their lives to this man, although the specificity of Gramsci's condition during most of his relationship with these two women, his utter helplessness in prison, his isolation and the strictures imposed on his gestural mobility may be seen to qualify his role and responsibility in these matters.[1] The two women are well known to Gramsci scholars: Giulia Schucht and Tatiana Schucht, two sisters and multi-culturally educated women of Russian descent, who crossed Gramsci's path only to be intricately linked with his destiny, which weighed heavily on them. Giulia Schucht was trained as a musician and Tatiana Schucht as a natural scientist. Giulia Schucht's active relationship with Gramsci was very short. In the span of a few years she meets Gramsci and bears him two sons. Gramsci barely knew the older boy and never knew the younger. After Gramsci's arrest, something like three years into their relationship, during most of which time they had anyhow, due to Gramsci's apparently all-consuming political responsibilities and tasks, lived apart, Giulia Schucht attempted to continue to live a normal life under abnormal conditions: away from Italy and thus from Gramsci's prisons, and in the Moscow of the late 1920s and the 1930s, she tries to raise her and Gramsci's sons according to her own progressive educational philosophies inspired by Rousseau and the fragmented, intermittent and tormented wishes conveyed to her by the letters of her imprisoned companion, as well as to survive emotionally and materially in an environment the character of which is still not very well known. What we do know is that she did not do well given the pressures of her situation, and some of the data I have consulted suggest that she suffered repeated and serious nervous breakdowns. As companion or wife of one of the greatest leaders of the twentieth-century working-class movement and one of the greatest theorists, she certainly did not enjoy much of an independent life. It is difficult to judge what she got out of her relationship with such a famous public man, given the fact that he managed to spend apparently only a very limited time with her, and that his imprisonment imposed a separation which, in the event, was never repealed. Some of the letters suggest that he intended to incorporate her intellectual abilities into some of his work, by asking for her co-operation and collaboration in the composition of articles which were to be signed, on his insistence, with both of their names.[2] Yet given the fact that none of these intentions ever materialized, and could not, under the circumstances, have materialized, the sense one is left with when thinking about Giulia Schucht, and coupled with surviving photographs of her, is one of immense sadness and defeat.[3]

Tatiana Schucht's relationship with Gramsci is of a different kind. Yet one wonders whether she fared much better than her sister, considering what could have been her due as an intelligent and independent woman of her time. When Gramsci is arrested in 1926, Tatiana Schucht has known him for only a short period, less than a year. With her young nephew (Gramsci's and Giulia's son) and her pregnant sister Giulia far away in the Soviet Union, she assumes, at the arrest of Gramsci, a set of necessary tasks, such as facilitating some of the prisoner's wishes concerning personal items, needs and legal counsel and contacts. In a way she acts as probably most close relatives would have acted under similarly trying circumstances. Yet the initial support Tatiana Schucht provides for Gramsci soon develops into a demanding, all-consuming, full-time activity. In spite of her own fragile disposition and a series of health problems, Gramsci's well-being, and perhaps also his eventual liberation, become the centre of Tatiana Schucht's life and she assiduously dedicates eleven years to this stressful and extraordinarily difficult endeavour. There is a possibility that Gramsci's political allies expressly endorsed her continuous contact with Gramsci, taking advantage of her status as sister-in-law which enabled her, in compliance with the inordinately stringent fascist regulations, to maintain contact by letter with Gramsci and even to visit him in prison. If this is so, Gramsci's political allies would have deployed her and her devotion to him, for many years, as a screen for political communiqués and consultations. In this scenario, she could have been used as a strategic pawn by a desperate and decimated Italian left. Or perhaps she consented to or even welcomed the political nature of such moves. Be that as it may, with Tatiana Schucht enabling Gramsci to maintain contact with his wife and his children in the Soviet Union and also with his political allies either in exile or underground, she soon becomes the most important person in Gramsci's prison life. From arranging the forwarding to Gramsci of desired reading materials and books to furnishing him with information on legal and medical issues, from responding to his personal needs for toiletries, clothes, food, or medicines to recopying his letters to her sister or other interested parties and vice versa, and from conveying in detail the content of her conversations with him during her visits to the prisons to attempting continuously to monitor his mental and physical health, Tatiana Schucht, for eleven years and it seems quite unflaggingly, does it all. Yet she also seems to have been aware of the importance of her mission, self-appointed or not, as the case may be, and beyond assisting the husband of her sister who in turn suffered ill health in a faraway country. When Gramsci's severely failing health, including several physical and mental crises, inexorably announces the ebbing stages of his life, she makes sure of securing Gramsci's prison notebooks for posterity. She assists him when he is transferred, under surveillance, to a clinic that suits Mussolini's nefarious designs, and she is next to him when he dies, minutely detailing the last few days, hours and minutes of Gramsci's life to his friend Sraffa, who will then disseminate this news to the political allies. Less than five years after Gramsci's death she also dies, by no means an old woman, one whose most important life activities, by a fluke of destiny, centred on assisting Gramsci in protecting himself from the effects of Mussolini's special political prisons. It is difficult to assess what she received in return for her selfless services. It looks as if she received little if anything during her lifetime, and gestures of recognition which would vindicate her unquestionably significant presence in his prison life, are, as far as I can tell, yet to come. Whatever she did, she did quietly, and in private, perhaps so for political reasons, but in any event hidden from the public eye. That posterity most probably owes the survival of Gramsci's prison notebooks to her is a testimony to her non-negotiable function in Gramsci's life. It is surely possible to view Tatiana Schucht's devotion to Gramsci as a general humanitarian gesture, the story of one human being selflessly giving to another under the trying political and historical circumstances of Italian fascism, with its vicious persecution of the left, with its attempted eradication of democratic norms and values, with Mussolini's impassioned desire to silence Gramsci, a charismatic and intelligent leader of the opposition, once and for all. Yet I find it difficult to see in her sacrifice only a general historical account and not a particular one, the particular story of a particular woman.

I write these lines not in the spirit of implicating Gramsci. Certainly, from what I can gather, Gramsci did not reflect much on the unusual care and services Tatiana Schucht provided for him. There is a certain routine, natural tone when he sets down his wishes in letters addressed to her. While he seldom neglects to thank her for her individual services, he also seldom if ever questions the grounds on the basis of which she should or did incessantly care for him for eleven years. Her care and services follow a rationality and expediency of their own, uninterrogated by Gramsci, who, after all, rarely lacks an interrogative will when it comes to other issues. Is this, from his point of view, what women are expected to do? And conversely, I do find him often, in his letters to Giulia Schucht and Tatiana Schucht, using a tone which is harsh, authoritarian and condescending. It is possible that his imposed isolation and paralysis contribute to such a style. Yet I also see him deeply committed to Giulia Schucht and their children, and suffering under her intermittent silence, the reasons for which are unclear. The precise dynamics of their relationship are difficult to make out, and perhaps it is, ultimately, none of our business. If I write a brief account of Gramsci's relations with these two women and the effects of these relations, as far as I can interpret them, on the women's lives, then I do so not in the spirit of condoning Gramsci, or of endorsing Tatiana Schucht's services as natural, but, on the contrary, in order to recall the presence of women so often neglected in the historiographical narratives of a famous life. If I refrain from particularly implicating Gramsci when it comes to his practices with women, then I do not follow a quite popular trend among cultural workers, of assiduously polishing the tainted mirrors of theoretical heroes.[4] Rather, the reason is that I do not expect Gramsci to think or act differently from the way he does when it comes to women. If, in spite of a few decades of intensive feminist discourses and practices, many contemporary men often display little feminist consciousness in the practices of their daily lives, despite all theoretical claims to the contrary, and if many of our contemporary women, even some of great repute as feminists, are at times incapable of basic forms of feminist solidarity when it comes to some very real male power relations that continue to marginalize women, so that it seems indeed that a new poverty of feminism has arrived, I find it difficult to insist on feminist practices when it comes to a thinker and man such as Gramsci whose experiences were not confronted, the way ours now are, with a series of continuous radical, complex and extensive feminist discourses.

This mixture of 'rationality' and 'expediency' that marks Gramsci's attitude towards the two important women in his life also filters through his discussion of feminism and sexuality in the context of his notes on 'Americanism and Fordism'. It should be pointed out that Gramsci was not particularly versed in the issues of feminism of his time, at least not more, but also not less, than most of those of his contemporaries whose chosen business was to deal with issues of political and economic equality and social justice. Out of hundreds and hundreds of notes on a multitude of issues, there are merely a few paragraphs in the *Prison Notebooks* that deal with feminist issues. These suggest, however, that Gramsci recognized, at least in theory, the non-negotiable and fundamental importance of women's complete emancipation for any liberatory agenda. The crucial lines, from my point of view, read as follows:

> Until women can attain not only a genuine independence in relation to men but also a new way of conceiving themselves and their role in sexual relations, the sexual question will remain full of unhealthy characteristics and caution must be exercised in proposals for new legislation. Every crisis brought about by unilateral coercion in the sexual field unleashes a 'romantic' reaction which could be aggravated by the abolition of organized legal prostitution. All these factors make any form of regulation of sex and any attempt to create a new sexual ethic suited to the new methods of production and work extremely complicated and difficult. However, it is still necessary to attempt to

create a new ethic.... The truth is that the new type of man demanded by the rationalization of production and work cannot be developed until the sexual instinct has been suitably regulated and until it has been rationalized.[5]

This passage is part of Gramsci's discussion of 'Americanism and Fordism', where he investigates, *inter alia*, the relationship of the rationalization of new production processes to human instincts, desires and needs. What he observes is that modern industrialists, such as Ford, by paying close attention to the sexual practices of their employees, have designed ways the better to discipline sexuality and other bodily drives in order to heighten the individual productivity of the workers on the assembly-line. In this context Gramsci also briefly mentions the function of prohibition in the 1920s in the USA. In contradistinction to received interpretations of this political and social phenomenon, Gramsci does not view the implementation of prohibition as a measure imparted by the puritanical sense of the North American people, but rather as a rational plan by the economic and political authorities in order to further the productivity of the individual workers by enforcing abstention and sobriety, by disciplining the desires of the body. What is interesting in Gramsci's treatment of feminism is that he does not approach this question from a merely economic or political point of view, from the standpoint of production as well as legislation, as the women's question was in general dealt with by the traditional left.[6] Sexuality figures in his account. This allows him not only to assess women's unequal status in our societies in terms of their economic exploitation and political marginalization from the public sphere, but also to point to women's material and symbolic function in the reproduction of the workforce necessary for production processes as a whole. Moreover, it allows him to focus on sexuality as a site of domination and oppression.

That Gramsci should not only examine the oppression of women in the public sphere, as an effect of economic organization and political institutions, but extend it to the private realm is not surprising. One of the most significant concepts of his critical theory, his concept of hegemony, was capable of probing relations of power on a microstructural as well as on a macrostructural level. With this concept he had attempted to extend relations of power beyond the hierarchical relation of state and citizen, where the state, in its coercive function, in the realm of army, police and legislation, as political society, that is, was able to discipline the bodies of its citizens. The extension of power and domination to other areas of society had led him to examine power relations in what he calls civil society, in the institutions, in religious organization, in educational systems as well as in families, and indeed in the practices of everyday life. If political society potentially disciplined the bodies, civil society disciplined above all the mind. Power was thus not only a relation which was operative between the state and the citizens, but also and beyond the state it was operative in the relation between civic institutions and the practices of everyday life. With the various strata of semi-professionals and professionals mediating between political and civil society and the ordinary people, validating the way of seeing and doing things of the class in power as natural, a consensus to the status quo arises 'spontaneously'. So Gramsci's concept of hegemony, which attempts to grasp the power relations in the interstices of everyday life, also has the potential of lending itself to probing relations of domination in the most intimate practices of everyday life, in sexual practices, that is, where different ways of experiencing, seeing and validating the body meet. In this sense Gramsci can stand as the forerunner of the famous dictum of second-wave feminism: the personal is political. Woman's autonomy, self-determination and dignity are thus in Gramsci's account not only contingent on economic independence from men, which is but one *quid pro quo* of her emancipation. Gramsci also mobilizes the notion of a feminist consciousness that insists on choice when it comes to sexual practices. That consciousness he ties to a new kind of ethics.

So far Gramsci seems to be an acceptable candidate for a feminist ticket. Change in legislation or in the political structure is but one strategy for changing the woman's condition. Hasty changes in legislation, which would criminalize prostitution, would, so the realist Gramsci argued, eliminate not prostitution, but the few rights prostitutes had gained for themselves: access to health care, which is extraordinarily important in light of the health hazards connected to their work, and protection from prosecution for the type of work they perform. Moreover, Gramsci insists on the centrality of sexuality, a woman's rights over her body, when it comes to the emancipation not only of women, but of society as a whole. However, when Gramsci ties the woman's inalienable rights of control over her sexuality and her body to processes of rationalization of production, when he believes that new and liberated forms of sexuality for women, and ways of validating these new forms of sexuality, a new ethics, are contingent on the demands of the sphere of production attentive to restraining the passions of the body, then he somehow loses his advantage in the feminist match. His insistence on the validation of sexuality as the crucial factor in the oppression of women as well as for resistance to oppression, which would place him alongside contemporary radical feminists such as Catherine MacKinnon, Mary Daly, Susan Griffin, or Andrea Dworkin, loses its persuasive power as soon as he relates sexuality to processes of rationalization in production and the need to discipline sexuality for economic and political purposes. No doubt, in terms of Gramsci's social and political assessment of these processes of production, with which he brackets, as discussed earlier, problems of alienation and reification, his account of the fact of sexual discipline makes sense. What makes less sense is his account of the need for it, his legitimation of sexual discipline and his lack of interest in distinguishing between different kinds of sexualities and their effects on the social and cultural level. The modernist intensification of the rationalization of production does not elicit new possibilities for sexual expression and freedom for women, but requires modern women to adjust to the requirements of disciplined structures of time and place and legitimate these requirements in appropriate ethics. Yet in effect, in Gramsci's narrative, women might merely exchange the constraints of agricultural-patriarchal structures on their sexuality with the constraints of industrial-corporative structures. So the promising concessions Gramsci makes to the liberation of feminine sexuality are severely curtailed by his deterministic view of progress, his belief in the liberatory potential of industrialization and above all his uncritical deployment, indeed, his 'forgetting', of one of his own powerful analytical tools in the demystification of power: the ubiquitous operations of hegemony, of certain ways of seeing and validating relations in multiple sites of political and social relations, in the public, but above all in the private sphere, in political, but above all in civil society, in the social, in the cultural, in the micro-spaces of everyday life. If the economic and political revolution had not occurred in the west, as he writes in a passage that made him famous, because 'the state was only an outer ditch, behind which there stood a powerful system of fortresses and earthworks', because there existed 'a sturdy structure of civil society' which unstintingly supported the trembling state, then, we might ask, why should there be reason to believe that the sexual revolution can occur?[7] Do not perhaps, behind the modernization of processes of industrialization and the adjustments of political society, whether on capitalist or socialist terms, latent but powerful systems of fortresses and earthworks continue to exist, sturdy structures of civil society that can, precisely because they dominate the private realm, extend their power over many gener-ations, muffle the liberatory sexual struggles while simultaneously perpetuating age-old practices of prejudice and discrimination? The history of feminism in the twentieth century would attest to the unusual theoretical validity of Gramsci's analysis and concept of civil society.[8] But Gramsci is mute on this point. His revolutionary insight into the workings of power relations in everyday life did not extend to the question of feminine sexuality.

Gramsci's brief notes on this topic constitute something of a micro-history of sexuality that anticipates, in the early 1930s, the histories of sexuality written much later in the twentieth century, such as the series of works by Michel Foucault.[9] For Gramsci, human sexuality has undergone fundamental changes reflecting the transformation from agricultural societies to industrial societies. Whereas in the context of agricultural communities, in the country, unbridled sexual desires often violently explode in rape and incest, in the context of industrialized communities and the cities the potential violence in-scribed in sexual drives has been suppressed, contained and civilized. Gramsci considers that an applaudable, rational, progressive development.[10] While he distinguishes, with Foucault, between discourses on sexuality that reflect on the status of sexuality in pre-industrial and in industrial societies, he sanctions, in contradistinc-tion to Foucault, the needs of modern industrialization rigorously to curtail sexual desires. Gramsci invites modern men and women to consent to the requirements of industrialization, indeed to create a new ethics which would morally legitimate the operations of sexual regulation. In Foucault's *History of Sexuality*, attempting to expose the manifold systems of power relations, the discourses on sexuality become operations of power, engulfing almost all facets of our modern and postmodern life. He, contrary to Gramsci, evokes an ethics of resistance to sexual domination, one that would resist the multiplicity of domination in multiple sites of social relation. The Foucauldian term for this kind of resistance is heterotopia. What Gramsci and Foucault share, or perhaps this is something Foucault adopted from Gramsci, is the notion that power and domination function in so far as those dominated consent to that domination. Without consent there is no domination. What Gramsci and Foucault also share is their understanding of the production of that consent. It is produced from within the systems and subsystems of social relations, in the interac-tions, in the microstructures that inform the practices of everyday life.

Where Gramsci and Foucault differ, however, is in what they have to say concerning the directedness of the production of that consent. For both authors, all people are ultimately producers of support for the status quo, in that they coerce others into assenting to systems of values and beliefs. Recall Gramsci's notion of legislation, his question as to who constitutes a legislator, whereby every person, including the most powerless on the social scale, is a legislator in his or her function as a parent, and thereby imposes rules and his or her underlying values on to their children.[11] While all individuals are sites of power, not all individuals quantitatively and qualitatively embody the same form of power. Some possess more and some possess less, and the directedness of power in power relations attempts to maintain the balance of power. So that directedness of power originates somewhere, and proceeds with a certain purpose. It is not purposeless. Indeed, if the exercises of power were undirected operations, merely dominative and hegemonic, there would have been no reason for Gramsci to develop his theory of intellectuals, and his notion of counter-hegemony.[12]

It would seem that Gramsci's insistence on the ubiquity of power is of secondary importance when compared to his analysis of the hierarchical structure of power relations. While power is ubiquitous, as Foucault would have it, equally ubiquitous are unequal relations of power. So the question for Gramsci is not so much, as it is for Foucault, to show that and how power exists, though Gramsci shows that as well. Equally important is why power exists. This aspect of Gramsci's thought would make him, so it seems, a prime candidate for a feminist agenda, possibly challenging the eminent place Foucault enjoys in feminist discourse. No doubt, many feminist theorists have found much inspiration in the conceptual sophistication and methods of analysis of Foucault's work. In particular, his analysis of the operations of power, such as his critical studies of the institutions of medicine, prisons and science, which have identified the body as a site of power through which docility and submission are accomplished, has been a useful way for feminist theory to understand the female body as a site of disciplinary power exerted by the male establishment of the medical fields and the scientific fields. Moreover, Foucault's emphasis on the functional partiality of discourses and language in the production of domination and in the marginalization and silencing of counter-discourses has also been an important source of insight for feminist theory. Language, the symbolic sphere, the tools of our intercommunicative practices are indeed implicated in the production and reproduction of hegemonic domination. Further-more, Foucault has called into question the legitimacy of ways of telling history, metanarratives which tell a linear story instead of a discontinuous one, and metanarratives which insist on telling the story from a western point of view, on telling the true story of how and why it all happened. Feminist theory could deploy aspects of this critique as well. The western point of view, the true discourse, was mostly a white and male discourse, often obfuscating, despite all its claims to objectivity and rationality, the experiences and ways of seeing of social groups that do not take part in the privileges of the dominant white power elite. Indeed, objectivity and rationality itself were dismantled by Foucault as constructions designed to secure hegemony. These are but a few Foucauldian positions which femin-ists could easily incorporate into their theoretical work. However, since Foucault's account of power gives 'no headquarters which set the direction', to use Nancy Hartsock's formulation, many feminist theorists have turned away from Foucault.[13] On the other hand, since Gramsci maps some of the locations of the headquarters of power, his theoretical model might be useful for staking out the operations of power in a way that goes beyond a mere declaration of the ubiquity of power. With Gramsci, so it seems, feminist theory can make out who is powerful and who is not. It would give women the opportunity, which has been seized on many occasions, yet this time against the background of Gramscian theory, to see all men as the perpetrators, those on the other side, who direct the operations of power in the interstices of political and civil society, in the service of producing a spontaneous consent to unequal gender relations, a consent to the sexuality of the status quo.

There is certainly a lot of feminist theory which has, mostly without Gramsci, precisely worked in that direction. By most accounts it is radical feminism that has insisted on that way of seeing things, whereby men, to put it simply, represent power and women the lack of power. I see no need to say more about this problematic, which is known to anyone who has some familiarity with the history of second-wave feminism in the western world. Let it suffice to state here that critical or legitimatory accounts of radical feminism continue to enrich in various versions and to various degrees our feminist theor-etical body. In a recent book entitled *The Oppositional Imagination*, Joan Cocks has, as many other feminist theorists have done on many occasions, refused to join the rank and file of radical feminism, and objected to dividing the world into black and white when it comes to power relations and access to power. Yet she was armed not only with Foucault when arguing for a more complex notion and analysis of the operations of power when dealing with issues of sexuality and gender. Gramsci was mobilized as well in this call for moderation, next to Edward Said and Raymond Williams. She argues forcefully that radical feminism offers only a blunt and crude understanding of power, a representation of dominative power which is far from being emancipatory.[14] This description of power neglects the very real existence of power relations among women, while simultaneously oversimplifying the fact that individual persons can occupy different positions along different axes of power at the same time. It is for this reason that power can be dominative and oppositional at the same time.[15] Cocks' reminder that power can be dominative and oppositional at the same time is not a new insight. The feminist movement, radical and non-radical feminists alike, have, so it seems to me, in the very act of dismantling patriarchal domination indicated its oppositional force. What I find more intriguing and useful is Cocks' calling into question the often presumed innate virtuousness of women and their lack of a will to (male?) power as implied by a good deal of radical feminism. This is a welcome theoretical gesture at a time when, in spite of the many irreversible gains we have made in public and private spaces, the general poverty of feminism in the 1980s has brought home none the less with inexorable force the fact that feminist solidarity often crumbles unexpectedly when access to power in whatever constellation dangles in front of some women's eyes. This in itself would require more complex and sophisticated analyses of relations of power.

What I would like to propose, then, next to Joan Cocks, is something like this. That equipped not only with some of Foucault's as well as Gramsci's conceptual frameworks and methods, but also with the analyses of more recent feminist research, we are in the position to continue to examine relations of power on a local and a global level, along with our function and position with regard to these relations. Most of the work of Foucault will be a reminder that we are all implicated in power, that, in many ways, power is gender blind. And indeed, as well-to-do members of western economic and political communities, as most of us theorists and writers are, we are in some ways implicated in the power these communities hold over the non-western and underdeveloped or developing parts of the world. From Gramsci's complex analyses we can adopt the notion that we are indeed part of many different 'structures of feeling', a partiality which carries a positive and negative potential. Our feminist analyses of power relations, of the way these power relations that often marginalize our specific experiences, forms of knowledge, ways of seeing or epistemologies, ways of judging or ethics, are represented in the discursive and symbolic realm, can contribute to understanding broader and global relations as well.

To be sure, the analysis of power understood in these broad terms cannot be carried out by individuals alone. These are collective projects, and in some respects they are already well under way. What I would plead for is a greater measure of co-operation and collaboration, rather than isolation and academic bickering, collaboration which the rapid dissemination of information technology more powerfully enables as each day passes. I would welcome the exploration of collective discourses, electronic or otherwise, that call into question and problematize the universalizability and relevance of our theories and concerns, such as the multiplicity or the disappearance of the subject, when for many minorities, including many women, access to self-determination, freedom of choice, dignity and some control over their bodies and their minds still belongs to the unattainable realm of a utopian fantasy. If my study of Gramsci inspires some readers to examine the possibilities of working in that direction, then this book will have achieved its aim.

Notes

1 GRAMSCI AND CRITICAL THEORIES

1 Georg Lukács, 'Art and Objective Truth', in *Writer and Critic and Other Essays*, ed. and tr. Arthur D. Kahn (Grosset & Dunlap Publishers, New York, 1971 [1974 edn], pp. 25–61, original German edn 1934.

2 Georg Lukács, 'Grösse und Verfall des Expressionismus', in Georg Lukács, *Werke*, vol. 4, *Probleme des Realismus I* (Luchterhand, Neuwied and Berlin, 1971a), pp. 101–49, original edn 1934.

3 Hans-Jürgen Schmitt, *Die Expressionismusdebatte: Materialien zu einer marxistischen Realismuskonzeption* (Suhrkamp, Frankfurt, 1973), pp. 192–231. This volume contains many of the important essays concerning this famous debate.

4 There are many excellent biographies of Gramsci. I recommend Alastair Davidson, *Antonio Gramsci: Towards an Intellectual Biography* (Merlin Press, London and Humanities Press, New Jersey, 1977), and James Joll, *Gramsci* (Fontana, Collins, Glasgow, 1977); Robert S. Dombroski, *Antonio Gramsci* (Twayne Publishers, Boston, Mass., 1989), offers a short but incisive annotated bibliography of Gramsci's works in general, including biographies. See also Giuseppe Fiori, *Life of a Revolutionary*, tr. Tom Nairn (E. P. Dutton & Co., New York, 1971), original Italian edn 1966.

5 It is also unclear whether Gramsci even knew about the events of June 1935 in Paris. In conjunction with the International Convention of Writers in Defence of Non-Fascist Culture, writers and critics marched alongside 60,000 French people against fascism and rallied for an anti-fascist popular front which would unite all the anti-fascist forces. Gramsci's portrait was among the emblems of that manifestation and writers such as Romain Rolland and Louis Aragon pleaded for Gramsci's liberation from fascist prisons. The notion of an anti-fascist popular front was among the key concepts Gramsci had been working on at the time of his arrest in 1926, yet it is difficult to make out whether the convention knew of or even relied in part on Gramsci's concept.

6 Gramsci's sister-in-law Tatiana Schucht, who was in continuous contact with him, had certainly been informed by Gramsci of some of the topics he was working on. This is apparent from their correspondence. And his

friend Piero Sraffa also knew about some of Gramsci's research projects in prison. It was, however, only after Gramsci's death in 1937 that they were able to learn more about his theoretical work, when both took charge of the writings he had composed in prison, known as the *Quaderni del carcere* or, in English, as the *Prison Notebooks*. As is well known, these notebooks were first transported to Gramsci's wife Giulia Schucht in Moscow; after the war they were taken back to Italy to be published by Editori Riuniti in a series of several volumes.

7 A notable exception is Giuliano Manacorda, 'Introduzione' (1975b), in Giuliano Manacorda's edition of *Marxismo e letteratura* by Antonio Gramsci (Editori Riuniti, Rome, 1975a), pp. 11–59. Yet his apologetic tone indicates quite well, I think, how uncomfortable he felt about his decision to look into Gramsci's activities as a literary critic, rather than as a political theorist. A classic when it comes to Gramsci's notes on literature is Niksa Stipčević, *Gramsci e i problemi letterari*, Civiltà letteraria del novecento, no. 11 (Mursia, Milan, 1968). And of more recent date (1989) Dombroski, op. cit. A formidable account of Gramsci's position as an intellectual and literary critic is Arshi Pipa's as yet unpublished manuscript entitled 'The Politics of Literature'. I thank Arshi Pipa for presenting me with a copy.

8 For Gramsci's discussion of hegemony see his scattered remarks throughout his *Prison Notebooks*, in particular pp. 206–76 of *Selections from the Prison Notebooks*, ed. and tr. Quintin Hoare and Geoffrey Nowell Smith (International Publishers, New York, 1971), hereafter referred to as *SPN*. A recent and very helpful introduction to the concept, which has fascinated many a mind, is Robert Bocock's *Hegemony* (Tavistock Publications, London and New York, 1986). For the use Althusser made of Gramsci's distinction between civil society and political society see Louis Althusser, *Lenin and Philosophy and Other Essays*, tr. Ben Brewster (Monthly Review Press, New York, 1971), in particular pp. 127–89, 'Ideology and Ideological State Apparatuses'.

9 Most sources I have consulted on Gramsci's political or social theory, as well as on his philosophy, prefer to view Gramsci in the context of western Marxism. Here I will refer to Walter L. Adamson, *Hegemony and Revolution: A Study of Antonio Gramsci's Political and Cultural Theory* (University of California Press, Berkeley, Los Angeles, Ca and London, 1980); Perry Anderson, 'The Antinomies of Antonio Gramsci', *New Left Review* 100 (1976–7), 5–81; Carl Boggs, *The Two Revolutions: Gramsci and the Dilemmas of Western Marxism* (South End Press, Boston, Mass., 1984); Maurice Finocchiaro, *Gramsci critico e la critica* (Armando Editore, Rome, 1988a); John Hoffman, *The Gramscian Challenge: Coercion and Consent in Marxist Political Theory* (Basil Blackwell, Oxford and New York, 1984); Franz Kaminski, Heiner Karuscheit and Klaus Winter, *Antonio Gramsci, Philosophie und Praxis: Grundlagen und Wirkungen der Gramsci-Debatte* (Sendler Verlag, Frankfurt, 1982); Sabine Kebir, *Die Kulturkonzeption Antonio Gramscis* (Damnitz Verlag GmbH, Munich, 1980); Richard Kilminster, *Praxis and Method: A Sociological Dialogue with Lukács, Gramsci and the Early Frankfurt School* (Routledge & Kegan Paul, Boston, Mass., London and Henley, Oxon., 1979); Chantal Mouffe (ed.), *Gramsci and*

Marxist Theory (Routledge & Kegan Paul, Boston, Mass., London and Henley, Oxon., 1979); Thomas Nemeth, *Gramsci's Philosophy: A Critical Study* (Harvester Press, Brighton, Sussex and Humanities Press, Atlantic Highlands, 1980); Anne Showstack Sassoon, *Gramsci's Politics* (Croom Helm, London, 1980); Roger Simon, *Gramsci's Political Thought: An Introduction* (Lawrence & Wishart, London, 1982). I recommend Roger S. Gottlieb (ed.), *An Anthology of Western Marxism: From Lukács and Gramsci to Socialist-Feminism* (Oxford University Press, New York and Oxford, 1989), for starters in this area, since it does contain introductions to the various western Marxist thinkers. Martin Jay, *Marxism and Totality: The Adventures of a Concept from Lukács to Habermas* (University of California Press, Berkeley and Los Angeles, Ca, 1984), is a classic and highly recommendable.

10 See, for instance, a most recent publication that again attempts to define Gramsci's politics, in spite of the title: Esteve Morera, *Gramsci's Historicism: A Realist Interpretation* (Routledge, London and New York, 1990).

11 Fredric Jameson, *Marxism and Form: Twentieth-Century Dialectical Theories of Literature* (Princeton University Press, Princeton, NJ, 1971), pp. 160–205, has written some of the more compelling and as yet unsurpassed pages in English on Lukács as literary theorist. I also recommend the chapter 'Western Marxism' in a book by Merleau-Ponty, where Lukács appears in the context of the philosophical issues of the 1920s: see Maurice Merleau-Ponty, *The Adventures of the Dialectic*, tr. Joseph Bien (Northwestern University Press, Evanston, Ill., 1973), pp. 30–59, original French edn 1955. Of utmost importance for understanding Lukács' position in a broader theoretical context that transcends the received rejection of his aesthetics is Lucien Goldmann, *Lukács and Heidegger: Towards a New Philosophy*, tr. William Q. Boelhower (Routledge & Kegan Paul, Boston, Mass., London and Henley, Oxon., 1977), original French edn 1960.

12 There are many outstanding anthologies and collections available on the Frankfurt School and those intellectuals who were close to that school. I recommend Andrew Arato and Eike Gebhardt (eds), *The Essential Frankfurt School Reader*, introduction Paul Piccone (Urizen Books, New York, 1978), since these editors wrote excellent introductions to the pertinent issues that concerned that school.

13 See Alfred Schmidt, *History and Structure: an Essay on Hegelian-Marxist and Structuralist Theories of History*, tr. Jeffrey Herf (MIT Press, Cambridge, Mass., 1981), p. 79, original German edn 1971.

14 For bibliographical information see: Marino Biondi, *Guida Bibliografica a Gramsci*, presentation Renato Zangheri (Libreria Adamo Bettini, Cesena, 1977); Phil Cozens, *Twenty Years of Antonio Gramsci: A Bibliography of Gramsci and Gramsci Studies Published in English, 1957–1977* (Lawrence & Wishart, London, 1977); and *Antonio Gramsci: A Bibliography*, Social Theory: a Bibliographic Series, no. 7 (Reference and Research Services, Santa Cruz, Ca, 1987). The above-mentioned Biondi bibliography is particularly relevant when it comes to indicating what kind and how much of and when Gramscian texts have been translated into the various languages. It is interesting to note that some of Gramsci's work was already available in France by the late 1950s. See Biondi, op. cit., p. 46. In comparison, editions of Gramsci in English did not get published until the

1970s. There should be little doubt that the earlier translations of Gramsci had an impact on the Gramsci reception in France. What Althusser has incorporated into his theory is in particular Gramsci's distinction between political and civil society, which Althusser tends to amalgamate in his notion of ideological state apparatuses. For an interesting study that looks at both Althusser's incorporation of Gramscian theories and their rejection see: Hermes Coassin-Spiegel, *Gramsci und Althusser: Eine Kritik der Althusserschen Rezeption von Gramsci's Philosophie* (Argument Verlag, Berlin, 1983). As far as Nicolas Poulantzas is concerned, I am referring to Perry Anderson's discussion of Poulantzas' notion of 'consent to the status quo', which he does not understand as class consciousness but rather as a way to deal with domination that transcends capitalist structures, in that religion, as it has existed throughout the centuries, often participated in the maintenance of a status quo. See Anderson, op. cit., pp. 5–81. Gramsci also extends that notion of consent in its form as religion to many historical epochs, and not only to the class consciousness of the proletariat. See my discussion of this problem on pp. 112–16 of this present study. For Poulantzas see his *Fascism and Dictatorship: The Third International and the Problem of Fascism*, tr. Judith White (New Left Books, London, 1974), original French edn 1970, where forms of domination are no longer the province of capitalism alone but are extended to other dictatorial regimes, including socialist countries.

15 See his *Marxism and Literature* (Oxford University Press, Oxford, 1977), pp. 108–12; his *Problems in Materialism and Culture* (Verso, London, 1988), pp. 37–42; and his *The Sociology of Culture* (Schocken Books, New York, 1982), pp. 214–18.

16 Among the German publications available on Gramsci, I cite the following: Gerhard Roth, *Gramscis Philosophy der Praxis: Eine neue Deutung des Marxismus* (Patmos Verlag, Düsseldorf, 1972), which is one of the few Gramscian texts available in German; and Christian Riechers, *Das Verhältnis der Philosophie der Praxis Antonio Gramscis zum Marxismus* (Europäische Verlagsanstalt, Frankfurt, 1970); Kaminski, Karuscheit and Winter, op. cit.; Kebir, op. cit.

17 For information on the formidable Gramsci reception in Italy see the above-mentioned bibliography by Biondi; also of help is Dombroski's recent (1989) *Antonio Gramsci*, op.cit.

18 See, for instance, Nestor Garcia Canelini, 'Gramsci con Bourdieu. Hegemonia, consumo y nuevas formas de organizacion popular', *Nueva Sociedad* 71 (l984), 69–78; and C. Maya, 'El concepto del estado en los "Cuadernos de la Carcel" ', *Cuadernos Politicos* 33 (1982), 7–19. See in particular Dora Kanoussi and Javier Mena, *La revolución pasiva: Una lectura de los Cuadernos de la Carcel* (Universidad Autonoma de Puebla, Puebla, Mexico, 1985).

19 See, for instance, Joan Cocks, *The Oppositional Imagination: Feminism, Critique and Political Theory* (Routledge, London and New York, 1989), where Gramsci joins the rank and file with Edward Said, Raymond Williams and Michel Foucault.

20 When I asked one of the last living members of the Frankfurt School, Professor Leo Lowenthal, at the request of my students and myself, to visit my class on 'Gramsci, Western Marxism, and Gender', at Berkeley in the

spring of 1990, Professor Lowenthal quickly let me know: 'To be candid with you, I don't know all that much about Gramsci.' No doubt, this was an understatement, particularly because it comes from an intellectual who, as many of us who know him can testify, indefatigably keeps informing himself about the state of the critical arts. Yet in some ways it speaks too, I think, of Gramsci's status in that regard.

21 See Ernesto Laclau and Chantal Mouffe, *Hegemony and Socialist Strategy: Towards a Radical Democratic Politics* (Verso, London and New York, 1985), where Gramsci is interestingly enlisted in the struggle for a radical democracy poststructurally conceived. The 'de-centring and autonomy of the different discourses and struggles, the multiplications of antagonisms and the construction of a plurality of spaces within which they can affirm themselves and develop, are the conditions *sine qua non* of the possibility that the different components of the classic ideal of socialism can be achieved .... this plurality of spaces does not deny, but rather requires, the overdetermination of its effects at certain levels and the consequent hegemonic articulation between them' (p. 192). Both authors have a long and solid standing among the critical community that has evolved around Gramsci.

22 In their outstanding 'General Introduction' to *SPN*, Hoare and Nowell Smith point to the fact that 'until all his work for the years between 1922 and 1926 has been published, and until more is known about his life and activity in Moscow (May 1922–November 1923) and in Vienna (December 1923–May 1924), it will not be possible to reconstruct fully his political biography for these crucial years' (p. xlvii). Almost twenty years after this statement, not much has changed, in my view, in the scholarship that reconstructs Gramsci's biography for these years.

23 For the exchanges between Italian Marxists and the Central Committee of the Soviet Communist Party, see the Gramsci–Togliatti exchange in Antonio Gramsci, *Selections from Political Writings 1921–1926*, ed. and tr. Quintin Hoare (International Publishers, New York, 1980a), pp. 426–40, which provides a glimpse of the level on which Gramsci was engaged in international leftist politics.

24 For an expedient introduction to the beginnings of Russian semiotics and structuralism see Ladislav Matejka, 'On the First Russian Prolegomena to Semiotics' in V. N. Vološinov, *Marxism and the Philosophy of Language*, tr. Ladislav Matejka and I. R. Titunik (Harvard University Press, Cambridge, Mass. and London, 1986), pp. 161–74; and in the same volume, I. R. Titunik, 'The Formal Method and the Sociological Method (M. M. Bakhtin, P. N. Medvedev, V. N. Vološinov) in Russian Theory and Study of Literature', pp. 175–200.

25 Fritz J. Raddatz, *Georg Lukács: In Selbstzeugnissen und Bilddokumenten* (Rowohlt, Hamburg, 1972), p. 66, points out that Lukács, while working as editor of the journal *Kommunismus* in Vienna in those years, had many an ideological debate with Italian leftists. It is unlikely, Raddatz concludes, that Lukács did not meet Gramsci at that point.

26 For Gramsci's view of futurism and his letter to Trotsky on the matter see *Selections from Cultural Writings*, ed. David Forgacs and Geoffrey Nowell Smith, tr. William Boelhower (Harvard University Press, Cambridge, Mass., 1985), pp. 46–54.

27 Peter Gorsen, 'Zur Dialektik des Funktionalismus heute: Das Beispiel des kommunalen Wohnungsbaus im Wien der zwanziger Jahre', in Jürgen Habermas (ed.), *Stichworte zur 'Geistigen Situation der Zeit'*, vol. 1, *Nation und Republik* (Suhrkamp, Frankfurt, 1982, first edn 1979), pp. 688–707.

28 Marcia Landy, 'Culture and Politics in the Works of Antonio Gramsci', in *Boundary 2* (Special Issue, *The Legacy of Antonio Gramsci*, ed. Joseph Buttigieg) 14, 3 (1986), 49–71.

29 Anne Showstack Sassoon, 'Introduction', in *Gramsci's Politics*, 2nd edn (Hutchinson, London and Melbourne, 1987), p. x.

30 Jean-François Lyotard, *The Postmodern Condition: A Report on Knowledge*, tr. Geoff Bennington and Brian Massumi, foreword Fredric Jameson (University of Minnesota Press, Minneapolis, Minn., 1984, original French edn 1979). Jürgen Habermas, *The Theory of Communicative Action*, vol. 1, *Reason and the Rationalization of Society*, tr. Thomas McCarthy (Beacon Press, Boston, Mass., 1984), vol. 2, *Lifeworld and System: A Critique of Functionalist Reason*, tr. Thomas McCarthy (Beacon Press, Boston, Mass., 1987) (vols 1 and 2, Beacon Paperback 1989), original German edn 1981.

31 See Mark Poster, *The Mode of Information: Poststructuralism and Social Context* (University of Chicago Press, Chicago, 1990).

32 My friend of many years, Ida Jeters, a critical information technology specialist, has instructed me on many occasions as to the democratic potential of information technology. I would like to thank her here for the many hours she has spent with me on these issues.

2 GRAMSCI, LUKÁCS AND MARXIST AESTHETICS

1 Antonio Gramsci, *Selections from the Prison Notebooks*, ed. and tr. Quintin Hoare and Geoffrey Nowell Smith (International Publishers, New York, 1971), pp. 382–6, hereafter referred to as *SPN*. Contrary to the Italian edition of Gramsci's work, the *Quaderni del carcere*, ed. Valentino Gerratana, 4 vols (Giulio Einaudi Editore, Turin, 1975), hereafter referred to as *Quaderni*, which indicates the sequence of the various notebooks, the English edition, being merely a selection from and not a reproduction of all of the notebooks, was not able to include this useful classificatory system.

2 Antonio Gramsci, *Il materialismo storico e la filosofia di Benedetto Croce* (Einaudi, Turin, 1948); a new revised edition with an introduction by Luciano Gruppo appeared from Editori Riuniti, Rome, 1975. As is quite well known, the bulk of Gramsci's prison writings appeared after the war in a series of seven volumes more or less topically arranged which attempted to accommodate an apparent logic in the unsystematicity of Gramsci's notes as well as the philosophical and political prerogatives of the editors. A new critical edition, the so-called Gerratana edition, published in 1975 under the auspices of the Gramsci Institute (Istituto Gramsci) in Rome, respected the original unsystematic order of the notebooks. Gramsci, *Quaderni*, op. cit.

3 A good example of the predominant topics of interest to Gramsci scholars until recently are the publications issued by the Gramsci Institute, Rome: Pietro Rossi (ed.), *Gramsci e la cultura contemporanea*, 2 vols (Editori Riuniti,

Rome, 1969, 1975). Intellectuals writing on Gramsci in Italy are well known to the liberal cultural community: Norberto Bobbio, Eugenio Garin, Ernesto Ragionieri, Natalino Sapegno, Paolo Spriano – to name but a few.

4 Giuliano Manacorda (ed.), 'Introduzione', in *Marxismo e letteratura* by Antonio Gramsci (Editori Riuniti, Rome, 1975), p. 11.

5 Sabine Kebir, *Die Kulturkonzeption Antonio Gramscis* (Damnitz Verlag GmbH, Munich, 1980), pp. 97–8. Since this study is not available in English, its author has not received the attention such work on Gramsci deserves. It is splendid, in spite of her unmistakably opting for an ideological reading of Gramsci's major concepts suitable to the ideological requirements of the former GDR. She is in my view the most knowledgeable Gramsci scholar in Germany.

6 Esteve Morera, *Gramsci's Historicism: A Realist Interpretation* (Routledge, London and New York, 1990), p. 3.

7 There is no complete edition of Gramsci available in English. Joseph Buttigieg is working on the translation of the *Quaderni del carcere*, to be published by Columbia University Press. The selections of Gramsci's writings in English commonly used are *SPN*. Geoffrey Nowell Smith also edited, together with David Forgacs, *Selections from Cultural Writings*, tr. William Boelhower (Harvard University Press, Cambridge, Mass., 1985), hereafter referred to as *SCW*. They include selections from Gramsci's pre-prison writings. In addition, there are two volumes available on Gramsci's political writings: *Selections from Political Writings 1910–1920*, ed. Quintin Hoare, tr. Jolin Mathews (Lawrence & Wishart, London, 1977) and *Selections from Political Writings 1921–1926*, ed. and tr. Quintin Hoare (International Publishers, New York, 1980a). There is also a selection entitled *The Modern Prince and Other Writings*, tr. Louis Marks (International Publishers, New York, 1957, 10th printing 1987), as well as Pedro Cavalcanti and Paul Piccone (eds), *History, Philosophy and Culture in the Young Gramsci* (Telos Press, St Louis, Miss., 1975). A very useful volume is David Forgacs' *The Gramsci Reader*, published by Lawrence & Wishart, London, 1988.

8 I am referring to Jean Hyppolite's *Genesis and Structure of Hegel's Phenomenology of the Spirit*, tr. Samuel Cherniak and John Heckman (Northwestern University Press, Evanston, Ill., 1974), original French edn 1946, followed by Alexandre Kojève's *Introduction to the Reading of Hegel: Lectures on the Phenomenology of the Spirit*, ass. Raymond Queneau, ed. Allan Bloom, tr. James H. Nichols, Jr (Cornell University Press, Ithaca, NY and London, 1969), original French edn 1947. There is no reason to believe that Kojève and Hyppolite were uninfluential in the preparation of poststructuralist readings of the Hegelian text, such as Jacques Lacan's, where Hegel's master-slave dialectic resurfaces in the inexorable ties between the imaginary and the symbolic, the symptom and the real. See also Jean Hyppolite's *Studies on Marx and Hegel*, tr. with introduction, notes and bibliography John O'Neill (Basic Books, New York and London, 1969), original French edn 1955.

9 I am referring here to the discourses on philosophy as a kind of writing. Useful discussions of this problem are Richard Rorty's *Consequences of*

Pragmatism (University of Minnesota Press, Minneapolis, Minn., 1982);
John Rajchman and Cornel West (eds), *Post-Analytic Philosophy* (Columbia University Press, New York, 1985); and Richard Rorty, J. B. Schneewind and Quentin Skinner (eds), *Philosophy in History* (Cambridge University Press, Cambridge, 1984).

10 Gramsci's letters from prison have appeared in a series of editions. An edition in Italian which includes almost all these letters is *Lettere dal carcere*, ed. Sergio Caprioglio and Elsa Fubini (Einaudi, Turin, 1965). In English there is *Letters from Prison*, ed., tr. and introduction Lynne Lawner (Noonday Press, Farrar, Straus & Giroux, New York, first edn 1973). See also Hamish Henderson (ed.), *Gramsci's Prison Letters: Lettere dal Carcere* (Zwan Publications, London, 1988). For an introduction to Gramsci's life and work I recommend Alastair Davidson, *Antonio Gramsci: Towards an Intellectual Biography* (Merlin Press, London, and Humanities Press, New Jersey, 1977) as well as Robert S. Dombroski, *Antonio Gramsci* (Twayne Publishers, Boston, Mass., 1989). A classic introduction is James Joll, *Gramsci* (Fontana, Collins, Glasgow, 1977). All of these contain excellent bibliographies for further study of Gramsci's life.

11 Nowell Smith's 'General Introduction' to the English edition of his writings on culture, *SCW*, illustrates this point on pp. 3–5.

12 Manacorda, 'Introduzione', op. cit., p. 12.

13 Hans-Jürgen Schmitt, *Die Expressionismusdebatte: Materialien zu einer marxistischen Realismuskonzeption* (Suhrkamp, Frankfurt, 1973) gives an excellent account of this debate.

14 For an introduction to Marxism and aesthetics see Maynard Solomon, *Marxism and Art* (Wayne State University Press, Detroit, Mich., 1979). See also Herbert Marcuse, *The Aesthetic Dimension: Toward a Critique of Marxist Aesthetics* (Beacon Press, Boston, Mass., 1978a), original German edn 1977; equally useful is Lee Baxandall and Stefan Morawski (eds), *Marx and Engels on Literature and Art* (Telos Press, St Louis, Miss., 1973).

15 Karl Marx, preface to the *Critique of Political Economy*, in *Selected Writings*, ed. David McLellan (Oxford University Press, Oxford and New York, 1988), pp. 388–93.

16 Friedrich Engels, preface to the English edition (1888) of *The Communist Manifesto*, in Karl Marx and Friedrich Engels, *The Communist Manifesto*, introduction and notes A.J.P. Taylor (Penguin Books, Harmondsworth, Mx, 1967), p. 62.

17 Marx, preface to the *Critique of Political Economy*, op. cit., pp. 389–90.

18 Benedetto Croce, *Historical Materialism and the Economics of Karl Marx*, tr. C.M. Meredith, introduction A. D. Lindsay (Macmillan, New York, 1914), original Italian edn 1900.

19 For a history of Marxism see Leszek Kolakowski, *Main Currents of Marxism*, vol. 3, *The Breakdown*, tr. P. S. Falla (Oxford University Press, Oxford, 1978), original Polish edn 1976.

20 For a substantial overview of the adventures of western Marxism see Martin Jay, *Marxism and Totality: The Adventures of a Concept from Lukács to Habermas* (University of California Press, Berkeley and Los Angeles, Ca, 1984).

21 Georg Lukács, *History and Class Consciousness: Studies in Marxist Dialectics*,

tr. Rodney Livingstone (MIT Press, Cambridge, Mass., 1971b), original German edn 1923.

22 For Labriola's specific form of Marxism, as well as Gramsci's relation to it, see Paul Piccone, *Italian Marxism* (University of California Press, Berkeley, Ca, 1983). For Lukács' indebtedness to Labriola see Fritz J. Raddatz, *Georg Lukács: In Selbstzeugnissen und Bilddokumenten* (Rowohlt, Hamburg, 1972), p. 43.

23 See ibid., p. 47.

24 *Quaderni*, p. 469.

25 *SPW*, pp. 277–322.

26 Karl Korsch, *Marxism and Philosophy*, tr. Fred Halliday (Monthly Review Press, New York and London, 1970), original German edn 1924.

27 For Althusser's discussion on humanism and Marxism, on the question of the scientificity of Marxism over and above a humanist Marxism, see his 'Marxism and Humanism' in Louis Althusser, *For Marx*, tr. Ben Brewster (Verso, London, 1977), pp. 219–49, original French edn 1965. For the Habermas/Luhmann debate on system theory see Jürgen Habermas and Niklas Luhmann, *Theorie der Gesellschaft oder Sozialtechnologie* (Suhrkamp, Frankfurt, 1971); see also Robert C. Holub, *Jürgen Habermas: Critic in the Public Sphere* (Routledge, London, 1991), in particular chapter 5. The literature by followers both of Habermas and of Lyotard on the issue is so extensive that it cannot be cited here. A good overview is provided by Robert C. Holub, op. cit., chapter 6. Suffice it to say that Habermas' belief in the possibility of communicative action, and thus the possibility of effecting social change, is countered by Lyotard's belief in the overdetermination of social action by complex systems of information and domination. I see these images as pertaining to a late twentieth-century version of the debate between dialectical materialism and historical materialism.

28 Raddatz, op. cit., p. 110.

29 For Gramsci's complex relation to Croce see his notes on Croce's philosophy, conveniently ordered in Gramsci *Il materialismo storico e la filosofia di Benedetto Croce* (Einaudi, Turin, 1948). On Gramsci's admiration for de Sanctis see his note on 'Back to de Sanctis' in *SCW*, pp. 91–3, and the many intermittent entries on de Sanctis in the *Quaderni*.

30 Francesco de Sanctis, *History of Italian Literature*, vol. 2, tr. Joan Redfern (Harcourt, Brace & Co., New York, 1931), p. 937, original Italian edn 1870–1.

31 See *Quaderni*, p. 5, and *SCW*, p. 3.

32 See *SCW*, pp. 278–98.

33 *Quaderni*, p. 3350.

34 The presence of Spinozism in Italian intellectual history, and in its amalgamation with Hegelianism, as it occurred in the later nineteenth century, is very fascinating. See Piccone, *Italian Marxism*, op. cit. Antonio Negri's *The Savage Anomaly: The Power of Spinoza's Metaphysics and Politics*, tr. Michael Hardt (University of Minnesota Press, Minneapolis, Minn., 1990), original Italian edn 1982, as well as his more recent *Lenta ginestra. Saggio sull'ontologia di Giacomo Leopardi* (Sugar Editori, Milan, 1987) are surely texts which can be read as part of that tradition.

35 *SCW*, pp. 278–98.

36 Gramsci, *Letters*, op. cit., pp. 79–81.
37 These explanations are based on Gramsci's discussion of the dynamics of popular culture, *SCW*, pp. 342–86.
38 *SCW*, pp. 199–286.
39 ibid., pp. 288–94.
40 ibid., pp. 289–90.
41 ibid., pp. 291–4.
42 ibid., p. 291.
43 ibid., p. 295.
44 *Quaderni*, pp. 937–8.
45 ibid., p. 949 and p. 943.
46 ibid., pp. 2206–8.
47 *SCW*, p. 294.
48 *Quaderni*, p. 2118.
49 *SCW*, p. 249.
50 ibid., pp. 293–4.
51 ibid., p. 296.
52 For the cultural politics of the immediate post-war era in Italy see Renate Holub, 'The Cultural Politics of the CPI from 1944–56', *Yale Italian Studies* 2 (1978), 261–83.
53 See Gianni Scalia, 'Manzoni a sinistra', *Italianistica* 1 (1973), 21–42; Robert S. Dombroski, 'The Ideological Question in Manzoni', *Studies in Romanticism* 20 (Winter 1981), 497–524, as well as his *L'apologia del vero: Lettura ed interpretazione dei 'Promessi Sposi'* (Liviana Editrice, Padua, 1984).
54 Lukács' extensive work on European realism, written in German and published in the late 1940s and 1950s, has appeared in some English editions. See Georg Lukács, *Studies in European Realism*, introduction Alfred Kazin (Grosset & Dunlap, New York, 1964); also *The Historical Novel*, tr. Hannah and Stanley Mitchell, introduction Fredric Jameson (University of Nebraska Press, Lincoln, Nebr. and London, 1983), original German edn 1955. As Lukács points out in 1948, many of his essays on realism had been written ten years earlier, thus in the period in which the expressionism/realism debate was taking place. See his *Studies in European Realism*, op. cit., p. 1.
55 See introduction to Schmitt, op. cit., pp. 7–37.
56 See his 'Es geht um den Realismus' in ibid., pp. 192–230, original edn 1937.
57 'Die Brecht-Polemik gegen Lukács' in ibid., pp. 302–37. See also Bertolt Brecht, *Gesammelte Werke 19: Schriften zur Literatur und Kunst 2* (Suhrkamp, Frankfurt, 1967c), pp. 290–331.
58 For Bloch's reaction to Lukács, see his 'Diskussionen über den Expressionismus' and Bloch and Eisler, 'Die Kunst zu erben' in Schmitt, op. cit., pp. 180–92 and pp. 258–64.
59 For a discussion of the relation between Lukács and Heidegger in this context see Lucien Goldmann, *Lukács and Heidegger: Towards a New Philosophy*, tr. William Q. Boelhower (Routledge & Kegan Paul, Boston, Mass., and Henley, Oxon., 1977), original French edn 1960.
60 See Georg Lukács, *The Destruction of Reason*, tr. Peter Palmer (Merlin Press, London, 1980), original German edn 1962.

61 See Bloch in Schmitt, op. cit., p. 187.
62 See ibid., pp. 186–8.
63 See Lukács, 'Es geht' in ibid., pp. 192–231.
64 See Lukács, *The Historical Novel*, pp. 68–73.
65 ibid., pp. 69–70.
66 ibid.
67 For Lukács' general theory of realism see *Studies in European Realism*, op. cit.
68 In a 1967 preface to *History and Class Consciousness* Lukács corrects himself on the issue of dialectics in nature. See his *History and Class Consciousness*, op. cit., pp. ix–xli.

3 THE INDUSTRIALIZATION OF CULTURE

1 Antonio Gramsci, *Selections from Cultural Writings*, ed. David Forgacs and Geoffrey Nowell Smith, tr. William Boelhower (Harvard University Press, Cambridge, Mass., 1985), p. 92, hereafter referred to as *SCW*.
2 One of the exceptions to this rule is, according to Gramsci, the poet Pascoli. See ibid., pp. 246–7.
3 On populism in France see ibid., p. 363.
4 ibid., p. 256.
5 ibid., pp. 115–16, on Manzoni's attitude in the context of Italian cultural and political history.
6 Sabine Kebir argues throughout her *Die Kulturkonzeption Antonio Gramscis* (Damnitz Verlag GmbH, Munich, 1980) that one of the key concepts of Gramsci's writings is the notion of anti-fascist popular alliances. This notion, she contends, derived from his political struggle, first and foremost informs his cultural writings. These are, in her view, the 'results of his politics of alliance' (p. 98).
7 Antonio Gramsci, 'On the Southern Question', in *The Modern Prince and Other Writings* (International Publishers, New York, 1957, 10th printing 1987), pp. 28–51.
8 Hans-Jürgen Schmitt, *Die Expressionismusdebatte: Materialien zu einer marxistischen Realismuskonzeption* (Suhrkamp, Frankfurt, 1973), in particular in the introduction, pp. 7–37.
9 See Albrecht Betz, 'Lukács als Literaturstratege', in *Verdinglichung und Utopie: Ernst Bloch und Georg Lukács zum 100. Geburtstag*, ed. Michael Löwy, Arno Münster and Nicolas Tertulian (Sender Verlag, Frankfurt, 1987), pp. 150–9.
10 Gramsci, 'On the Southern Question', op. cit., p. 36.
11 It is interesting in this context to compare Gramsci's notion of the complexity of the 'structures of acceptance', which are related to mechanisms of consent, to Wilhelm Reich's essays on the needs, feelings, beliefs and participation of the masses. See in particular his 'What is Class Consciousness' in *An Anthology of Western Marxism: From Lukács and Gramsci to Socialist Feminism*, ed. Roger S. Gottlieb (Oxford University Press, New York and Oxford, 1989), pp. 145–67.
12 A more detailed discussion of Gramsci's materialism would have to take into account his probable indebtedness to the Italian materialist tra-

dition, in particular Labriola and the Spaventa brothers, whose reading of Hegel, for instance, is not without Spinozistic nuances. See Paul Piccone, *Italian Marxism* (University of California Press, Berkeley, Ca, 1983), for crucial information on the forms of materialist philosophy in Italy. Gramsci's 'Spinozism' would also have to be viewed, however, in its relation to Bergsonianism, in that Gramsci's imagery reveals not only a physical model, matter in motion, but also a physiological one. In an unpublished manuscript, 'The Politics of Literature', Arshi Pipa speaks of Gramsci's 'organic imagery', or 'genetic imagery'.

13 Esteve Morera, *Gramsci's Historicism: A Realist Interpretation* (Routledge, London and New York, 1990), p. 39.

14 I am referring to Herbert Marcuse's *The Aesthetic Dimension: Towards a Critique of Marxist Aesthetics* (Beacon Press, Boston, Mass., 1978a), original German edn 1977. Adorno's more recent aesthetic programme was published posthumously in Theodor W. Adorno, *Aesthetic Theory*, ed. Gretel Adorno and Rolf Tiedemann, tr. C. Lenhardt (Routledge & Kegan Paul, London and New York, 1984), original German edn 1970.

15 There are some studies which I found helpful in preparing this section on Gramsci's activities as a theatre critic: Edo Bellingeri, *Dall'intellettuale al politico. Le 'Cronache Teatrali' di Gramsci* (Dedalo libri, Bari, 1975); Guido Davico Bonino, *Gramsci e il teatro* (Giulio Einaudi Editore, Turin, 1972); and also Niksa Stipčevič, *Gramsci e i problemi letterari*, Civiltà letteraria del novecento, no. 11 (Mursia, Milan, 1968), in particular pp. 89–146. Gramsci's theatre reviews are included in Antonio Gramsci, *Cronache Torinesi (1913–1917)*, ed. Sergio Caprioglio (Giulio Einaudi Editore, Turin, 1980b), pp. 735–855.

16 Gramsci's discussion of the so-called 'Catholic' literature occurs in connection with what he calls 'Father Bresciani's progeny', literature written in the style and the spirit of the nineteenth-century historical novelist Antonio Bresciani which not only ironically or nostalgically portrays the life of the common people, but also resists forms of social and cultural transformation. The *SCW* contains a good deal of material from the articles Gramsci wrote on this topic and includes a helpful introduction to the issue. See pp. 298–341.

17 'The life of the peasantry occupies a large space in literature, but here, too, not as work and toil but as "folklore"', writes Gramsci in a section in which he discusses the absence of an adequate presentation of labour and work in Italian literary circles. See ibid., pp. 212–13.

18 ibid., p. 80.

19 See Antonio Gramsci, *Quaderni del carcere*, ed. Valentino Gerratana, 4 vols (Giulio Einaudi Editore, Turin, 1975), p. 1419, hereafter referred to as *Quaderni*. The section is entitled 'Objectivity and Reality of the External World' and appears in Notebook 11 entitled 'Introduction to the Study of Philosophy'. See also an earlier and shorter version of this idea on p. 874 of the *Quaderni*.

20 For Horkheimer's discussion of this problem see his 'On the Problem of Truth' in Andrew Arato and Eike Gebhardt (eds), *The Essential Frankfurt School Reader*, introduction Paul Piccone (Urizen Books, New York, 1978), pp. 407–44, original German edn 1935.

21 Giuliano Manacorda, 'Introduzione' in *Marxismo e letteratura* by Antonio Gramsci (Editori Riuniti, Rome, 1975b), p. 12.

22 Given the immense suggestiveness of Gramsci's theory it should come as no surprise that intellectuals such as Raymond Williams and Edward Said have had little problem in also adopting Gramsci's point of view on the issue when they set out, in their respective studies, to interrogate the relations that obtain between centre and margin and their conditions of possibility. For Williams' appreciation of Gramsci's contribution to an understanding of the operations of cultural formations see his explicit notes on Gramsci in *Marxism and Literature* (Oxford University Press, Oxford, 1977), pp. 108–12; *Problems in Materialism and Culture* (Verso, London, 1988), pp. 37–42; *The Sociology of Culture* (Schocken Books, New York, 1982), pp. 214–18. Yet Williams' theoretical indebtedness far exceeds his express statements on the matter. For Edward W. Said, see his *Orientalism* (Vintage Books, New York, 1979), where he makes good use of Gramsci in his introduction. See also his *The World, the Text, and the Critic*, (Harvard University Press, Cambridge, Mass., 1983), where Gramsci's presence is felt throughout. While there is no doubt that Williams seems theoretically closer to Gramsci than Said, the latter incorporating many Foucauldian points of view into his work, there is also no doubt that Said's most salient political edge clashes with Foucault but not with Gramsci. For an interesting discussion of the Gramsci/Williams/Said/Foucault axis see Joan Cocks, *The Oppositional Imagination: Feminism, Critique and Political Theory* (Routledge, London and New York, 1989).

23 Gramsci refers to a portrayal of the Italian peasant in a cultural microhistory on pp. 722–3 of the *Quaderni*. That portrayal is clearly no match for Pirandello's.

24 *SCW*, pp. 70–3.

25 ibid., p. 72.

26 ibid.

27 ibid.

28 Walter Benjamin, 'Literaturgeschichte und Literaturwissenschaft' in *Der Stratege im Literaturkampf: Zur Literaturwissenschaft*, ed. Hella Tiedemann-Bartels (Suhrkamp, Frankfurt, 1974), pp. 7–15, original edn 1931.

29 See ibid., p. 14.

30 For Horkheimer see his 'Traditional and Critical Theory' in *Critical Sociology: Selected Readings*, ed. Paul Connerton (Penguin Books, Harmondsworth, Mx, 1976), pp. 206–24, original German edn 1937.

31 Theodor Adorno and Max Horkheimer, 'The Culture Industry: Enlightenment as Mass Deception', in *Dialectic of Enlightenment*, tr. John Cumming (New York: Continuum Publishers, 1972), pp. 120–67, original German edn 1947.

32 Very useful introductions to the issues the Frankfurt School concerned itself with are supplied by Arato and Gebhardt in their *Essential Frankfurt School Reader*, op. cit.

33 *SCW*, pp. 64–70.

34 See the new edition of Antonio Gramsci, *Letteratura e vita nazionale*, introduction Edoardo Sanguineti (Editori Riuniti, Rome, 1987), pp. 353–69.

35 *SCW*, pp. 56–70.

36 ibid., p. 60.

37 ibid., pp. 54–6.

38 ibid., p. 55.

39 ibid.

40 For Herbert Marcuse see his 'Some Social Implications of Modern Technology' in Arato and Gebhardt, op. cit., pp. 138–61. For Adorno and Horkheimer see their 'The Culture Industry: Enlightenment as Mass Deception' in their *Dialectic of Enlightenment*, op. cit.

41 Bertolt Brecht, 'Theatersituation 1917–1927', in *Gesammelte Werke 15: Schriften zum Theater 1* (Suhrkamp, Frankfurt, 1967a), pp. 125–6.

42 ibid., p. 125.

43 Bertolt Brecht, 'Ueber Film', in *Gesammelte Werke 18: Schriften zur Literatur und Kunst 1* (Suhrkamp, Frankfurt, 1967b), p. 137.

44 I am referring to Stipčevič, *Gramsci e i problemi letterari*, but other critics should also be considered. Since the issue of Gramsci's Crocean heritage is discussed in practically all the studies of him that have appeared, I will refrain from taking it up myself.

45 That Gramsci owes much to Croce, Italy's foremost idealist philosopher, is part and parcel of much current Gramsci scholarship. Since Gramsci also owes much to Marx, it should come as no surprise that the 'idealist-materialist' or the 'subjective-objective' tension predominates exegetical efforts in terminology and problematization. Rather than following this undoubtedly useful path, I have preferred not to overlook Croce, but to regard those elements which are or appear 'Crocean' in the Gramscian text as modes of thinking which transcend Croce the author. Rather I find it difficult not to consider that which appears as 'Crocean' as part of modernizing forms of cultural texts, as structures of thinking that re-emerge in some forms and to some degree in the aesthetics of authors such as Marcuse and Adorno; I also find it difficult not to consider that which appears 'Crocean' as part of a structure of thinking which is not unrelated to the formation of structuralist sensibilities as well. (Consider Croce's autonomously functioning 'distinctions' in relation to Althusser, for instance.)

46 *Quaderni*, p. 1677.

47 ibid., p. 1821. See also *SCW*, p. 99.

48 See *Quaderni*, pp. 1821, 2122, 2195, 1677.

49 ibid., p. 2122.

50 ibid., p. 2194.

51 ibid., p. 2195.

52 Walter Benjamin, 'The Work of Art in the Age of Mechanical Reproduction' in *Illuminations: Essays and Reflections*, ed. and introduction Hannah Arendt (Schocken Books, New York, 1968), pp. 217–53, original German edn 1955.

53 Walter Benjamin, 'The Author as Producer', in *Reflections: Essays, Apho-*

risms, Autobiographical Writings, ed. Peter Demetz, tr. Edmund Jephcott (Schocken Books, New York, 1978), pp. 220–39.

54 For Benjamin's critique of 'high culture', see his *Der Stratege im Literaturkampf.*

4 GRAMSCI'S THEORY OF CONSCIOUSNESS

1 Antonio Gramsci, *Selections from Cultural Writings*, ed. David Forgacs and Geoffrey Nowell Smith, tr. William Boelhower (Harvard University Press, Cambridge, Mass., 1985), pp. 136–47, contains the major prison notes on Pirandello. Hereafter referred to as *SCW*.

2 ibid., pp. 81–6.

3 ibid., pp. 138–40.

4 ibid., p. 138.

5 See Bertolt Brecht, 'Theatersituation 1917–1927', in *Gesammelte Werke 15, Schriften zum Theater 1* (Suhrkamp, Frankfurt, 1967a), p. 136, where he appreciates Piscator's theatrical apparatus. For the way in which Brecht conceives of his own theatre see ibid., p. 126, where he appears both as producer and director. For Brecht's discussion of his preference for a speculative audience, rather than an emotional one, see ibid., p. 140.

6 *SCW*, pp. 144–5.

7 ibid.

8 ibid., p. 145.

9 ibid., p. 144.

10 See Niksa Stipčevič, *Gramsci e i problemi letterari*, Civiltà letteraria del novecento, no. 11 (Mursia, Milan, 1968).

11 Georg Lukács, *Soul and Form*, tr. Anne Bostock (MIT Press, Cambridge, Mass., 1974), pp. 22–33, original German edn 1911; and his *History and Class Consciousness: Studies in Marxist Dialectics*, tr. Rodney Livingstone (MIT Press, Cambridge, Mass., 1971b), original German edn 1923.

12 *SCW*, p. 145.

13 ibid.

14 ibid.

15 See Martin Jay, *Marxism and Totality: The Adventures of a Concept from Lukács to Habermas* (University of California Press, Berkeley and Los Angeles, Ca, 1984), p. 159, fn. 39, where Jay also refers to Adamson's *Hegemony and Revolution* in order to support his case. See, in this context, Antonio Gramsci, *Quaderni del carcere*, ed. Valentino Gerratana, 4 vols (Giulio Einaudi Editore, Turin, 1975), pp. 287–8, hereafter referred to as *Quaderni*, and Gabriele Carletti, 'Gramsci e la critica della teoria psicoanalitica', *Trimestre* 13–14, 14–1 (1980–1), 71–99.

16 Raymond Williams is one of our contemporary critics who indefatigably evokes Gramsci's originality in most of his writings. Gramsci's outstanding status as a theorist in Britain owes much to Williams.

17 The non-distinction between civil and political society has become a major issue in pro-Althusserian and anti-Althusserian debates. For Althusser, see both his *Lenin and Philosophy and Other Essays*, tr. Ben Brewster (Monthly Review Press, New York, 1971) and *For Marx*, tr. Ben Brewster (Verso, London, 1977), original French edn 1965.

Notes

18 Raymond Williams, *Marxism and Literature* (Oxford University Press, Oxford, 1977), pp. 108–15.
19 *SCW*, p. 183, and *Quaderni*, pp. 2341–51.
20 *SCW*, p. 389.
21 ibid.
22 ibid., p. 409.
23 ibid.
24 ibid., pp. 386–427.
25 ibid., p. 126.
26 ibid., p. 379; and *Quaderni*, pp. 1676–7.
27 'Oratory, Conversation, Culture' in *SCW*, pp. 380–5.
28 'Popular Literature' in ibid., pp. 379–80.
29 'The Operatic Conception of Life' in ibid., pp. 377–8.
30 'Statistics' in ibid., pp. 365–6.
31 'Influence of French Romantic Serials' in ibid., pp. 345–6.
32 'Various Types of Popular Novel' in ibid., pp. 359–62.
33 ibid., p. 359.
34 'The Heroes of Popular Literature' in ibid., p. 350.
35 ibid.
36 '*Guerin Meschino*' in ibid., pp. 350–1.
37 ibid., pp. 356–7.
38 ibid., p. 349.
39 ibid., pp. 349–50.
40 Paul Breines, 'Notes on Lukács' "The Old Culture and the New Culture"', in Bart Grahl and Paul Piccone (eds), *Towards a New Marxism* (Telos Press, St Louis, Miss., 1973), p. 9.
41 See *Quaderni*, pp. 2303–5, where Gramsci speaks of a '*classe media*' or a 'middle-class formation'. In *Quaderni*, pp. 302–3, where Gramsci designs the contours of a 'history of the subaltern classes', he speaks of the proletarians of the middle ages, whom he differentiates from the '*popolo*' – probably referring to the '*popolo minuto*' as compared to the '*popolo grasso*', the unskilled workers on the margins as compared to the urban bourgeoisie of the city states. Notes on the Taylorized worker are in *Quaderni*, pp. 288–90 and in *SCW*, pp. 262–4.
42 *SCW*, p. 34.
43 ibid., pp. 34–7.
44 See Walter Benjamin, 'Dienstmädchenromane des vorigen Jahrhunderts' in *Aussichten: Illustrierte Aufsätze* (Frankfurt, Suhrkamp, Inseltaschenbuch, 1977), p. 48: 'For the moment it is still difficult to approach these rather unpolished works. It is somewhat strange to think seriously of books which have never been part of a "library". Let us not forget that a book used to be an object of use-value, even a nutrient. These ones here [i.e. the *Dienstmädchenromane*] used to be eaten with one bite. Let us study the chemistry of the nutritional content of these novels!'
45 See ibid. See also his 'Der Autor als Produzent' or 'The Author as Producer' in *Reflections: Essays, Aphorisms, Autobiographical Writings*, ed. Peter Demetz, tr. Edmund Jephcott (Schocken Books, New York, 1978), pp. 220–39, where Benjamin contends that a genuine dialectical approach

to culture has no use whatsoever for isolating individual cultural products.

46 Benjamin, 'Dienstmädchenromane', op. cit., p. 46.
47 'The Book Fair' in *SCW*, p. 364.
48 For Benjamin see his essay 'The Author as Producer' in *Reflections*, op. cit., where he understands the newspaper as an instrument by which the people themselves would be able to intervene in the affairs of the day; in this they would not only be readers, but they could also become writers.
49 'Types of Periodicals' in *SCW*, pp. 412–18.
50 ibid., p. 417.
51 ibid.
52 'Journalism: Intellectual Movements and Centres' in ibid., pp. 405–6.
53 'Serial Novels' in ibid., pp. 34–7.
54 For a discussion of discursive practices in Italy in the 1970s see Renate Holub, 'Towards a New Rationality? Notes on Feminism and Current Discursive Practices in Italy', *Discourse* 4 (1982), 89–107.
55 *SCW*, p. 371.
56 ibid.
57 ibid., p. 373.
58 ibid., pp. 373–4.
59 ibid., p. 374.
60 *Quaderni*, p. 2133.
61 Ernst Bloch, 'Anticipatory Consciousness', in *The Principle of Hope*, tr. Neville Plaice, Stephen Plaice and Paul Knight, 3 vols (MIT Press, Cambridge, Mass., 1986), pp. 45–339, original German edn 1972.
62 Antonio Gramsci, *Selections from the Prison Notebooks*, ed. and tr. Quintin Hoare and Geoffrey Nowell Smith (International Publishers, New York, 1971), p. 303.

5 PHENOMENOLOGY, LINGUISTICS, HEGEMONY

1 Antonio Gramsci, *Lettere dal carcere*, ed. Sergio Caprioglio and Elsa Fubini (Einaudi, Turin, 1965), p. 248, hereafter referred to as *LC*. Most of the time I found it easiest to translate the passages myself rather than quoting from the two English editions of the letters that exist. For one thing, many of the letters I cite have not been included in the English editions, and for another, I prefer to paraphrase or translate loosely rather than literally. However, I have consulted all the letters available in English, and my translating has often been facilitated by these existing translations. When my own translation was very close to one included in the English editions of the letters, I usually adapted my version to the existing translation and quoted accordingly.
2 *LC*, p. 255, 9 February 1929.
3 Antonio Gramsci, *Quaderni del carcere*, ed. Valentino Gerratana, 4 vols (Giulio Einaudi Editore, Turin, 1975), p. 5, hereafter referred to as *Quaderni*.
4 See Antonio Gramsci, *Selections from Cultural Writings*, ed. David Forgacs and Geoffrey Nowell Smith, tr. William Boelhower (Harvard University

Press, Cambridge, Mass., 1985), pp. 147–50, hereafter referred to as *SCW*.

5 See his letters to Tatiana Schucht: 2 February 1931; 17 August 1931; 7 September 1931; 20 September 1931; 22 February 1932; 21 March 1932; all in *LC*.

6 See Frank Rosengarten, 'Gramsci's "Little Discovery": Gramsci's Interpretation of Canto X of Dante's Inferno', in *Boundary 2* (Special Issue, *The Legacy of Antonio Gramsci*, ed. Joseph Buttigieg) 14, 3 (1986), 71–91; an earlier version of this article, presented at the MLA 1979 in San Francisco, also holds to the father-son parallels between the two Cavalcantis and Gramsci and his father.

7 Hamish Henderson (ed.), *Gramsci's Prison Letters: Lettere dal Carcere* (Zwan Publications, London, 1988), p. 193. See 22 February 1932, to Tatiana Schucht, *LC*, p. 575.

8 ibid.

9 *SCW*, pp. 151–2.

10 *LC*, p. 492.

11 ibid., p. 490.

12 For an outstanding introduction to the methodology of phenomenology see Paul Piccone, 'Phenomenological Marxism', in Bart Grahl and Paul Piccone (eds), *Towards a New Marxism* (Telos Press, St Louis, Miss., 1973), pp. 133–58.

13 The history and chronology of Soviet semiotics and linguistics in the 1920s and 1930s is very complex. It is, therefore, difficult to establish whether Gramsci anticipated some of the insights of Soviet linguistics or how he was exposed to it. Klaus Bochmann, 'Sprache als Kultur und Weltanschauung. Zur Sprachauffassung Antonio Gramscis', in Antonio Gramsci, *Notizen zur Sprache und Kultur* (Gustav Kiepenheuer Verlag, Leipzig and Weimar, 1984), pp. 7–39, has suggested that in many ways Gramsci's social linguistics precedes the work of Vološinov. As I have shown in the previous chapters, I am not so much interested in establishing 'influences', but prefer rather to proceed homologically.

14 The extent to which Gramsci operates with a conceptual apparatus that is similar to semiotics and narratology becomes apparent when reading a rather recent publication by Cesare Segre, *Teatro e romanzo* (Einaudi Editore, Turin, 1984). This well-known Italian theorist analyses in this book the structural similarities of diegetic and mimetic discourses against the background of Russian formalism, Prague structuralism and the theoretical advances made in this area in France and Italy.

15 See in particular ibid., as well as Segre's *Le strutture e il tempo* (Einaudi, Turin, 1974), which takes into consideration, next to narrative and drama, the structure of poetic models as well. Also of interest is the appendix 'On the Functions of Language in Theater' which Roman Ingarden included in his *The Literary Work of Art: An Investigation on the Borderlines of Ontology, Logic, and Theory of Literature*, tr. and introduction George G. Grabowicz (Northwestern University Press, Evanston, Ill., 1973), pp. 377–96.

16 *SCW*, p. 153.

17 Roland Barthes, *The Pleasure of the Text*, tr. Richard Miller (Hill & Lang, New York, 1975), original French edn 1973.

18 *SCW*, p. 152.

19 See his *How To Do Things With Words*, ed. J. O. Urmson and Marina Sbisà, 2nd edn 1976 (Harvard University Press, Cambridge, Mass., 1962).

20 Dialogicity of language refers to various linguistic theories, above all to those of Mikhail Bakhtin, *The Dialogic Imagination*, ed. Michael Holquist, tr. Caryl Emerson and Michael Holquist (University of Texas Press, Austin, Tex., 1981) and V. N. Vološinov, *Marxism and the Philosophy of Language*, tr. Ladislav Matejka and I.R. Titunik (Harvard University Press, Cambridge, Mass. and London, 1986), in particular chapter 3 on verbal interaction, pp. 83–98. Yet I am also thinking of Emile Benveniste, *Problems in General Linguistics*, tr. Mary Elizabeth Meek (University of Miami Press, Coral Gables, Fla, 1971), original French edn 1966, who emphasizes both the subjectivity (the I) and the intersubjectivity (the you) residing in the linguistic act.

21 For Vladimir Propp see his *Morphology of the Folktale*, 1st edn tr. Laurence Scott, introduction Svatava Pirkova-Jakobson, 2nd edn rev., ed. and preface Louis A. Wagner, new introduction Alan Dundes (University of Texas Press, Austin, Tex. and London, 1968, 1979), original Russian edn 1928.

22 *LC*, p. 492.

23 There are quite a few instances in Gramsci's *Prison Notebooks* where he distinguishes a work of art from other human activities, where he upholds, that is, the separation between art and life generally attributed to modern (idealist) aesthetic theory. These passages have not gone unnoticed, and critics in general understand them as vestiges of Croce's influence on Gramsci. See the controversies concerning Gramsci's 'Croceanism' in Pietro Rossi (ed.), *Gramsci e la cultura contemporanea*, 2 vols (Editori Riuniti, Rome, 1969, 1975), in particular pp. 265–305. See also pp. 27–51 of Rocco Musolini, 'Gramsci e il metodo della critica letteraria', in *Marxismo ed estetica in Italia* (Editori Riuniti, Rome, 1971).

24 *LC*, p. 492.

25 ibid.

26 ibid., p. 493.

27 ibid., pp. 464–9.

28 Franco Lo Piparo, *Lingua Intellettuali Egemonia in Gramsci* (Laterza, Rome-Bari, 1979), is a highly recommendable book on Gramsci and linguistics. A good introduction to this topic has also been provided by Bochmann, op. cit.

29 See his notes on this issue in *SCW*, pp. 167–88.

30 I am referring to Vološinov, op. cit.

31 *SCW*, p. 153.

32 ibid.

33 ibid., pp. 153–4.

34 Vološinov, op. cit., p. 35.

35 ibid., p. 82.

36 ibid., p. 117.

37 Quoted from Ladislav Matejka, 'On the First Russian Prolegomena to Semiotics', in Vološinov, op. cit., p. 168.

38 ibid., p. 169.

39 Lo Piparo points out that Matteo Bartoli, Gramsci's teacher in linguistics, published, towards the end of his life, a volume of his writings which he understood as a linguistics of space, *Saggi di linguistica spaziale*. See Lo Piparo, op. cit., pp. 63–6.

40 ibid., p. 105; Bochmann, op. cit., and *SCW*, pp. 183–4.

41 In his essay 'On the Southern Question', Gramsci reflects on the position of the northern workers, exploited by capitalism, with respect to the southern peasants, also exploited by capitalism. The question for him is why did these two social classes, both subject to the hegemony of capitalism with its industries and banks, not enter into an alliance against capitalism and the fascist formation it supported in the 1920s. What Gramsci highlights here is not only that peasants and workers speak a similar language with respect to the capitalists. They also resent their exploitation. Yet, on the other hand, the workers in the north speak a different language from the peasants in the south in that they have assimilated, in the practices of everyday life, northern points of view which reflect the position and ideology of the capitalist – a position and ideology profitable to the capitalist, but not to the northern worker. As, for instance, when northern workers maintain that people in the south are lazy by nature, criminal, backward and so forth. By the same token Gramsci explains how the intellectuals in the south, belonging to the rural petty and middle bourgeoisie, speak the language of the south with respect to the north, as well as the language of national Italian bureaucracy (three-fifths of the Italian bureaucracy of the time was staffed by southerners), in addition to the language that mediates between the peasants and the landowners, thereby cementing an agrarian bloc that benefits the north. And they speak the language of the history of Italian culture as well. All of these languages, positions and consciousnesses, which contributed to the volatility of the southern intellectual, interface now and interfaced then in the period of the fascists' takeover of power. They opted for fascism. See Gramsci, *The Modern Prince and Other Writings*, tr. Louis Marks (International Publishers, New York, 1957, 10th printing 1987), pp. 29–51.

42 For Merleau-Ponty see his *The Primacy of Perception*, tr. and introduction James M. Edie (Northwestern University Press, Evanston, Ill., 1964), pp. 3–12. And his 'The Intertwining – The Chiasm' in *The Visible and the Invisible*, ed. Claude Lefort, tr. Alfonso Lingis (Northwestern University Press, Evanston, Ill., 1968), pp. 130–56, original French edn 1964.

43 See Alfred Schutz, *The Phenomenology of the Social World*, tr. George Walsh and Frederick Lehnert, introduction George Walsh (Northwestern University Press, Evanston, Ill., 1967), original German edn 1932.

44 *LC*, p. 7.

45 ibid.

46 ibid., p. 3.

47 ibid., pp. 300–1. As usual, I consulted Lynne Lawner's edition of Gramsci's *Letters from Prison* (Noonday Press, Farrar, Straus & Giroux, New

York, 1973), pp. 154–5, hereafter referred to as Lawner, *Letters*, and some expressions were inspired by her.

48 *LC*, p. 301.
49 Lawner, *Letters*, pp. 61–4.
50 ibid., p. 111.
51 ibid., p. 188.
52 ibid., p. 268.
53 ibid., p. 266.
54 Letter to Tatiana Schucht, ibid., pp. 156–7.
55 Paul Piccone, in the above-mentioned essay on 'Marxism and Phenomenology', views Gramsci as one of the figures to be learned from in the context of a phenomenological Marxism. The trajectory of the Italian version of phenomenology is yet to be made out in its complexity, in its relation to the Italian and non-Italian philosophical traditions, that is. It would surely include figures such as Antonio Banfi and Enzo Paci, as well as Luigi Pagliari. For pioneering work in this area published in English see Peter Carravetta, 'An Introduction to the Hermeneutics of Luigi Pareyson', *Differentia* 3–4 (1989), 217–41.

6 GRAMSCI AND THE AGE OF INFORMATION TECHNOLOGY

1 A beautiful collection of some hitherto unpublished letters is Antonio A. Santucci (ed.), *Nuove lettere di Antonio Gramsci, con altre lettere di Piero Sraffa*, preface Nicola Badaloni (Editori Riuniti, Rome 1986). This collection, better than most others, gives an insight into Sraffa's dedication to saving a friend and one of the leaders of the Italian working-class movement from the fascist prisons. Since Tatiana Schucht regularly informed Sraffa of the contents of Gramsci's letters to her, Sraffa assumed the objectively almost impossible role of monitoring Gramsci's psychological well-being via suggestions to Tatiana Schucht which she in turn incorporated into her letters to Gramsci. Sraffa also constituted a link between Gramsci (via Tatiana Schucht) and the outside political world. The precise nature of Gramsci's interactions with the political world (via Schucht via Sraffa) is somewhat hazy. In her *Per Gramsci* (Il Mulino, Bologna, 1974), pp. 372–90, Maria Antonietta Macciocchi, describing her visit in the 1970s to an old Piero Sraffa residing in Cambridge, Britain, unmistakably suggests that the haziness surrounding Gramsci's political relations while in prison is unlikely to be dispelled.
2 See Nicola Badaloni, 'Preface', in Santucci, op. cit., p. 13, fn. 10. By many accounts, Gramsci's mental and physical health began seriously to deteriorate by the summer of 1931, by his fifth year in prison, that is.
3 Mark Poster, *Critical Theory and Poststructuralism: In Search of a Context* (Cornell University Press, Ithaca, NY and London,1989), as well as his *The Mode of Information: Poststructuralism and Social Context* (University of Chicago Press, Chicago, 1990).
4 From 1914 on Gramsci worked as a journalist for a variety of newspapers and journals. Among these are the weekly *Grido del popolo*, an organ of the socialist federation of Turin, the directorship of which he would assume in the politically tumultuous years of 1917–18. In addition, he wrote as a

cultural critic and polemicist for the Piedmont edition of *Avanti*, the paper of the Socialist Party. His journal *La città futura*, which he launched for young socialists, lasted only one number. His most important journalistic venture is his work with *Ordine Nuovo*, a cultural weekly of the socialists, founded on 1 May 1919, which became a daily by 1 January 1921 under the directorship of Gramsci. By 1924, the *Ordine Nuovo* had become a bi-monthly, whereas *L'Unità* (12 February 1924) would become the daily paper of the Italian working class. It still exists and carries this name today.

5 Many other journals and their producers should be mentioned here, and the function both fulfilled in cultural politics of the time. Among these are *Lacerba, La Voce, Leonardo*, some of which were quite short-lived. For an overview of the cultural scene under consideration see Nicola Badaloni and Carlo Muscetta (eds), *Labriola, Croce, Gentile* (Editori Laterza, Bari, 1978).

6 Gramsci's trajectory as intellectual in the years 1914–21 (the young Gramsci) is traced in a variety of studies. Among these I recommend: Walter L. Adamson, *Hegemony and Revolution: A Study of Antonio Gramsci's Political and Cultural Theory* (University of California Press, Berkeley and Los Angeles, Ca and London, 1980) and Alastair Davidson, *Antonio Gramsci: Towards an Intellectual Biography* (Merlin Press, London and Humanities Press, New Jersey, 1977). Edo Bellingeri, *Dall'intellettuale al politico. Le 'Cronache Teatrali' di Gramsci* (Dedalo libri, Bari, 1975) focuses on Gramsci's theatrical criticism. Pedro Cavalcanti and Paul Piccone (eds), *History, Philosophy and Culture in the Young Gramsci* (Telos Press, St Louis, Miss., 1975) include writings from the young Gramsci in English, and Sergio Caprioglio's edition of Antonio Gramsci, *Cronache Torinesi 1913–1917* (Giulio Einaudi Editore, Turin, 1980b), has Italian versions of these early writings.

7 Antonio Gramsci, 'Culture and Class Struggle', in *Selections from Cultural Writings*, ed. David Forgacs and Geoffrey Nowell Smith, tr. William Boelhower (Harvard University Press, Cambridge, Mass., 1985), p. 32, originally published in *Grido del Popolo*, 25 May 1918. Hereafter referred to as *SCW*.

8 ibid., p. 33.

9 Gramsci's tirades against the 'indifferents' stem from his article entitled 'Gli Indifferenti', published in *La città futura*. See Cesare Colombo (ed.), *Gramsci e il suo tempo*, introduction Mario Spinella, text Francesca Occhipinti (Longanesi & Co., Milan, 1977), p. 39.

10 Piero Gobetti represents, in some sense, the liberal counterpart to Gramsci. He, like Gramsci, participated in the construction of a new cultural democratic life for Italy after World War I. He launched journals and founded a publishing house and, not unlike Gramsci, he suffered a very premature death at the hands of fascist squads. Attacked and mutilated by fascists for his commitment to democratic practices, Gobetti went into exile in France, where he soon died of the wounds inflicted on him by the fascists. Yet Gobetti also represents a liberal counterpart to Croce, whose attitude towards the fascists was never quite as one-linear as many of his biographers would have us believe. See Colombo, op. cit., p. 66. Gramsci

speaks eloquently of Gobetti in one of his major essays, 'On the Southern Question' in *The Modern Prince and Other Writings*, tr. Louis Marks (International Publishers, New York, 1957, 10th printing 1987), pp. 48–50.

11 ibid., pp. 28–51.

12 ibid., pp. 44–7.

13 ibid., p. 32.

14 ibid., p. 31.

15 Gramsci is thinking of Benedetto Croce here, but also of Giustino Fortunato; ibid., p. 42.

16 ibid.

17 ibid., p. 43.

18 Antonio Gramsci, *Selections from the Prison Notebooks*, ed. and tr. Quintin Hoare and Geoffrey Nowell Smith (International Publishers, New York, 1971), p. 8, hereafter referred to as *SPN*.

19 ibid., 8.

20 Anne Showstack Sassoon, 'The People, Intellectuals and Specialized Knowledge', in *Boundary 2* (Special Issue, *The Legacy of Antonio Gramsci*, ed. Joseph Buttigieg) 14 (3) (Spring 1986), 137–68.

21 For a very informative overview of progressive intellectual movements in Italy in the nineteenth century see Paul Piccone, *Italian Marxism* (University of California Press, Berkeley, Ca, 1983).

22 Gramsci, 'On the Southern Question', op. cit., p. 50.

23 ibid., p. 12.

24 ibid.

25 ibid., pp. 8–10.

26 *SPN*, p. 8.

27 Gramsci's notes on the history of the Italian intellectual in general contain a sharp critique. In his analysis of the attitude of the Italian intellectuals during humanism and the Renaissance, he points to the unrealistic nature of many major intellectuals during the period. While other European countries engaged in economic, political, social and cultural centralization, as did France and Britain, for instance, Italy postponed its transformation. Its intellectuals, notes Gramsci, were cosmopolitan in outlook rather than focusing on national issues. See his many notes on the issue, in particular the 'Quaderno 12' of his *Quaderni del carcere*, ed. Valentino Gerratana, 4 vols (Giulio Einaudi Editore, Turin, 1975), pp. 1513–52; also pp. 652–3, 906, 1054, 1828–9, 1910, 1913, 1935, 2350.

28 *SPN*, pp. 8–10.

29 ibid., p. 5.

30 ibid., p. 9.

31 ibid., p. 10.

32 ibid., p. 323.

33 ibid.

34 ibid.

35 ibid.

36 ibid., p. 266.

37 For a discussion of Vico's notion of the intellectual see Renate Holub, 'Giambattista Vico's Theory of Poetics and Aesthetics', unpublished dissertation (University of Wisconsin, Madison, Wisc., 1983), available

from University Microfilms International, Ann Arbor, Mich., 1983, in particular chapter 5, 'On the Historicity of Poetry'. There has been, of late, a discussion among intellectual historians dealing with Italy concerning the specificity of an Italian trajectory in philosophy and theory marked by a penchant towards practical and social philosophy rather than epistemology, metaphysics, or science. Among these intellectual historians is Edmund Jacobitti, who has been tracing a distinct trajectory from Machiavelli to Vico and to Gramsci. His book on the topic is forthcoming. Similarly, in recent discussions of postmodernism in Italy, the specificity of Italian postmodernism, represented mostly by the 'Pensiero debole', is viewed as an attempt to insist on a minimum of practical philosophy rather than abandoning ethics and metaphysics altogether. For an assessment of this phenomenon in the late twentieth century see Giovanna Borradori, *Recoding Metaphysics: The New Italian Philosophy* (Northwestern University Press, Evanston, Ill., 1988), in particular her introduction, as well as Renate Holub, 'For the Record: the Non-Language of Italian Feminist Philosophy' in *Romance Language Annual* 1 (1990), 133–40, which emphasizes the practical nature of Italian philosophy in the realm of feminism. A distinctly practically oriented way of philosophizing as supported by Italian feminism is also at issue in Renate Holub, 'Towards a New Rationality? Notes on Feminism and Current Discursive Practices in Italy' in *Discourse* 4 (1982), 89–107. For a discussion of the complexity of this issue which posits more than one trajectory of Italian philosophy on the basis of the concept and the historical event of humanism see Renate Holub, 'Critical Il/literacy: Humanism, Heidegger, Anti-Humanism', *Differentia* 3–4 (1989), 73–90. A different point of view concerning Italian contemporary philosophy is presented by Peter Carravetta, 'Repositioning Interpretive Discourse', *Differentia* 2 (1988), 83–127.

38 In the introduction to the second edition of her excellent *Gramsci's Politics* (Hutchinson, London and Melbourne, 1987), pp. ix–xxi, Anne Showstack Sassoon puts it like this: 'Gramsci may be enormously suggestive, but he is also very difficult.... [His] argument is much more complex than the one usually presented. His writings cannot be "applied". They do not constitute a manual' (pp. ix and x).

39 In her introduction to the Hutchinson edition of ibid., Sassoon makes reference to the use of some of the Gramscian concepts, such as passive revolution, in political theory as it develops in the Latin American world. See fn. 8, p. xx.

40 Much debate surrounds the two terms of modernism and postmodernism. David Harvey, *The Condition of Postmodernity* (Basil Blackwell Ltd, Oxford and Cambridge, 1989) has recently rehearsed many of the debates, in particular on pp. 38–65.

41 See ibid., where Harvey puts the case like this: 'Yet we still live, in the West, in a society where production for profit remains the basic organizing principle of economic life' (p. 121). I have profited immensely from the various parts of this book, in particular from Harvey's discussion of the transformations in the economic sector.

42 Poster, *Critical Theory and Poststructuralism*, pp. 3–11.

43 Ernesto Laclau and Chantal Mouffe, *Hegemony and Socialist Strategy:*

Towards a Radical Democratic Politics (Verso, London and New York, 1985), pursue this vision by relying in large parts on Gramsci. Focusing on the importance of hegemony as the expression of the amalgamation of politics and culture, of coercion and consent, shows that political alternatives, or counter-hegemonies, will arise not from political action in the traditional sense but from the politicization of the cultural sphere. The emphasis thus shifts from politics to culture, from political organization to social and cultural formations.

44 In a recent publication, Fredric Jameson reiterates the political nature of Adorno's project in *Late Marxism. Adorno, or, The Persistence of the Dialectic* (Verso, London, 1990).

45 For an introduction to the most pertinent issues in information technology, including how they relate to non-western cultures, see a collection of essays edited by Tom Forester, *The Information Technology Revolution* (MIT Press, Boston, Mass., 1985). Colin Norman, *The God That Limps: Science and Technology in the Eighties* (A Worldwatch Institute Book, W.W. Norton & Co., New York and London, 1981), is a critique of some technological advances, and its premiss is extendable to information technology. Arnold Pacey, *The Culture of Technology* (MIT Press, Boston, Mass., 1983) examines current technology from the perspective of under-developed countries, and Theodore Roszak, *The Cult of Information: The Folklore of Computers and the True Art of Thinking* (Pantheon, New York, 1986), sceptically views the application of computer technology in the production of critical thinking. Stewart Brand, *The Media Lab: Inventing the Future at M.I.T.* (Viking Penguin, New York, 1987), is a delightful account of information technologies and media technologies as they develop at MIT.

46 Yoneji Masuda, 'Computopia', in Forester, op. cit., pp. 620–34.

47 This vision is also related to the notion of the 'Big Brother society' and to Marshall McLuhan. In humanistic circles, Jean-François Lyotard carries the day with his notion of a steady homogenization of a society submitted to almost total surveillance and control, in that the information society self-regulates the production and reproduction of facts and interpretation. See his *The Postmodern Condition: A Report on Knowledge*, tr. Geoff Bennington and Brian Massumi, foreword Fredric Jameson (University of Minnesota Press, Minneapolis, Minn., 1984), pp. 11–14. See also various versions of systems theory, in particular Niklas Luhmann, *Legitimation durch Verfahren* (Luchterhand, Neuwied, 1969) and his *The Differentiation of Society*, tr. Stephen Holmes and Charles Latmore (Columbia University Press, New York, 1982).

48 See his 'Answering the Question: What is Postmodernism', in *The Postmodern Condition*, op. cit., pp. 71–82.

49 With respect to the latter I am referring to systems theory as we know it from Luhmann. See Jürgen Habermas and Niklas Luhmann, *Theorie der Gesellschaft oder Sozialtechnologie* (Suhrkamp, Frankfurt, 1982), for the Habermas–Luhmann debate. With respect to the few intellectuals who seem to know what can be done I am referring to the theory of the intellectual as propounded by Lyotard, in *The Postmodern Condition*, op. cit., pp. 71–82, as well as by Michel Foucault: see his 'Intellectuals and Power' in

Language, Counter-Memory, Practice: Selected Essays and Interviews, ed. and introduction Donald F. Bouchard, tr. Donald F. Bouchard and Sherry Simon (Cornell University Press, Ithaca, NY, 1977), pp. 205–18; as well as his 'Two Lectures' in *Power/Knowledge: Selected Interviews and Other Writings 1972–1977*, ed. Colin Gordon, tr. Colin Gordon, Leo Marshall, John Mepham and Kate Soper (Pantheon, New York, 1980), pp. 78–109.

50 See Chris Freeman, 'Long Waves of Economic Development' in Forester, op. cit., pp. 603–16.

51 Harvey, op. cit., p. 150.

52 Barbara Ehrenreich, *Fear of Falling: The Inner Life of the Middle Class* (HarperCollins, New York, 1989), uses this term on p. 209.

53 Juan Rada, 'Information Technology and the Third World', in Forester, op. cit., pp. 571–89.

54 ibid., p. 581.

55 *SPN*, p. 8.

56 See Stephen Gill, 'Intellectuals and Transnational Capital', in Ralph Miliband and Leo Panitch (eds), *The Retreat of the Intellectuals: Socialist Register 1990* (Merlin Press, London, 1990), pp. 290–310.

57 I would like to refer again to Gill's 'Intellectuals and Transnational Capital', pp. 290–310, for further details and explanations.

58 See Andrew Ross, *No Respect: Intellectuals and Popular Culture* (Routledge, New York and London, 1989), in particular pp. 209–32. See also Andrew Ross (ed.) *Universal Abandon? The Politics of Postmodernism* (University of Minnesota Press, Minneapolis, Minn., 1988). In the same vein, consider Jim Merod, *The Political Responsibility of the Critic* (Cornell University Press, Ithaca, NY, 1987).

59 Ross, *No Respect: Intellectuals and Popular Culture*, p. 229.

60 ibid.

61 As a text for interested readers I recommend *The Chomsky Reader*, ed. James Peck (Pantheon Books, New York, 1987), in particular because of its apposite essay on 'The Responsibility of Intellectuals', pp. 59–137.

62 Russell Jacoby, *The Last Intellectuals: American Culture in the Age of Academe* (Noonday Press, New York, 1987).

63 Chomsky, op. cit., p. 28.

64 ibid.

65 Louis Althusser, *Lenin and Philosophy and Other Essays*, tr. Ben Brewster (Monthly Review Press, New York, 1971) and his *For Marx*, tr. Ben Brewster (Verso, London, 1977).

66 Lyotard, op. cit., in particular his discussion of the legitimation of performativity.

67 See Jürgen Habermas, *The Theory of Communicative Action*, vol. 1, *Reason and the Rationalization of Society*, tr. Thomas McCarthy (Beacon Press, Boston, Mass., 1984), and in particular vol. 2, *Lifeworld and System: A Critique of Functionalist Reason*, tr. Thomas McCarthy (Beacon Press, Boston, Mass., 1987) (vols 1 and 2, Beacon Paperback 1989).

68 Nancy Fraser, 'What's Critical about Critical Theory? The Case of Habermas and Gender', in Seyla Benhabib and Drucilla Cornell (eds),

Feminism as Critique (University of Minnesota Press, Minneapolis, Minn., 1987), pp. 31–56.
69 Seyla Benhabib, 'The Generalized and the Concrete Other', in ibid., pp. 76–95.

7 IN LIEU OF A CONCLUSION

1 Perhaps the best introduction not to these women's relationship to Gramsci, but to Gramci's relationship with Tatiana Schucht and Giulia Schucht are his letters, most of them collected in *Lettere dal carcere*, ed. Sergio Caprioglio and Elsa Fubini (Einaudi, Turin, 1965, fifth edn 1975). An English edition of this particular collection is still to come. What is available in English is a collection, *Letters from Prison*, ed., tr. and introduction Lynne Lawner (Noonday Press, Farrar, Straus & Giroux, New York, 1989), first edn by Harper & Row, 1973. Some Italian feminists have attempted, in the 1970s, to reconstruct Gramsci's relationship to the sisters Schucht, including an older sister, Olga. See Adele Cambria, *Amore Come Rivoluzione* (Sugar Edizioni, Milan, 1976). Working exclusively with the letters, both published and unpublished, in particular with the unpublished letters written by the women, which Gramsci's editors have not thought of including in the editions of his letters, Cambria suggests a complex relationship among the three sisters, which in turn would explain why rather than remaining beside Gramsci in Italy, Giulia Schucht returned to Moscow shortly before his arrest. The complexities of the relations among the three Schucht sisters were presented in a play, *Nonostante Gramsci*, which Cambria reproduced in *Amore Come Rivoluzione*, pp. 207–73. For a comment on this play see Teresa de Lauretis, 'Gramsci Notwithstanding, or, The Left Hand of History', in her *Technologies of Gender* (Indiana University Press, Bloomington and Indianapolis, Ind., 1987), pp. 84–95. Antonio A. Santucci (ed.), *Nuove lettere di Antonio Gramsci, con altre lettere di Piero Sraffa*, preface Nicola Badaloni (Editori Riuniti, Rome, 1986), emphasizes the genuine feelings Gramsci seems to have had for Giulia Schucht while simultaneously commenting on the efforts of Gramsci's friends to get him out of prison. Most published Gramsci biographies do not pay any particular attention to the women in his life. For initial familiarization with the major dates and encounters in Gramsci's life see Giuseppe Fiori, *Life of a Revolutionary*, tr. Tom Nairn (New York, E.P. Dutton & Co., 1971), original Italian edn 1967.
2 See Cambria, op. cit., p. 71: in almost all his letters, first from Vienna and then from Italy, Gramsci emphasizes that he would like Giulia with him, not only for emotional reasons, but also for political ones. So from Vienna: 'You have got to know that when you come, you will of course be working, and you will help me with my work.' And again from Vienna, this time in reference to a translation: 'You are going to help me out, aren't you? We will both put our names on it.'
3 For a collection of photographs of Gramsci and his family, and illustrating his political life, see Cesare Colombo (ed.), *Gramsci e il suo tempo*, introduction Mario Spinella, text Francesca Occhipinti (Longanesi & Co., Milan, 1977).

4 What I am referring to are the discussions on Heidegger's involvement with Nazism, as well as on Paul de Man's so-called wartime journalism, that we have witnessed over the last few years.

5 Antonio Gramsci, *Selections from the Prison Notebooks*, ed. and tr. Quintin Hoare and Geoffrey Nowell Smith (International Publishers, New York, 1971), p. 296, hereafter referred to as *SPN*. For additional entries on the question of feminism see Antonio Gramsci, *Quaderni del carcere*, ed. Valentino Gerratana, 4 vols (Giulio Einaudi Editore, Turin, 1975), pp. 531, 902–3 and 2149–50.

6 Examples of this kind would be Engels, *The Origin of the Family*, introduction Michele Barrett (Penguin, Harmondsworth, Mx, 1985), August Bebel, *Die Frau und der Sozialismus*, ed. Monika Seifert (Fackelträger-Verlag Schmidt-Küster GmbH, Hanover, 1974), original edn 1896, as well as many other documents from within and outside first-wave feminism.

7 Gramsci, *SPN*, p. 238.

8 I think that this concept is also extraordinarily powerful in analysing recent developments in eastern Europe. The explosion of racist sentiments in many eastern European countries, a sentiment which had been successfully repressed by state regulations as long as political society stayed intact, can be explained by the notion of civil society, of powerful systems of fortresses and earthworks, sturdy structures in the recesses of which racism has never been eradicated.

9 There are many points of contact between the work of Gramsci and that of Michel Foucault. So far as I know, an extended study which would examine more closely the relatedness of their texts has still to be written. With respect to some aspects of the relation between Gramsci and Foucault see R. Radhakrishnan, 'Toward an Effective Intellectual: Foucault or Gramsci', in Bruce Robbins (ed.), *Intellectuals: Aesthetics, Politics, Academics* (University of Minnesota Press, Minneapolis, Minn., 1990), pp. 59–99.

10 Gramsci, *SPN*, pp. 294–8.

11 ibid., p. 265.

12 See Norberto Bobbio, 'Gramsci and the Conception of Civil Society', one of the most important essays on this topic, published as 'Gramsci e la concezione della società civile' in Pietro Rossi (ed.), *Gramsci e la cultura contemporanea*, 2 vols (Editori Riuniti, Rome, 1969, 1975), vol. 1, pp. 75–101.

13 Nancy Hartsock, 'Foucault on Power: a Theory for Women?', in Linda J. Nicholson (ed.), *Feminism/Postmodernism* (Routledge, New York and London, 1990), pp. 157–76.

14 Joan Cocks, *The Oppositional Imagination: Feminism, Critique and Political Theory* (Routledge, London and New York, 1989), p. 19.

15 ibid., p. 6.

Bibliography

Adamson, Walter L. (1980) *Hegemony and Revolution: A Study of Antonio Gramsci's Political and Cultural Theory*, University of California Press, Berkeley and Los Angeles, Ca. and London.

Adorno, Theodor W. (1984) *Aesthetic Theory*, ed. Gretel Adorno and Rolf Tiedemann, tr. C. Lenhardt, Routledge & Kegan Paul, London and New York, original German edn 1970.

—— and Horkheimer, Max (1972) 'The Culture Industry: Enlightenment as Mass Deception', in Theodor W. Adorno and Max Horkheimer, *Dialectic of Enlightenment*, tr. John Cumming, Continuum Publishers, New York, pp. 120–67, original German edn 1947.

Althusser, Louis (1971) *Lenin and Philosophy and Other Essays*, tr. Ben Brewster, Monthly Review Press, New York.

—— (1977) *For Marx*, tr. Ben Brewster, Verso, London, original French edn 1965.

Anderson, Perry (1976–7) 'The Antinomies of Antonio Gramsci', *New Left Review* 100, 5–81.

Antonio Gramsci: A Bibliography (1987), Social Theory: a Bibliographic Series, no. 7, Reference and Research Services, Santa Cruz, Ca.

Arato, Andrew and Gebhardt, Eike (eds) (1978) *The Essential Frankfurt School Reader*, introduction Paul Piccone, Urizen Books, New York.

Austin, J. L. (1962) *How To Do Things With Words*, ed. J. O. Urmson and Marina Sbisà, 2nd edn 1976, Harvard University Press, Cambridge, Mass.

Badaloni, Nicola and Muscetta, Carlo (eds) (1978) *Labriola, Croce, Gentile*, Editori Laterza, Bari.

Bakhtin, Mikhail (1981) *The Dialogic Imagination*, ed. Michael Holquist, tr. Caryl Emerson and Michael Holquist, University of Texas Press, Austin, Tex.

Barthes, Roland (1975) *The Pleasure of the Text*, tr. Richard Miller, Hill & Lang, New York, original French edn 1973.

Baxandall, Lee and Morawski, Stefan (eds) (1973) *Marx and Engels on Literature and Art*, Telos Press, St Louis, Miss.

Bebel, August (1974) *Die Frau und der Sozialismus*, ed. Monika Seifert, Fackelträger-Verlag Schmidt-Küster GmbH, Hanover, original edn 1896.

233

Bibliography

Bellingeri, Edo (1975) *Dall'intellettuale al politico. Le 'Cronache Teatrali' di Gramsci*, Dedalo libri, Bari.

Benhabib, Seyla (1987) 'The Generalized and the Concrete Other', in Seyla Benhabib and Drucilla Cornell (eds), *Feminism as Critique*, University of Minnesota Press, Minneapolis, Minn., pp. 76–95.

Benjamin, Walter (1968) *Illuminations: Essays and Reflections*, ed. and introduction Hannah Arendt, Schocken Books, New York, pp. 217–53, original German edn 1955.

—— (1974) *Der Stratege im Literaturkampf: Zur Literaturwissenschaft*, ed. Hella Tiedemann-Bartels, Suhrkamp, Frankfurt.

—— (1977) 'Dienstmädchenromane des vorigen Jahrhunderts', in *Aussichten: Illustrierte Aufsätze*, Suhrkamp, Inseltaschenbuch, Frankfurt, pp. 46–54.

—— (1978) *Reflections: Essays, Aphorisms, Autobiographical Writings*, ed. Peter Demetz, tr. Edmund Jephcott, Schocken Books, New York.

Benveniste, Emile (1971) *Problems in General Linguistics*, tr. Mary Elizabeth Meek, University of Miami Press, Coral Gables, Fla, original French edn 1966.

Betz, Albrecht (1987) 'Lukács als Literaturstratege', in *Verdinglichung und Utopie: Ernst Bloch und Georg Lukács zum 100. Geburtstag*, ed. Michael Löwy, Arno Münster and Nicolas Tertulian, Sender Verlag, Frankfurt, pp. 150–9.

Biondi, Marino (1977) *Guida bibliografica a Gramsci*, presentation Renato Zangheri, Libreria Adamo Bettini, Cesena.

Bloch, Ernst (1973) 'Diskussionen über den Expressionismus', in Hans-Jürgen Schmitt, *Die Expressionismusdebatte: Materialien zu einer marxistischen Realismuskonzeption*, Suhrkamp, Frankfurt, pp. 180–92.

—— (1986) 'Anticipatory Consciousness', in *The Principle of Hope*, tr. Neville Plaice, Stephen Plaice and Paul Knight, 3 vols, MIT Press, Cambridge, Mass., pp. 45–339, original German edn 1972.

—— and Eisler, Hanns (1973) 'Die Kunst zu erben', in Hans-Jürgen Schmitt, *Die Expressionismusdebatte: Materialen zu einer marxistischen Realismuskonzeption*, Suhrkamp, Frankfurt, pp. 258–64.

Bobbio, Norberto (1969, 1975) 'Gramsci e la concezione della società civile', in Pietro Rossi (ed.), *Gramsci e la cultura contemporanea*, 2 vols, Editori Riuniti, Rome, pp. 75–101.

Bochmann, Klaus (1984) 'Sprache als Kultur und Weltanschauung. Zur Sprachauffassung Antonio Gramscis', in Antonio Gramsci, *Notizen zur Sprache und Kultur*, Gustav Kiepenheuer Verlag, Leipzig und Weimar, pp. 7–39.

Bocock, Robert (1986) *Hegemony*, Tavistock Publications, London and New York.

Boggs, Carl (1984) *The Two Revolutions: Gramsci and the Dilemmas of Western Marxism*, South End Press, Boston, Mass.

Bonino, Guido Davico (1972) *Gramsci e il teatro*, Giulio Einaudi Editore, Turin.

Borradori, Giovanna (1988) *Recoding Metaphysics: The New Italian Philosophy*, Northwestern University Press, Evanston, Ill.

Brand, Stewart (1987) *The Media Lab: Inventing the Future at M.I.T.*, Viking Penguin, New York.

Brecht, Bertolt (1967a) 'Theatersituation 1917–1927', in *Gesammelte Werke 15: Schriften zum Theater 1*, Suhrkamp, Frankfurt, pp. 125–6.

—— (1976b) *Gesammelte Werke 18: Schriften zur Literatur und Kunst 1*, Suhrkamp, Frankfurt.

—— (1967c) *Gesammelte Werke 19: Schriften zur Literatur und Kunst 2*, Suhrkamp, Frankfurt.

—— (1973) 'Die Brecht-Polemik gegen Lukács', in Hans-Jürgen Schmitt, *Die Expressionismusdebatte: Materialien zu einer marxistischen Realismuskonzeption*, Suhrkamp, Frankfurt, pp. 302–37.

Breines, Paul (1973) 'Notes on Lukács' "The Old Culture and the New Culture"', in Bart Grahl and Paul Piccone (eds), *Towards a New Marxism*, Telos Press, St Louis, Miss., pp. 3–21.

Cambria, Adele (1976) *Amore Come Rivoluzione*, Sugar Edizioni, Milan.

Canelini, Nestor Garcia (1984) 'Gramsci con Bourdieu. Hegemonia, consumo y nuevas formas de organizacion popular', *Nueva Sociedad* 71, 69–78.

Carletti, Gabriele (1980–1) 'Gramsci e la critica della teoria psicoanalitica', *Trimestre* 13–14, 14–1, 71–99.

Carravetta, Peter (1988) 'Repositioning Interpretive Discourse', *Differentia* 2, 83–127.

—— (1989) 'An Introduction to the Hermeneutics of Luigi Pareyson', *Differentia* 3–4, 217–41.

Cavalcanti, Pedro and Piccone, Paul (eds) (1975) *History, Philosophy and Culture in the Young Gramsci*, Telos Press, St Louis, Miss.

Chomsky, Noam (1987) *The Chomsky Reader*, ed. James Peck, Pantheon Books, New York.

Coassin-Spiegel, Hermes (1983) *Gramsci und Althusser: Eine Kritik der Althusserschen Rezeption von Gramsci's Philosophie*, Argument Verlag, Berlin.

Cocks, Joan (1989) *The Oppositional Imagination: Feminism, Critique and Political Theory*, Routledge, London and New York.

Colombo, Cesare (ed.) (1977) *Gramsci e il suo tempo*, introduction Mario Spinella, text Francesca Occhipinti, Longanesi & Co., Milan.

Coward, Rosalind and Ellis, John (1977) *Language and Materialism: Developments in Semiology and the Theory of the Subject*, Routledge & Kegan Paul, Boston, Mass., London and Henley, Oxon.

Cozens, Phil (1977) *Twenty Years of Antonio Gramsci: A Bibliography of Gramsci and Gramsci Studies Published in English, 1957–1977*, Lawrence & Wishart, London.

Croce, Benedetto (1914) *Historical Materialism and the Economics of Karl Marx*, tr. C. M. Meredith, introduction A. D. Lindsay, Macmillan, New York, original Italian edn 1900.

Davidson, Alastair (1977) *Antonio Gramsci: Towards an Intellectual Biography*, Merlin Press, London and Humanities Press, New Jersey.

de Lauretis, Teresa (1987) 'Gramsci Notwithstanding, or, The Left Hand of History', in *Technologies of Gender*, Indiana University Press, Bloomington and Indianapolis, Ind., pp. 84–95.

de Sanctis, Francesco (1931) *History of Italian Literature*, vol. 2, tr. Joan Redfern, Harcourt, Brace & Co., New York, original Italian edn 1870–1.

del Noce, Augusto (1978) 'L'influenza di De Sanctis su Gramsci', in *De Sanctis e il realismo*, 2 vols, Giannini Editore, Naples, vol. 2, pp. 1315–45.

235

Diamond, Irene and Quinby, Lee (eds) (1988) *Feminism and Foucault: Reflections on Resistance*, Northeastern University Press, Boston, Mass.

Dombroski, Robert S. (Winter 1981) 'The Ideological Question in Manzoni', *Studies in Romanticism* 20, 497–524.

—— (1984) *L'apologia del vero: Lettura ed interpretazione dei 'Promessi Sposi'*, Liviana Editrice, Padua.

—— (1989) *Antonio Gramsci*, Twayne Publishers, Boston, Mass.

Ehrenreich, Barbara (1989) *Fear of Falling: The Inner Life of the Middle Class*, HarperCollins, New York.

Engels, Friedrich (1985) *The Origin of the Family*, introduction Michele Barrett, Penguin, Harmondsworth, Mx.

Femia, Joseph V. (1981) *Gramsci's Political Thought: Hegemony, Consciousness, and the Revolutionary Process*, Clarendon Press, Oxford.

Finocchiaro, Maurice (1988a) *Gramsci critico e la critica*, Armando Editore, Rome.

—— (1988b) *Gramsci and the History of Dialectical Thought*, Cambridge University Press, Cambridge and New York.

Fiori, Giuseppe (1971) *Life of a Revolutionary*, tr. Tom Nairn, E. P. Dutton & Co., New York, original Italian edn 1966.

Forester, Tom (ed.) (1985) *The Information Technology Revolution*, MIT Press, Boston, Mass.

Forgacs, David (ed.) (1988) *The Gramsci Reader*, Lawrence & Wishart, London.

Foucault, Michel (1977) *Language, Counter-Memory, Practice: Selected Essays and Interviews*, ed. Donald F. Bouchard, tr. Donald F. Bouchard and Sherry Simon, Cornell University Press, Ithaca, NY.

—— (1978) *The History of Sexuality: An Introduction*, Pantheon, New York.

—— (1980) *Power/Knowledge: Selected Interviews and Other Writings 1972–1977*, ed. Colin Gordon, tr. Colin Gordon, Leo Marshall, John Mepham and Kate Soper, Pantheon, New York.

Fraser, Nancy (1987) 'What's Critical about Critical Theory? The Case of Habermas and Gender', in Seyla Benhabib and Drucilla Cornell (eds), *Feminism as Critique*, University of Minnesota Press, Minneapolis, Minn., pp. 31–56.

Freeman, Chris (1985) 'Long Waves of Economic Development', in Tom Forester (ed.), *The Information Technology Revolution*, MIT Press, Boston, Mass., pp. 603–16.

Gill, Stephen (1990) 'Intellectuals and Transnational Capital' in Ralph Miliband and Leo Panitch (eds), *The Retreat of the Intellectuals: Socialist Register 1990*, Merlin Press, London, pp. 290–310.

Goldmann, Lucien (1977) *Lukács and Heidegger: Towards a New Philosophy*, tr. William Q. Boelhower, Routledge & Kegan Paul, Boston, Mass., London and Henley, Oxon, original French edn 1960.

Gorsen, Peter (1982) 'Zur Dialektik des Funktionalismus heute: Das Beispiel des kommunalen Wohnungsbaus im Wien der zwanziger Jahre', in Jürgen Habermas (ed.), *Stichworte zur 'Geistigen Situation der Zeit'*, vol. 1, *Nation und Republik*, Suhrkamp, Frankfurt, first edn 1979, pp. 688–707.

Gottlieb, Roger S. (ed.) (1989) *An Anthology of Western Marxism: From Lukács and Gramsci to Socialist-Feminism*, Oxford University Press, New York and Oxford.

Grahl, Bart and Piccone, Paul (1973) *Towards a New Marxism*, Telos Press, St Louis, Miss.

Gramsci, Antonio (1926) 'On the Southern Question', in *The Modern Prince and Other Writings*, International Publishers, New York, 1957, 10th printing 1987, pp. 28–51.

—— (1948) *Il materialismo storico e la filosofia di Benedetto Croce*, Einaudi, Turin.

—— (1957) *The Modern Prince and Other Writings*, tr. Louis Marks, International Publishers, New York, 10th printing 1987.

—— (1965) *Lettere dal carcere*, ed. Sergio Caprioglio and Elsa Fubini, Einaudi, Turin.

—— (1971) *Selections from the Prison Notebooks*, ed. and tr. Quintin Hoare and Geoffrey Nowell Smith, International Publishers, New York.

—— (1973) *Letters from Prison*, ed., tr. and introduction Lynne Lawner, Noonday Press, Farrar, Straus & Giroux, New York.

—— (1975) *Quaderni del carcere*, ed. Valentino Gerratana, 4 vols, Giulio Einaudi Editore, Turin.

—— (1977) *Selections from Political Writings 1910–1920*, ed. Quintin Hoare, tr. Jolin Mathews, Lawrence & Wishart, London.

—— (1980a) *Selections from Political Writings 1921–1926*, ed. and tr. Quintin Hoare, International Publishers, New York.

—— (1980b) *Cronache Torinesi 1913–1917*, ed. Sergio Caprioglio, Giulio Einaudi Editore, Turin, pp. 735–855.

—— (1985) *Selections from Cultural Writings*, ed. David Forgacs and Geoffrey Nowell Smith, tr. William Boelhower, Harvard University Press, Cambridge, Mass.

—— (1987) *Letteratura e vita nazionale*, introduction Edoardo Sanguineti, Editori Riuniti, Rome, pp. 353–69.

Habermas, Jürgen (1984, 1987) *The Theory of Communicative Action*: (1984) vol. 1, *Reason and the Rationalization of Society*, tr. Thomas McCarthy, Beacon Press, Boston, Mass.; (1987) vol. 2, *Lifeworld and System: A Critique of Functionalist Reason*, tr. Thomas McCarthy, Beacon Press, Boston, Mass.; vols 1 and 2, Beacon Paperback 1989; original German edn 1981.

—— and Luhmann, Niklas (1971) *Theorie der Gesellschaft oder Sozialtechnologie*, Suhrkamp, Frankfurt, 1982 edn.

Hartsock, Nancy (1990) 'Foucault on Power: a Theory for Women?', in Linda J. Nicholson (ed.), *Feminism/Postmodernism*, Routledge, New York and London, pp. 157–76.

Harvey, David (1989) *The Condition of Postmodernity*, Basil Blackwell Ltd, Oxford and Cambridge.

Henderson, Hamish (ed.) (1988) *Gramsci's Prison Letters: Lettere dal Carcere*, Zwan Publications, London.

Hoare, Quintin and Nowell Smith, Geoffrey (eds and trs) (1971) 'General Introduction' to Antonio Gramsci, *Selections from the Prison Notebooks*, International Publishers, New York, pp. xvii–xcvi.

Hoffman, John (1984) *The Gramscian Challenge: Coercion and Consent in Marxist Political Theory*, Basil Blackwell, Oxford and New York.

Holub, Renate (1978) 'The Cultural Politics of the CPI from 1944–56', *Yale Italian Studies* 2, 261–83.

—— (1982) 'Towards a New Rationality? Notes on Feminism and Current Discursive Practices in Italy', *Discourse* 4, 89–107.

—— (1983) 'Giambattista Vico's Theory of Poetics and Aesthetics', unpublished dissertation, University of Wisconsin, Madison, Wisc. (available University Microfilms International, Ann Arbor, Mich.).

—— (1989) 'Critical Il/literacy: Humanism, Heidegger, Anti-Humanism', *Differentia* 3–4, 73–90.

—— (1990) 'For the Record: the Non-Language of Italian Feminist Philosophy', *Romance Language Annual* 1, 133–40.

Holub, Robert C. (1991) *Jürgen Habermas: Critic in the Public Sphere*, Routledge, London.

Horkheimer, Max (1976) 'Traditional and Critical Theory', in *Critical Sociology: Selected Readings*, ed. Paul Connerton, Penguin Books, Harmondsworth, Mx, pp. 206–24, original German edn 1937.

—— (1978) 'On the Problem of Truth', in *The Essential Frankfurt School Reader*, ed. Andrew Arato and Eike Gebhardt, introduction Paul Piccone, Urizen Books, New York, pp. 407–44, original German edn 1935.

Hyppolite, Jean (1969) *Studies on Marx and Hegel*, tr., with introduction, notes and bibliography John O'Neill, Basic Books, New York and London, original French edn 1955.

—— (1974) *Genesis and Structure of Hegel's Phenomenology of the Spirit*, tr. Samuel Cherniak and John Heckman, Northwestern University Press, Evanston, Ill., original French edn 1946.

Ingarden, Roman (1973) 'On the Functions of Language in Theater', in *The Literary Work of Art: An Investigation on the Borderlines of Ontology, Logic, and Theory of Literature*, tr. and introduction George G. Grabowicz, Northwestern University Press, Evanston, Ill., pp. 377–96.

Jacoby, Russell (1987) *The Last Intellectuals: American Culture in the Age of Academe*, Noonday Press, New York.

Jameson, Fredric (1971) *Marxism and Form: Twentieth-Century Dialectical Theories of Literature*, Princeton University Press, Princeton, NJ.

—— (1990) *Late Marxism. Adorno, or, The Persistence of the Dialectic*, Verso, London.

Jay, Martin (1984) *Marxism & Totality: The Adventures of a Concept from Lukács to Habermas*, University of California Press, Berkeley and Los Angeles, Ca.

Joll, James (1977) *Gramsci*, Fontana, Collins, Glasgow.

Kaminski, Franz, Karuscheit, Heiner and Winter, Klaus (1982) *Antonio Gramsci, Philosophie und Praxis: Grundlagen und Wirkungen der Gramsci-Debatte*, Sendler Verlag, Frankfurt.

Kanoussi, Dora and Mena, Javier (1985) *La revolución pasiva: Una lectura de los Cuadernos de la carcel*, Universidad Autonoma de Puebla, Puebla, Mexico.

Kebir, Sabine (1980) *Die Kulturkonzeption Antonio Gramscis*, Damnitz Verlag GmbH, Munich.

Kilminster, Richard (1979) *Praxis and Method: A Sociological Dialogue with Lukács, Gramsci and the early Frankfurt School*, Routledge & Kegan Paul, Boston, Mass., London and Henley, Oxon.

Kojève, Alexandre (1969) *Introduction to the Reading of Hegel: Lectures on the*

Phenomenology of the Spirit, ass. Raymond Queneau, ed. Allan Bloom, tr. James H. Nichols, Jr, Cornell University Press, Ithaca, NY and London, original French edn 1947.

Kolakowski, Leszek (1978) *Main Currents of Marxism*, vol. 3, *The Breakdown*, tr. P. S. Falla, Oxford University Press, Oxford, original Polish edn 1976.

Korsch, Karl (1970) *Marxism and Philosophy*, tr. Fred Halliday, Monthly Review Press, New York and London, original German edn 1924.

Labriola, Antonio (1908) *Essays on the Materialist Conception of History*, tr. Charles H. Kerr, C. H. Kerr & Co., Chicago, original Italian edn 1896.

Laclau, Ernesto and Mouffe, Chantal (1985) *Hegemony and Socialist Strategy: Towards a Radical Democratic Politics*, Verso, London and New York.

Landy, Marcia (1986) 'Culture and Politics in the Works of Antonio Gramsci', in *Boundary 2* (Special Issue, *The Legacy of Antonio Gramsci*, ed. Joseph Buttigieg) 14, 3, 49–71.

Lo Piparo, Franco (1979) *Lingua Intellettuali Egemonia in Gramsci*, Laterza, Rome-Bari.

Löwy, Michael (1976) *Pour une sociologie des intellectuels révolutionnaires: L'évolution politique de Lukács 1909–1929*, Presses Universitaires de France, Paris, 1976.

Luhmann, Niklas (1969) *Legitimation durch Verfahren*, Luchterhand, Neuwied.

—— (1982) *The Differentiation of Society*, tr. Stephen Holmes and Charles Latmore, Columbia University Press, New York.

Lukács, Georg (1937) 'Es geht um den Realismus', in Hans-Jürgen Schmitt (ed.), (1973) *Die Expressionismusdebatte: Materialien zu einer marxistischen Realismuskonzeption*, Suhrkamp, Frankfurt, pp. 192–230.

—— (1964) *Studies in European Realism*, introduction Alfred Kazin, Grosset & Dunlap, New York.

—— (1971a) 'Grösse und Verfall des Expressionismus', in *Werke*, vol. 4, *Probleme des Realismus I*, Luchterhand, Neuwied and Berlin, pp. 101–49, original edn 1934.

—— (1971b) *History and Class Consciousness: Studies in Marxist Dialectics*, tr. Rodney Livingstone, MIT Press, Cambridge, Mass., original German edn 1923.

—— (1971) [1974 edn]) 'Art and Objective Truth', in *Writer and Critic and Other Essays*, ed. and tr. Arthur D. Kahn, Grosset & Dunlap Publishers, New York, pp. 25–61, original German edn 1934.

—— (1974) *Soul and Form*, tr. Anne Bostock, MIT Press, Cambridge, Mass., original German edn 1911.

—— (1980) *The Destruction of Reason*, tr. Peter Palmer, Merlin Press, London, original German edn 1962.

—— (1983) *The Historical Novel*, tr. Hannah and Stanley Mitchell, introduction Fredric Jameson, University of Nebraska Press, Lincoln, Nebr. and London, original German edn. 1955.

Lyotard, Jean-François (1984) *The Postmodern Condition: A Report on Knowledge*, tr. Geoff Bennington and Brian Massumi, foreword Fredric Jameson, University of Minnesota Press, Minneapolis, Minn., original French edn 1979.

Macciocchi, Maria Antonietta (1974) *Per Gramsci*, Il Mulino, Bologna.

Manacorda, Giuliano (ed.) (1975a) *Marxismo e letteratura* by Antonio Gramsci, Editori Riuniti, Rome.

—— (1975b) 'Introduzione', in *Marxismo e letteratura* by Antonio Gramsci, Editori Riuniti, Rome, pp. 11–59.

Marcuse, Herbert (1978a) *The Aesthetic Dimension: Toward a Critique of Marxist Aesthetics*, Beacon Press, Boston, Mass., original German edn 1977.

—— (1978b) 'Some Social Implications of Modern Technology', in Andrew Arato and Eike Gebhardt (eds), *The Essential Frankfurt School Reader*, introduction Paul Piccone, Urizen Books, New York, pp. 138–61.

Marx, Karl (1988) *Selected Writings*, ed. David McLellan, Oxford University Press, Oxford and New York.

—— and Engels, Friedrich (1967) *The Communist Manifesto*, introduction and notes A. J. P. Taylor, Penguin Books, Harmondsworth, Mx.

Masuda, Yoneji (1985) 'Computopia', in Tom Forester (ed.), *The Information Technology Revolution*, MIT Press, Boston, Mass., pp. 620–34.

Matejka, Ladislav (1986) 'On the First Russian Prolegomena to Semiotics', in V.N. Vološinov, *Marxism and the Philosophy of Language*, tr. Ladislav Matejka and I. R. Titunik, Harvard University Press, Cambridge, Mass. and London, pp. 161–74.

Maya, C. (1982) 'El concepto del estado en los "Cuadernos de la Carcel" ', *Cuadernos Politicos* 33, 7–19.

Merleau-Ponty, Maurice (1964) *The Primacy of Perception*, tr. and introduction James M. Edie, Northwestern University Press, Evanston, Ill.

—— (1968) 'The Intertwining – The Chiasm', in *The Visible and the Invisible*, ed. Claude Lefort, tr. Alfonso Lingis, Northwestern University Press, Evanston, Ill., pp. 130–56, original French edn 1964.

—— (1973) *The Adventures of the Dialectic*, tr. Joseph Bien, Northwestern University Press, Evanston, Ill., original French edn 1955.

Merod, Jim (1987) *The Political Responsibility of the Critic*, Cornell University Press, Ithaca, NY.

Morera, Esteve (1990) *Gramsci's Historicism: A Realist Interpretation*, Routledge, London and New York.

Mouffe, Chantal (ed.) (1979) *Gramsci and Marxist Theory*, Routledge & Kegan Paul, Boston, Mass., London and Henley, Oxon.

Musolini, Rocco (1971) 'Gramsci e il metodo della critica letteraria', in *Marxismo ed estetica in Italia*, Editori Riuniti, Rome, pp. 27–51.

Negri, Antonio (1987) *Lenta ginestra. Saggio sull'ontologia di Giacomo Leopardi*, Sugar Editori, Milan.

—— (1990) *The Savage Anomaly: The Power of Spinoza's Metaphysics and Politics*, tr. Michael Hardt, University of Minnesota Press, Minneapolis, Minn., original Italian edn 1982.

Nemeth, Thomas (1980) *Gramsci's Philosophy: A Critical Study*, Harvester Press, Brighton, Sussex and Humanities Press, Atlantic Highlands, NJ.

Norman, Colin (1981) *The God That Limps: Science and Technology in the Eighties*, A Worldwatch Institute Book, W. W. Norton & Co., New York and London.

Pacey, Arnold (1983) *The Culture of Technology*, MIT Press, Boston, Mass.

Piccone, Paul (1973) 'Phenomenological Marxism', in Bart Grahl and Paul Piccone (eds), *Towards a New Marxism*, Telos Press, St Louis, Miss., pp. 133–58.

—— (1983) *Italian Marxism*, University of California Press, Berkeley, Ca.

Pipa, Arshi (1990) 'The Politics of Literature', unpublished manuscript.

Poster, Mark (1989) *Critical Theory and Poststructuralism: In Search of a Context*, Cornell University Press, Ithaca, NY and London.

—— (1990) *The Mode of Information: Poststructuralism and Social Context*, University of Chicago Press, Chicago.

Poulantzas, Nicolas (1974) *Fascism and Dictatorship: The Third International and the Problem of Fascism*, tr. Judith White, New Left Books, London, original French edn 1970.

Propp, Vladimir (1968, 1979) *Morphology of the Folktale*, 1st edn tr. Laurence Scott, introduction Svatava Pirkova-Jakobson, 2nd edn rev., ed. and preface Louis A. Wagner, new introduction Alan Dundes, University of Texas Press, Austin, Tex. and London, original Russian edn 1928.

Rada, Juan (1985) 'Information Technology and the Third World', in Tom Forester (ed.), *The Information Technology Revolution*, MIT Press, Boston, Mass., pp. 571–89.

Raddatz, Fritz J. (1972) *Georg Lukács: In Selbstzeugnissen und Bilddokumenten*, Rowohlt, Hamburg.

Radhakrishnan, R. (1990) 'Toward an Effective Intellectual: Foucault or Gramsci', in Bruce Robbins (ed.), *Intellectuals: Aesthetics, Politics, Academics*, University of Minnesota Press, Minneapolis, Minn., pp. 59–99.

Rajchman, John and West, Cornel (eds) (1985) *Post-Analytic Philosophy*, Columbia University Press, New York.

Reich, William (1989) 'What is Class Consciousness', in *An Anthology of Western Marxism: From Lukács and Gramsci to Socialist Feminism*, ed. Roger S. Gottlieb, Oxford University Press, New York and Oxford, pp. 145–67.

Riechers, Christian (1970) *Das Verhältnis der Philosophie der Praxis Antonio Gramscis zum Marxismus*, Europäische Verlagsanstalt, Frankfurt.

Robbins, Bruce (ed.) (1990) *Intellectuals: Aesthetics, Politics, Academics*, University of Minnesota Press, Minneapolis, Minn.

Rorty, Richard (1982) *Consequences of Pragmatism*, University of Minnesota Press, Minneapolis, Minn.

—— Schneewind, J. B. and Skinner, Quentin (eds) (1984) *Philosophy in History*, Cambridge University Press, Cambridge.

Rosengarten, Frank (1986) 'Gramsci's "Little Discovery": Gramsci's Interpretation of Canto X of Dante's Inferno', in *Boundary 2* (Special Issue, *The Legacy of Antonio Gramsci*, ed. Joseph Buttigieg) 14, 3, 71–91.

Ross, Andrew (ed.) (1988) *Universal Abandon? The Politics of Postmodernism*, University of Minnesota Press, Minneapolis, Minn.

—— (1989) *No Respect: Intellectuals and Popular Culture*, Routledge, New York and London.

Rossi, Pietro (ed.) (1969, 1975) *Gramsci e la cultura contemporanea*, 2 vols, Editori Riuniti, Rome.

Roszak, Theodore (1986) *The Cult of Information: The Folklore of Computers and the True Art of Thinking*, Pantheon, New York.

Roth, Gerhard (1972) *Gramscis Philosophy der Praxis: Eine neue Deutung des Marxismus*, Patmos Verlag, Düsseldorf.

Said, Edward W. (1979) *Orientalism*, Vintage Books, New York.

—— (1983) *The World, the Text, and the Critic*, Harvard University Press, Cambridge, Mass.

Santucci, Antonio A. (ed.) 1986 *Nuove lettere di Antonio Gramsci, con altre lettere di Piero Sraffa*, preface Nicola Badaloni, Editori Riuniti, Rome.

Sassoon, Anne Showstack (1980) *Gramsci's Politics*, Croom Helm, London.

—— (1986) 'The People, Intellectuals and Specialized Knowledge', in *Boundary 2* (Special Issue, *The Legacy of Antonio Gramsci*, ed. Joseph Buttigieg) 14, 3, 137–68.

—— (1987) 'Introduction', *Gramsci's Politics*, 2nd edn, Hutchinson, London and Melbourne, pp. ix–xxi.

Scalia, Gianni (1973) 'Manzoni a sinistra', *Italianistica* 1, 21–42.

Schmidt, Alfred (1981) *History and Structure: an Essay on Hegelian-Marxist and Structuralist Theories of History*, tr. Jeffrey Herf, MIT Press, Cambridge, Mass., original German edn 1971.

Schmitt, Hans-Jürgen (1973) *Die Expressionismusdebatte: Materialien zu einer marxistischen Realismuskonzeption*, Suhrkamp, Frankfurt.

Schutz, Alfred (1967) *The Phenomenology of the Social World*, tr. George Walsh and Frederick Lehnert, introduction George Walsh, Northwestern University Press, Evanston, Ill., original German edn 1932.

Segre, Cesare (1974) *Le strutture e il tempo*, Einaudi, Turin.

—— (1984) *Teatro e romanzo*, Einaudi, Turin.

Simon, Roger (1982) *Gramsci's Political Thought: An Introduction*, Lawrence & Wishart, London.

Solomon, Maynard (1979) *Marxism and Art*, Wayne State University Press, Detroit, Mich.

Somai, Giovanni (1979) *Gramsci a Vienna: Ricerche e documenti 1922/1924*, Argalia Editore, Urbino.

Spriano, Paolo (1979) *Antonio Gramsci and the Party: The Prison Years*, tr. John Fraser, Lawrence & Wishart, London.

Stipčević, Niksa (1968) *Gramsci e i problemi letterari*, Civiltà letteraria del novecento, no. 11, Mursia, Milan.

Titunik, I. R. (1986) 'The Formal Method and the Sociological Method (M. M. Bakhtin, P. N. Medvedev, V. N. Vološinov) in Russian Theory and Study of Literature', in V. N. Vološinov, *Marxism and the Philosophy of Language*, tr. Ladislav Matejka and I. R. Titunik, Harvard University Press, Cambridge, Mass. and London, pp. 175–200.

Vološinov, V. N. (1986) *Marxism and the Philosophy of Language*, tr. Ladislav Matejka and I. R. Titunik, Harvard University Press, Cambridge, Mass. and London.

Williams, Raymond (1977) *Marxism and Literature*, Oxford University Press, Oxford.

—— (1982) *The Sociology of Culture*, Schocken Books, New York.

—— (1988) *Problems in Materialism and Culture*, Verso, London.

Index

243

244

245